For the passengers and crew
of Argonaut Hotel Golf,
who fell to earth on
Sunday, 4 June 1967.

Stephen Morrin

SIX MILES FROM HOME

AUSTIN MACAULEY PUBLISHERS™

LONDON • CAMBRIDGE • NEW YORK • SHARJAH

A CIP catalogue record for this title is available from the British Library.

ISBN 9781528905572 (Paperback)
ISBN 9781528958028 (ePub e-book)

www.austinmacauley.com

First Published (2020)
Austin Macauley Publishers Ltd
25 Canada Square
Canary Wharf
London
E14 5LQ

This book would have been all but impossible and certainly not seen the light of day without the cooperation, support and approval of a great many people and organisations. First and foremost, I would like to record my sincere thanks to Vivienne Thornber, David Ralphs and Harold Wood for their kind permission to tell their remarkable and fortuitous stories of survival and recovery.

Of the many relatives and friends of those who lost their lives in the disaster, I would particularly like to express my gratitude and admiration to the following who related to me their longstanding and painful memories with great fortitude: John Pollard, Barbara Bishop, Jill Wood, Pauline O'Sullivan, Maralyn Bradley, Helen Cuthew and Susan Newgas.

Amongst the many members of the emergency services involved on the day and in the aftermath, my thanks go to the following for generously sharing with me their graphic first-hand accounts: John Heath, Charles Hunt, Geoff Burgess, Roger Gaskell, Bernard Sharrocks, Mike Conroy, Stephen Clegg and Mike Phillips.

I am grateful to David Thorpe for his consistent support throughout the entirety of the project and for furnishing me with background information on Hotel Golf's stewardess, Julia Partleton.

I would also like to extend my gratitude to the late Reverend Arthur Connop, MBE, chaplain to the Stockport Borough Police Force, Fire Service, Ambulance Service and Stockport Infirmary. I thank him for his kind counsel, advice and friendship over many years. It was through his personal involvement with the victims' families and survivors that he was able to give me invaluable insights into the human aspects of the tragedy.

A special mention goes to the late Brian Donohoe, one of the first civilian rescuers on the scene. I thank him for recounting his selfless rescue attempts on the day and joined with me on the approaching 30th anniversary of the disaster to fulfil his original vision for a permanent memorial to be erected on the site. Also, for their help in the memorial – which is very much part of this story – I thank Ann Coffey MP and Sir Andrew Stunell; also Joe Smith and Vanessa Brook of Stockport MBC Community Services for their enthusiastic and unstinting efforts during the early summer of 1998.

Another person I must not forget to mention is the late aviation historian and author Brian Robinson. I thank him for his encouragement, assistance, unlimited access to his extensive archival material and more than once pointing me in the right direction. He saved me months, if not years, of valuable research.

Thanks to Hilary Jones for her contagious sense of humour, encouragement and advice on simply how to hang on in there when I was flagging and reminding me that writing this story was important and not to give up.

I am immensely grateful to Steve Moss, a Senior Inspector at the Air Accident Investigation Branch, Farnborough. He went to great lengths to provide me with a wealth of technical documentation pertaining to the investigation and subsequent public inquiry which gave me new insights into the accident and are published here for the first time, without which this book would have been all the poorer.

Thanks, are also due to fellow aviation historian and author Malcolm Finnis for his contribution on the Air Ferry DC-4 accident, which prominently features in this story. I would also like to record my gratitude to the late esteemed aviation writers Bill Gunston and Stephen Barlay for their valuable suggestions and advice. I am greatly indebted to Jan Garvey for her diligent proofreading skills and her helpful and critical comments.

My appreciation extends to many others for their generous help in researching this book. There were so many that I shall simply list their names rather than attempt to specify their precise nature in which they were of assistance. They are: Arthur and Bertha Thorniley, Bobbie Marlow, Robert Marlow, the late Captain Tony Belcher, Ruth Oliver, the late Barry Bevans, David Hamilton, the late Bob Greaves, Ernie Taylor, John Prince, Eileen Payne, Peter Dewhurst, Tony Bellshaw, Joan Lomas, Brian Taylor, John Perkins, Margaret Finnigan, Chris McNeill, Barry Matkin, Jim Lovelock, Stewart Rigby, Robert and Chris Hamnett, Geoff Rowland, Gordon Smith, Arthur Wright, Ron Needham, Peter Eyre, Phil Hodgson, Alan Faulkner, Jackie Martinez, Susan Maddocks and Jacqueline Collins.

To everyone I might have failed to mention, my apologies. It is through all their efforts, hard work and contributions that the tragic and complex story of the Stockport air disaster can be accurately told. I hope they all feel that it was worth it.

Table of Contents

Introduction

At ten o'clock on the morning of Sunday 4 June 1967, a British Midland Airways Canadair C-4 Argonaut airliner – radio call sign Hotel Golf – packed with returning holidaymakers from Palma, Majorca, turned onto the approach to Ringway Airport, Manchester. To Captain Harry Marlow and his First Officer Chris Pollard monitoring the controls, it seemed a perfectly normal and routine let down. The light drizzle and low cloud base prevailing presented no kind of hazard. Yet eight minutes later, the airliner lay a tangled, twisted exploding wreck in Stockport town centre.

On that Sunday morning, the slow suburban pace of Stockport life suddenly stopped short to be replaced by unimaginable horror and terror. Of the 84 passengers and crew on board, only 12 were fortunate to escape with their lives. Mercifully, and indeed miraculously, there were no casualties on the ground; an extraordinary outcome considering the circumstances of the accident. At the time, it was the worst Argonaut accident in terms of fatalities and it was, and still remains to this day, the worst urban air disaster ever to occur in the UK. Considering the enormity of the tragedy in terms of death and destruction, it also remains one of the least known and least remembered.

Air disasters by their very nature are terrible things and the Stockport accident was no exception. Now, some fifty years after Hotel Golf plunged from the sky to bring such destruction and loss of life, the following narrative gives for the first time the full story of this truly horrific disaster and its aftermath so long lost in the annals of civil aviation history. It also gives an insight into the minds of the survivors, the bereaved and all those ordinary Stockport citizens, who suddenly without warning, were caught up in a catastrophe of massive proportions.

In the main, the following story is told by those who lived through the events. Although it is by no means a blow-by-blow account of all those involved – though many are included here – it is based on a collection of many interviews undertaken by the author over a twenty-year period. Apart from first-hand accounts, this book draws on numerous other sources: witness statements, correspondence, personal archives, newspaper, radio and television reports, together with the mass of technical documentation that was generated during the subsequent investigation and Public Inquiry. In fact, such is the volume of information unearthed; I have had to apply a certain amount of selectivity in order to keep the contents of this book in the bounds of manageable proportions.

Despite my many years of research, this book cannot be called, in the truest sense, a 'definitive' account, simply because all my sources, whether they be verbal or written, have their shortcomings. Even amongst those I personally interviewed, there were many discrepancies and contradictory recollections which cannot always be reconciled as to how the events unfolded on the day, who took part and in what order they occurred. These divergent viewpoints are the inevitable result of people trying to recall traumatic and shocking events which happened so long ago. This, of course, does not mean that their personal accounts are any the less true and are given here unabridged as told to me. The reader will, therefore, find some minor inconsistencies in the narrative, which I hope will not cause too much confusion. Fifty years on, it is vital that the truth doesn't become distorted with constant retelling and hearsay.

The following account also details the human side of the tragedy and how it changes lives forever. It is an intimate story of how the survivors recovered physically and mentally, and how the relatives of the victims struggled to come to terms with the magnitude of their loss and get on with the rest of their lives in an era where post-traumatic stress and counselling hadn't been heard of.

It was during my lengthy research that I uncovered startling new evidence regarding another accident to a British registered DC-4 airliner in almost identical circumstances six years earlier, which, if the authorities governing air safety had acted upon, would, without a shadow of a doubt have averted the Stockport disaster and the needless deaths of 72 men, women and children. This new evidence is so damning that it throws open the entire conduct of the original investigation and the findings of the Public Inquiry and to this day still leaves many questions unanswered.

After more than two decades of research, I believe I have gathered more than enough evidence to voice my views and theories on what I am certain really occurred on that fateful Sunday morning over Stockport, and more importantly – why?

I hope the reader can feel confident with the following narrative, which is, after half a century, as close to what really happened before, during and in the aftermath of a tragic aircraft accident that should never have happened.

I have no doubt that a certain number of former British Midland Airways employees and others in the aviation fraternity will be unhappy about how the airline has been portrayed in this book. For my part, I make no apologies; as an aviation historian, I have a duty to present the facts as they are known to me – distasteful as they may be – and do so in the interests of civil aviation history. In what has been a very challenging project, I have tried my utmost to remain impartial and I leave it entirely to the reader to make their own assessment based on the facts and details presented here.

This book is as complete as I can make it, and everything that follows is to the best of my knowledge a true and accurate account; needless to say, any errors that may occur in this somewhat complex story are mine, and mine alone.

Stephen R Morrin
Stockport
Cheshire 2018

Prologue

Are you old enough to remember the early summer of 1967? For those who do, it had so far proved an eventful year, full of incident and where tragedy seemed to be the order of the day. In January, disaster struck on a chilly overcast day in the Lake District, when 45-year-old Donald Campbell was killed as his jet-powered boat *Bluebird,* took off at 300 mph during an attempt to break his own water speed record. The boat somersaulted through the air before plunging into Coniston Water in full view of his horrified support crew watching from the shoreline.

In the same month, the American space programme claimed its first victims, when a horrific accident struck the first manned Apollo spacecraft during a simulated countdown on the launch pad at Cape Kennedy. Three astronauts died when fire broke out in the Command Module; they were Gus Grissom, the second American in space, Edward White, famous for his 'walk in space' in 1965, and Roger Chaffee, a relative newcomer to the programme.

Quite suddenly, the astronauts reported a fire inside the spacecraft which spread so rapidly that before the crew on the inside, or the launch personnel on the outside could open the hatch, the occupants were dead and the spacecraft devastated.

The Apollo tragedy was a major setback to the challenge President Kennedy laid down before Congress in 1961, when he told the world that the United States had set itself the goal of landing a man on the moon and returning him safely to Earth before the end of the decade.

If the Soviets thought they had stolen a lead over their rivals in the race to the moon, they too were in for a shock. On 23 April, cosmonaut Vladimir Komarov was launched into Earth orbit to test out the new Soyuz spacecraft. From the very start it was a troublesome flight and when the control system malfunctioned, it was decided to abort the mission. Although the spacecraft came through the fireball of re-entry intact, the main and reserve parachutes failed to deploy and the spacecraft slammed into the Russian Steppes at 400 mph killing Komarov instantly. The accident effectively brought the Soviet manned space programme to a shuddering halt. Now both contenders in the space race were in serious trouble. The moon in 1967 now seemed a long way off.

In February, Jack Ruby, the killer of President Kennedy's alleged assassin, Lee Harvey Oswald, dies in the same Dallas Hospital in which Oswald died and in which President Kennedy was pronounced dead. There was much speculation at the time and since regarding the true circumstances of Ruby's death and his role in the shooting of Oswald which has created generations of doubters and spawned a plethora of conspiracy theories.

In March, there occurred an environmental disaster of massive proportions when the Liberian-registered giant super tanker, *Torrey Canyon*, ran aground on the Seven Sisters Reef off Land's End, spilling its 117-ton cargo of crude oil into the sea, producing a slick that covered 260 square miles. The environmental damage caused was massive. Belated emergency measures were taken 10 days later when RAF and

Royal Navy aircraft dropped high explosives on the wreck to sink it and burn off the remaining oil. Six hours of continuous bombardment were a success, but it was far too late; by then more than 100 miles of the Cornish coastline were contaminated causing irreparable damage to wildlife.

Still on a maritime theme, but on a happier note, 65-year-old Francis Chichester sailed into Plymouth on 28 May in his 53-foot ketch Gipsy Moth IV at the end of his epic solo circumnavigation of the world. He was escorted into the harbour in the approaching dusk by an armada of 500 small boats as 250,000 well-wishers lined the shoreline. The following month, Chichester was dubbed Sir Francis by the Queen at Greenwich using Sir Francis Drake's sword in recognition of his outstanding achievement. His feat has been equalled or bettered many times since, but no subsequent yachtsman has had such an inspiring impact on the national mood.

In the world of aviation, the British Concorde prototype was taking final shape at the Filton factory near Bristol as was the French version at Toulouse – both would be rolled out by the end of the year. In the United States, the Boeing Company delivers its 1,000[th] groundbreaking Boeing 707 to American Airlines, making it the most successful jet airliner ever produced and which is credited with ushering in the jet age.

On the sporting front, World Heavyweight boxing champion, Muhammad Ali, refuses to be inducted into the US Army and is later stripped of his title. The 100 to 1 outsider, Foinavon, gallops home to win the Grand National at Aintree, and in May, Glasgow Celtic becomes the first British football team to win the European Cup by beating Inter Milan 2-1 in the merciless heat of the Estadio Nacional in Lisbon. That season Jock Stein's talented Celtic side, brimming with confidence and reputation, won every tournament they entered. At home, Manchester United are crowned First Division Champions and Tottenham Hotspur beat Chelsea in the first ever all London FA Cup Final at Wembley.

Also in May, the headlines were taken up by the marriage of rock and roll icon Elvis Presley to 21-year-old Priscilla Beaulieu in Las Vegas. The couple first met in West Germany in 1959 where Presley was serving his time in the army. The wedding caused scenes of mass hysteria across the United States and elsewhere amongst Presley's devoted teenage fans.

In America, the long hot humid summer of 67 was marked by civil unrest when racial rioting erupted in Detroit, Newark, Milwaukee and many other cities, resulting in mass violence, arson, looting and death. They were caused in the main by the dissatisfaction of American blacks with their way of life and living conditions and they felt powerless and disenfranchised.

In the world of popular music, 20-year-old barefoot beauty Sandie Shaw made it a first for Britain by winning the Eurovision Song Contest in Vienna with *Puppet on a String,* which lifts the nation and soars to No 1 in the UK and most countries in Europe. She was already a huge star on the continent, ensuring Eurovision success of a song she personally disliked. Other singles charting in that first week in June included: *Carrie Anne,* by Manchester-based group the Hollies; *She'd Rather Be with Me,* The Turtles; *Silence is Golden,* The Tremeloes; whilst British pop diva and former child film star, Petula Clark, advises us: *Don't Sleep* in *the Subway.*

The biggest and most influential pop group of all time, The Beatles, had just released probably the most eagerly awaited and acclaimed album in the history of popular music – *Sergeant Pepper's Lonely Hearts Club Band,* which their producer, George Martin, called: 'an undisciplined, sometimes self-indulgent trip into an unknown world'. The highly bureaucratic BBC, bastion of the Establishment and guardian of the country's morals, immediately bans the track *A Day in the Life,* because they claim, it contains 'overt' references to drugs. Despite this, the album is a spectacular success and remained at number one in Britain for 27 weeks and in America for 19. It was also the year that Paul McCartney meets Linda Eastman and discloses that the Beatles have taken acid – LSD.

To cater for the massive demand for non-stop pop music over the airwaves, an armada of 'pirate' radio ships dropped anchor just outside British territorial waters beyond the jurisdiction of the British authorities. Taking over from the unreliable Radio Luxembourg, they broadcast continuous pop music twenty-four hours a day, seven days a week, causing a revolution in the British music scene. For their ardent listeners, it was a breath of fresh air. With slick American style DJs and jingles, the public's response was immediate and overwhelming with tens of millions tuning in to the kind of music they wanted to hear. The British government took a dim view of course, portraying these illegal broadcasters as nothing more than gangsters and quickly introduced the Marine Broadcasting Act. Despite uproar from the public, the Act finally became law on 14 August 1967 and one by one, the stations fell silent. The pirates had caused such a shake-up in radio broadcasting that the staid and stuffy BBC had no option but to bow to what public opinion demanded and launched the all-pop Radio One in the autumn. To give the station credibility, the Corporation stole shamelessly from the pirate stations it replaced by employing many of their DJs such as Tony Blackburn, Kenny Everett, Emperor Rosko and others. Ex Radio Caroline disc jockey, Simon Dee, even starred in his own TV chat show, *Dee Time*, on BBC1. Dee's ascension to the level of Swinging '60s icon was meteoric but, thanks in part to Dee's own arrogance, it was short lived.

The summer of 1967 was also the 'Summer of Love' and 'Flower Power', perfectly summed up in Scott McKenzie's dreamy *San Francisco (Be sure to wear some flowers in your hair)*. During that fabled summer, Hippie psychedelia reached its peak, flooding the 'alternative' fashion world with Kaftans, Afghan coats, body paint and flowers in the hair. Their cannabis induced mantra preached: 'turn on, tune in, drop out', and 'make love not war'. The Hippies believed that through music, hallucinogenic drugs and 'free love' they could change the world. For a time, they did with seemingly unstoppable momentum, but it was not to last – by the autumn, it was all but over.

There can be no denying that a revolution of change was in the air that summer, but try your hardest, you were unlikely to find it on the streets of the provincial towns and cities of the North of England where life was much more tranquil and untouched and where change often came slowly.

One such northern outpost was the industrial town of Stockport in Cheshire, situated just a few miles to the south east of its sprawling neighbour Manchester. For the town's 142,000 inhabitants, that early summer seemed much like any other, but what was to occur here on a wet, oppressively warm Sunday morning in June of that watershed year would rock the town on its heels, making headlines that sent shockwaves around the world for all the wrong reasons.

Sunday 4 June dawned as just another unremarkable summer's day. A day that began so normally, so peacefully, yet in the blink of an eye, ended in absolute horror. It was a Sunday the town's clergy were preparing for their morning services, but suddenly, they had to forget the theology and struggle to make sense of shocking fact. So many dead, so quickly, so completely – just six miles from home and safety.

What follows is the truly remarkable and cataclysmic story of British Midland Airways flight BD 542. It proved in the end to be a totally avoidable accident that needlessly took the lives of seventy-two passengers and crew and changed forever the lives of many more.

Chapter One
The Sky Is Falling

"Oh my God... He's coming down!"

Police Constable – Bill Oliver

In the late 1960s, the industrial sprawl of Stockport came straight out of an L S Lowry painting, indeed the artist was a frequent visitor to the town to sketch and put brush to canvas capturing – sometimes depressingly – the gritty realism of the working-class North. With its network of tightly packed streets, cotton mills, tired old factories and a skyline sprouting a forest of belching factory chimneys, it was a scene that until recent years defined the town, making it undistinguishable from scores of others dotted across the north of England, all brought into being by the industrial revolution.

Lying on elevated ground, at the point where the Goyt and Tame rivers converge to create the Mersey, Stockport is situated some seven miles southeast of its larger neighbour Manchester. In the early 1800s, like most other bustling industrial towns, it was a vast urban environment characterised by substandard dwellings, much of which were overcrowded with no running water or internal sanitation and where frequent outbreaks of typhoid and cholera were not uncommon. The nineteenth century philosopher, Friedrich Engels, who visited the town in 1844, was particularly scathing about the standard of the housing and environmental conditions that the workers and their families had to endure. He was moved to comment that: "Stockport is renowned throughout the entire district as one of the duskiest, smokiest holes in the whole industrial area, and looks, indeed, especially when viewed from the railway viaduct, excessively repellent." But far more repulsive, he said, "'are the cottages and cellar dwellings of the working class, which stretch in long rows through all parts of the town." Another visitor described the town as: "An irregular, ill-built, badly lighted, dirty place, which no traveller passing through ever wished to see again." Even in the mid-1960s, the coal-fuelled dirty atmosphere of industry still cast a permanent, yellow haze over the town that at times blotted out the sun.

Without question, the most striking landmark running north-south through the town and dominating the western approaches is the enormous railway viaduct, which has cast a shadow over the landscape since its completion in 1840. This breath-taking feat of Victorian civil engineering brought rail transport from Manchester to Stockport and later right through to Birmingham and onwards to London. Standing above the Mersey valley, this colossus rises 111 feet above the river giving passing passengers an unobstructed bird's eye view over the smoky industrial landscape. Its statistics are striking: 1,786 feet long, 53 feet wide, with 22 main arches of 63-foot span as well as 4 arches of 22-foot span. It contains a staggering 11 million bricks and took 600 men working day and night almost two years to construct this monstrous edifice. At the time of its completion, it was the largest railway viaduct in the world, and today, it remains the largest brick-built structure in Europe. By 1885, the viaduct was carrying on average 250 passenger and 140 goods trains a day, spewing smoke and soot into the already polluted skies on their journey south. In the 1960s, this monolithic structure, like much of the townscape, was blackened with the accumulation of 130 years of industrial grime and would have given even the most casual of visitors the impression that Stockport was just another drab northern town with its fair share of gritty and grimy landscape.

Just a ten-minute leisurely walk east of the town centre lay the untidy urban sprawl of Portwood, a less than salubrious area. This depressing residential district was, in 1967, overshadowed by a massive gasholder, known locally as the 'Green Giant' because of its insipid green colour scheme. This colossus, standing at 255 feet high with a diameter of 136 feet, was a landmark feature and could be seen from miles around. Running a close second to this green monster, both in height and bulk, was the nearby Millgate Power Station cooling tower, which, before it was modified made the Portwood district a place of eternal drizzle.

Proliferating all around these industrial structures were tightly packed square courts of sooty black terrace housing that seemed to stretch into dreary infinity. With their side-by-side outside toilets and the inevitable corner shops and public houses to provide for the daily needs of this close-knit community, it made life just about bearable. Poorly planned and constructed in the early part of the nineteenth century by speculative builders to provide accommodation for the ever-growing number of mill and factory workers gravitating to the town, they were responsible for some of the worst excesses in housing conditions in the country. These two up two down, meaner than mean dwellings would endure right through to the late 1960s, by which time Portwood was a notorious area of crumbling slums unfit for human habitation. It was only then that the town's planners came along with radical plans for the wholesale demolition of the area, far beyond anything Herman Goering's Luftwaffe had achieved in six years of war.

Portwood is famous as the birthplace of the British Champion tennis player, Fred Perry. Prior to Andy Murray's historic win in 2013, Perry was the last British player to win the men's Wimbledon Championships way back in 1936; a Blue Plaque now marks the house in Carrington Road where he was born in 1909.

Figures from the entertainment field originating from the town include the comedy actor Peter Butterworth well known for his appearances in the 'Carry On' films; actress and TV presenter Yvette Fielding; comedian Jason Manford and impressionist Mike Yarwood who, in the '60s and '70s, was regarded as something of a TV superstar. Those from the sphere of literature include writer Christopher Isherwood, whose work later inspired the film *Cabaret*, and the famed journalist and broadcaster, Joan Bakewell, now Baroness Bakewell, who, like Isherwood legged it out of town when still young to further their careers.

Readers of a certain age may well remember the voluptuous Stockport lass Norma Sykes who famously became known as Sabrina. She was the stereotypical buxom 'dumb blond' with an impossibly proportioned body – 42-inch bust and 19-inch wasp like waist – she accomplished above the hips what Elvis accomplished below. In her time, she was a pinup, actress, singer, cabaret star and a sex queen who didn't like to be touched. She dated princes, charmed dictators, the public and the press and generated more myths, lies and legends than anyone else of her era. Sabrina passed away at her Hollywood home in November 2017 aged 80.

Just a short walk to the south of Portwood lies an area called the Carrs, a tiny steep sided triangular valley of land bordered by Hopes Carr, Churchgate and Waterloo Road. It was this small compact area that gave birth to Stockport's first industrial community that was instrumental in shaping the town's future economic development.

The rise of industry at this particular location was due entirely to the abundant supply of water from the Tin Brook that meandered below on its way to join the Mersey. It was here that the first mechanised silk mills in the British Isles were established in the eighteenth century, and later, due to the dampness of the air, converted to cotton spinning. In 1744, the sparkling waters of the Tin brook were dammed to form a 12-foot deep reservoir; the impounded water feeding the waterwheels of the mills. This became a Mecca for the locals – boating in the summer and ice-skating in the winter. Later, with the availability of cheap and efficient steam engines, waterpower became redundant and the reservoir was drained. With the later steep decline of the cotton industry, the rich legacy of the former mill buildings found various other industrial and commercial uses, but the Carrs economic dynamism as an industrial powerhouse was well and truly over; by the 1960s the area had further declined becoming semi-derelict, dirty and overgrown with an overall air of decay.

The calamitous event that was to occur here at nine minutes past ten on a damp Sunday morning in the early summer of 1967 would add yet another dimension to its long and renowned history.

Sunday, 4 June 1967 began much like any other. Overnight rain had splattered in from the west and the new day dawned with little promise. Everyone would have welcomed a little sunshine and cheer but there was very little to come that day – this was going to be a Sunday unlike any other.

By ten o'clock, the rain had abated giving way to a steady dispiriting drizzle that swept in waves over the rooftops blurring the irregular and gaunt urban skyline. The streets were almost deserted and lifeless with the weather keeping most people indoors, apart from a handful of hardier folks who braved the rain to step out for the Sunday newspapers along with faithful churchgoers on their way to morning worship.

In the dank streets of family homes radiating out in all directions from the town centre, housewives cleared away the breakfast dishes and began preparations for Sunday lunch, on what was seemingly going to be just another ordinary uneventful day. For others, capitalising on the fact that this was a Sunday – a work free day for most – took the opportunity to lie in bed for an hour or two.

As the morning began to unfurl, the town stretched and eased itself into a new day as it always had; there was nothing to suggest to anyone that this seemingly unremarkable tranquil Sunday morning, in this unremarkable northern town, was soon, very soon, going to be ripped apart by unimaginable horror. Everyone, it seemed, was preoccupied with the mundane tasks of day-to-day living, all blissfully unaware that the impending events were at that very moment being played out above the turbulent grey sky that pressed down over the town. In a few minutes, death and destruction would rain from the sky unannounced and uninvited. The cataclysmic events to come would shake everyone out of their Sunday morning lethargy, rock the town to its very foundations and make it the darkest hour and blackest day in its long history.

There were few people up and about that morning to see Patrick Finnigan and his 10-year-old son, Martin, making their way along Upper Brook Street towards the town centre. Clutching the lapels of his raincoat tightly to his throat, he leaned into the slanting drizzle and strode briskly along the terraced street. A few paces behind young Martin half walked, half ran, as he struggled to keep up with his father's hurried pace. Patrick, a caretaker for a local engineering company on Hopes Carr, made this ritual journey every Sunday morning to undertake a few odd jobs and stoke and fire up the boiler ready for the start of business the following day.

A few minutes past ten, they reached the end of the street and crossed over a deserted Waterloo Road. Safely on the other side, they took their usual short cut by squeezing through a narrow gap between a dilapidated two-storey brick warehouse and the end of the iron railings that overlooked the Carr valley. Picking their way along a muddy meandering path behind a local contractor's garage, they carefully negotiated tussocks of grass, nettle beds and the odd rusty bike frame. At this time of year, the new and popular phenomenon of the inclusive package tour holiday season was well underway and nearing its peak, but neither father nor son hardly spared an upward glance at the procession of droning airliners that nosed down through the grey overcast as they aimed westward in their descent towards Manchester's Ringway Airport some six miles distant.

Emerging onto the cobbles of Hopes Carr, they arrived at the front door of the building. As Patrick fumbled with his keys to open up, Martin stood patiently waiting on the pavement outside – the next few minutes would turn out to be the most dramatic and terrifying in the youngster's life. If both father and son had set out from home just a minute later that morning, then it is quite possible they would have been caught up in a national calamity and in all probability not lived to tell the tale.

Two hundred yards away in the town's bright and modern police headquarters on Lee Street, a lone sergeant looking bored was manning the front desk. Sunday mornings were always, in his long experience, a lack lustre shift and he found it somewhat tedious dealing with the usual mundane aspects of police work – lost dogs, minor traffic offences and the familiar faces of local housewives who, about to cook Sunday lunch, approached the desk with a handful of loose change asking for shillings for the gas meter.

Elsewhere in the station, a shift change was taking place, with police officers about to go on duty and those who had just finished their stint on nights took the opportunity to put their feet up and gossip amongst themselves over a steaming mug of tea in the station canteen. Soon, very soon, like a bolt out of the blue, their jovial mess room banter would be abruptly silenced when the alarm sounded, an alarm that would hurl them into a hideous catastrophe far removed from anything they had experienced in the whole of their police service. The horrors they were about to encounter would be a real test of their training and character.

Just around the corner from police headquarters on Middle Hillgate, stood the imposing edifice of the Salvation Army Citadel; known locally as the 'Fortress', it had been their base since 1884. With its melodramatic motto 'Blood and Fire', the Corps first opened fire in the town two years earlier occupying a temporary wooden building located at Waterloo Circus – ironically, the epicentre of this story. Outside the Citadel, in the falling drizzle, tambourines jingled along with the discordant sounds of euphoniums and cornets as the band – an integral part of the Salvation Army's tradition and ministry – tuned up in readiness to march off and play at a local old folk's home. It was all part of their Sunday morning ritual of taking traditional hymns, music and the Gospel message to people in their own environment. All were oblivious that in the next few minutes, their routine plans would be thrown into utter chaos as they suddenly found themselves catapulted into a kaleidoscope of unimaginable horror and carnage; a catastrophe of such magnitude that by the end of the day would shake and test their faith in the Almighty.

One policeman not taking refreshments in the canteen was motorcycle patrolman Bill Oliver. At 10:05, he was to be found in the police station's central yard preparing his motorbike in readiness to commence his tour of duty. When he arrived at police headquarters earlier that morning, he was expecting nothing more – with it being a Sunday – a relatively easy non-eventful shift. Attired in his protective black leather motorcycle jacket, boots, white crash helmet and matching leather gauntlets he kick-started his machine into life. With a twist of throttle, he gunned the bike up the ramp, turned sharp left into Edward Street coming to an immediate halt at the traffic lights which were against him. As he waited, the unremitting drizzle quickly misted his Perspex visor, with his right gauntlet-gloved hand he casually flipped it up to see the way ahead. The lights changed and he crossed over Middle Hillgate and entered Waterloo Road directly ahead. Cruising down the incline of the deserted road, something in his peripheral vision immediately caught his attention. Glancing up and to the right, he saw an astounding and shocking sight.

Emerging over the corrugated metalled roof of a local factory, like an airborne leviathan, was the unbelievable and terrifying sight of a four-engined airliner with engines throbbing bearing down towards him. Instinctively, he hit the brakes hard and fishtailed to a stop. Sitting astride his machine, he watched transfixed, stunned and unbelieving, yet at the same time fascinated by the unfolding drama. Slowly, almost sedately, the airliner floated over the road, so slow it seemed to hang in the air; its passage casting a dark shadow over the glistening roadway. He experienced time distorting, with seconds feeling like minutes. "It was so close I felt I could reach out and touch it." As he took all this in, the thunderous sound of the pounding engines abruptly ceased, the nose dropped and with a terrible finality plunged towards the ground. Realising that total disaster was imminent, he uttered an exclamation of alarm and horror: "Oh my God… He's coming down!"

Fearing it would crash directly in his path, he gunned the throttle accelerating in a slithering right-hand turn into the mouth of Canal Street. Screeching to a stop, he just had time to glance over his shoulder to catch a fleeting glimpse of the giant tailfin disappearing behind the buildings opposite. Simultaneously came the dreadful murderous sound of impact followed a millisecond later by a screaming cacophony of metal being brutally torn apart; the sickening noise of disintegration seemed to last an eternity. A second later, a cloud of dust and dense black smoke mushroomed up over the roofline. Apart from the crackle of isolated fires here and there, an ominous deathly silence fell over the scene – a silence that could almost be felt.

It was 10:09 British Summer Time.

This dramatic photograph was taken just a few minutes after impact (Philip Dunn/Rex Features.)

In the surrounding streets of family homes confusion reigned, first with a moment of dazed stillness, then, in response to the terrifying crash, curtains twitched, noses pressed against window glass, front doors tentatively opened a few inches, housewives in dressing gowns, their hair in curlers with arms folded cautiously emerged onto their doorsteps. Craning their necks, they looked down the street in fearful astonishment at the bubbling column of thick black smoke spiralling skywards.

Clearing the factory roof by a mere fifty feet, the airliner's first point of impact came when the port wing scythed into the gable end of the brick warehouse, completely severing it at the root and tearing away the forward side of the fuselage ejecting a handful of passengers – some still strapped in their seats. Luggage catapulted from the breeched under floor cargo hold, cart wheeling across the ground, bursting and scattering their contents. The nose then impacted the edge of the embankment sending an explosion of wet earth over the cockpit windows. The airliner reared up a dozen feet before slamming down hard on a long low prefabricated garage, demolishing the centre section and crushing a dozen cars and vans beneath. All around bits of aircraft, bricks, masonry and splintered timbers cascaded in all directions.

A rush of wind howled down the cabin as the fuselage exploded and disintegrated. Hand luggage, holiday souvenirs and a miscellany of loose items thrashed violently around the cabin in a vortex of chaos bombarding the terrified passengers. So extreme had been the downward force of the impact, the cabin floor shattered tearing seats from their attachments which violently concertinaed forward breaking the legs of the passengers as they flailed into the seat structure in front.

The Argonaut airliner exploded some ten minutes after impact ending the lives of those still trapped inside (author's archive).

Sliding forward a few feet, the aircraft came to an abrupt stop when the starboard wing slammed into the back wall of the Hopes Carr electricity sub station, exposing and seriously damaging the transformers which immediately caught fire causing the electricity supply to fail over a large area of the town centre, including the Police Headquarters, which automatically transferred over to emergency generators. The cockpit, apart from a few shards of metal and cables, was all but severed from the fuselage and lay crumpled against the sidewall of the sub station within ten feet of two underground petrol storage tanks, each almost full, threatening even more disastrous consequences. Inside the flight deck, the two unconscious pilots, still strapped to their broken seats, were pinned hard up against the disrupted instrument panel and controls; their crisp white flight shirts stained crimson with blood. The tail section, partially detached from the fuselage, was left projecting precariously over the edge of the ravine. From the first point of impact to the aircraft coming to rest was a mere 75 feet; all this violent destruction, death and injury was concertinaed into just a few seconds. Death came quickly for many of the passengers on board, but at least forty-five survived the terrifying impact – albeit with serious leg and head injuries. They didn't know it then but their ordeal was far from over – the real horrors were soon to come.

Moments before the airliner struck the ground, stewardess Julia Partleton was standing on the pitching floor of the galley struggling to pour a glass of water for a passenger who was feeling unwell. Suddenly, she found herself being tossed violently around the galley partitions and the next instant was hurled through a breech in the cabin wall when the aircraft impacted the ground. Regaining consciousness, she found herself lying on her back in the wet undergrowth in excruciating pain. Trying to make some sort of sense of what had happened, she fully opened her eyes and was shocked to see the leviathan tail fin directly above pointing towards the leaden sky; its fabric covered rudder and elevators fiercely ablaze. On looking down, she was shocked to see her shredded uniform burning and her nylon stockings fused deep into the sticky burnt flesh of her legs. With the pungent odour of aviation fuel and the crackling of fires in the surrounding hawthorn and elder, she made an agonised effort get away from the danger. Rolling on the ground to smother her burning uniform, she began to slip and tumble down the shrub-covered slope of the ravine towards the meandering stream below. On reaching the bottom, despite the severity of her injuries, she managed with a supreme effort to clamber over a six-foot high chain-link fence and attract the attention of a group of factory workers who were now frantically making their way down the opposite embankment to her rescue.

Patrick Finnegan had just unlocked the front door of the premises and was about to step over the threshold when he heard the horrendous heart-stopping sound of the airliner slewing into the ground just yards away – he grabbed the door jam to steady himself as the building shook. His young son, Martin, standing outside witnessed it all. Thunderstruck, ashen-faced and shaking with fear he screamed out: "DAD, THE SKY IS FALLING!"

Teenage brothers, Robert and Chris Hamnett, also had the fright of their young lives when they witnessed the airliner's horrifying fall to earth. Just like any other Sunday morning, they were to be found strolling along Spring Gardens on their way to attend the morning service at St Mary's church in the Market Place. Approaching the junction of Waterloo Road – pushing and shoving each other and generally larking about as youngsters do – their ears pricked up to the thunderous roar of the approaching aircraft which, within seconds, increased to an ear-splitting crescendo. They stopped dead in their tracks and on turning around were astounded to see the stricken airliner emerge over the rooftops on its terminal curving dive to earth. "It was massive." Robert told me… "It thundered right over us. It was so low we instinctively threw ourselves to the ground."

Seconds later, they heard and felt the sickening concussion of impact. Hurriedly getting to their feet, they raced down Waterloo Road abruptly stopping on reaching the wrought iron railings overlooking the ravine. They stared in shocked disbelief. There across on the far embankment was the heart-stopping and surreal sight of the crumpled airliner surrounded by a halo of dust and smoke. Frozen with fear, they stared wide-eyed in a paralysing hypnotic trance, unable to comprehend the enormity of what they were witnessing. Just like P C Bill Oliver, the harrowing experience gave both teenagers a strange feeling of dislocation with reality. Robert continues:

We just stood there rooted to the spot petrified with fear. It was impossible to believe what was there in front of us. Then, as the smell of aviation fuel drifted back towards us, we saw movement in the burning undergrowth just below the tail – it was the stewardess. She was frantically rolling on the ground trying to douse the flames of her burning uniform, then she began to slip and tumble down the slope of the ravine towards the stream below.

In all, we only stayed at the scene for a few minutes, and, strange as it might sound considering the horrifying event we had just witnessed, we continued on our way to church in shock. When we arrived and told people what had just happened, they didn't believe us…no one believed us.

Inside the wrecked fuselage, it was a scene of absolute chaos and carnage. Many of the passengers were stripped of their clothing and were shoeless due the massive forces they endured in the crash. The majority of those still alive and conscious were totally incapacitated with broken and shattered lower limbs preventing them from making any attempt to escape the smouldering wreck under their own steam. They reacted only with stunned silence and bewilderment. A handful with lesser injuries and able bodied enough to help themselves did nothing. They sat slumped and motionless in the remains of their disrupted seats staring blankly ahead too traumatised to cry out for help.

It is a misconception, held by many, that in an air crash people panic and pandemonium ensues – this is one of the biggest myths. We are all accustomed to seeing this sort of panic and chaos in disaster films but that kind of fear and hysteria almost never happens in reality. Surprisingly, the opposite is true, most people do nothing, they sit around waiting for instructions and help to arrive. The majority of air crash victims are likely to respond in this way with what is called negative panic.

A typical example of negative panic occurred in 1961. A Viscount touched down at Boston Logan airport and during the landing roll out, completely severed the tail off a Douglas DC-6 attempting to take off without clearance from another runway. The Viscount's fuel tanks were ruptured in the collision; fuel began to flow freely, fire was imminent and the DC-6 on losing its tail tipped on its nose.

The automatic air-stairs of the Viscount deployed normally. The stewardess begged and screamed at the passengers to evacuate the aircraft, she fought with them, tried to physically to drag them from their seats, but nobody was ready or willing to leave the aircraft. A man struggled to find his hand luggage first. A number of women complained to her that it was far too cold outside to be made to leave without their coats. A man stopped at the bottom of the stairs and, standing in the middle of a growing pool of aviation fuel, wanted to light a cigarette to settle his nerves before he would move on.

Similar scenes were going on in the meantime aboard the DC-6. The stewardess was crying in her helplessness knowing that all hell may break out at any moment. But people were just slow to react. An overweight women got herself trapped in the doorway when she resisted a four-foot jump from the rear of the aircraft. The stewardess had to kick her hard behind the knees to make her sit down and then people below pulled the women out by force.

When fire breaks out, some people become even more inert. After a Northeast Airlines DC-6 crash-landed at Rikers Island, New York in 1957 shortly after taking off from La Guardia Airport, fire immediately broke out. It spread slowly and there was little damage to the fuselage that passengers could evacuate without difficulty, yet, out of 102 people on board, twenty died from burning and asphyxia. Rescuers were on the scene within minutes and found several had died still strapped in their seats. Others sat idly by waiting for help to arrive as the toxic gases of combustion filled the cabin without making any attempt to break open the clearly marked escape hatches.

Inside the shattered cabin of the Argonaut, fifty-year-old Albert Owen from Eastham on the Wirral, who miraculously came through the ordeal without serious injury, was one of those suffering from negative panic. For a minute, he sat inert in the remains of his seat staring blankly ahead at the thousands of dust motes swirling in the light streaming in through the breach in the cabin wall. Dazed and shocked, he listened intently to the groans and creaks of the settling wreckage as his eyes darted around the dark interior trying to comprehend the distressing scene around him. Then, a painful question struck him: 'Eva... Eva, where is she?' He frantically called out for his wife, who just moments before was seated beside him – she and her seat were nowhere to be seen in the chaos. Anxious seconds passed as he listened intently for a response, but none came. He didn't know it then, but she was already dead, killed instantly by a ruptured heart on impact; her body now lay hidden under a pile of injured and dead passengers.

When tendrils of silver-grey smoke began snaking down the cabin, his heart raced as he tried to decide what to do next. With trembling hands, he eventually found the strength to unfasten his seat belt, flinging it aside he felt his legs – to see if they were still there – then forced his aching and bruised body free from the twisted remains of his seat. Groping around, trying to establish his surroundings, he breathlessly began to make his torturous way forward over a sea of clutter and humanity towards the light.

On finally reaching the front of the cabin, he poked his blooded head through the jagged rent and momentarily froze on seeing the ghastly panorama of devastation all around; bodies, parts of bodies, seats, burst suitcases and splintered timbers amidst a sea of rubble. Swinging his legs out of the fuselage, he dropped feet first onto the demolished remains of the garage below. Swaying slightly, he inhaled deeply the dusty air taking a moment to regain his equilibrium. Uncertain what to do next, he looked around the desolate scene and became aware of vague shadowy figures and distant voices in the haze of dust and smoke. He staggered towards them seeking help.

After witnessing the horrors of the crash, Bill Oliver, realising the true gravity of the situation, had the presence of mind to radio the nearby police headquarters to sound the alert. He then gunned his machine across Waterloo Road into Hopes Carr coming to a screeching halt alongside the blazing sub station. Dismounting, he was transfixed by the horrific spectacle of total devastation. A chill shiver ran down his back as he realised that this was a disaster of massive proportions, the enormity of which was barely forming in his mind. The destruction and carnage before him were beyond his comprehension. There was an eerie, all pervading stillness around the scene, broken only by the hiss and metallic clicking of the battered engines rapidly cooling on the sodden ground.

Through the dissipating dust cloud, he saw the crumpled cockpit lying on the forecourt pointing straight at him like some Roswellian spacecraft from another world. Then in an instant, his attention switched to the passenger cabin immediately behind, and saw to his horror through the gaping hole at least twenty badly injured passengers, slumped in their seats staring at him with fearful imploring eyes. He then became aware of movement. Emerging out of the dust cloud, he saw the blooded and dishevelled figure of survivor Albert Owen staggering mechanically like a puppet towards him.

Chapter Two

Rescue

"Men of retiring timidity are cowardly only in dangers which affect themselves, but the first to the rescue when others are in danger."

Jean Paul Richer

Ernie Taylor lived with his wife, Kath, at number 19 Upper Brook Street, a pleasant, red brick Victorian terrace house in a quiet residential street that branched off Waterloo Road. What should have been a quiet and relaxing Sunday morning for the couple, suddenly without warning, changed to one of terrible enormity. Ernie describes how the shocking events unfolded:

I had not long been up and was in the back kitchen making some toast and coffee, when I heard this tremendous roar approaching – it was like nothing I had ever heard before. At first, I thought it was a heavy lorry or petrol tanker travelling out of control down Waterloo Road which runs past the end of the street. Out of curiosity, I opened the kitchen's back door, poked my head out and was met by the sound of rolling thunder that shook the house rattling the doors and windows. My immediate thought was: *Has that petrol tanker crashed through the railings on Waterloo Road, plunged into the ravine and exploded?*

Dressed in just a flimsy T-shirt, jeans and slippers, he immediately abandoned his breakfast preparations and raced down the passageway that ran along the rear of the terrace. Breathlessly, he emerged onto Waterloo Road to be confronted with a scene of appalling devastation. Ernie continues:

There was thick, black smoke rising from the far embankment. It was only when I crossed the road and the smoke momentarily parted that I saw the surreal image of a gigantic aeroplane tail fin projecting over the edge of the ravine. I realised then, of course, that this was no petrol tanker that had crashed; the unimaginable had happened – it was an airliner full of people!

There were small fires attacking the half-demolished gable end of the warehouse building where the wing had appeared to have struck. From my position, standing alongside the railings overlooking the ravine, there was no direct way for me to reach the aircraft, so I sprinted along Waterloo Road past the burning building, turned sharp right into Hopes Carr and immediately came upon what I can only describe as a shocking panorama of chaos and destruction.

The centre section of the garage building had completely collapsed with the main body of the aircraft lying on top of crushed cars and vans. I saw that the cockpit had broken away somewhat from the fuselage and was resting against the side of the partly demolished sub station and the whole area around was strewn with rubble and debris.

When I first arrived on the scene, I distinctly remember looking around and there wasn't a soul about, then out of nowhere, motorcycle patrolman Bill Oliver roared up behind me and skidded to a halt. Almost immediately, local people, who like me, had heard the crash suddenly appeared, quickly followed by a handful of breathless police officers who had raced down from the nearby police station. Apart from the crackle of small fires here and there and the creaking of metal, it was strangely quiet and still.

Meanwhile, at police headquarters, John Heath, a 23-year-old constable attached to the Stockport Police Traffic Department, had just come on duty and was detailed that morning to act as observer on one of the force's Zephyr patrol cars. When he left home that morning, he was expecting nothing more than a quiet routine shift. What he was about to experience would have far-reaching and life-changing consequences. Forty-years after the event, he told me how that quiet Sunday morning quickly turned into a hideous nightmare.

I came on duty at ten o'clock and was in the station yard fuelling the car prior to going out on patrol. As I was refuelling the vehicle and my partner was completing the petrol allocation book, we heard the noise of a tremendous crash nearby. We both instinctively knew something was seriously amiss. With no time for deliberation, we jumped into the patrol car and sped off up the station ramp, turned sharp left into Edward Street and sped through the traffic lights on Middle Hillgate.

As we entered Waterloo Road, a young man, clearly distressed, came running along the pavement towards us waving his arms above his head. He stopped by my open window and breathlessly blurted out that a motor coach had blown up on the garage forecourt just around the corner. We continued the short distance and on turning left into Hopes Carr, we were shocked to be confronted with the appalling scene of an air crash but, even then, I did not fully comprehend the true enormity of the incident.

There was a considerable amount of smoke and dust around the immediate area and, standing beside his motorcycle, I saw my colleague, Bill Oliver, and half a dozen civilians milling about. We dived out of the car and ran over to Bill who was desperately trying to maintain radio contact with the control room. My driver, who was also failing to get a radio signal, immediately volunteered to drive the short distance back to headquarters to report the incident in more detail.

John Heath stood and stared open-mouthed at the incredulous sight of the crumpled remains of the downed airliner with no more apparent comprehension than the rest of those standing around – it was a maelstrom of unimaginable horror. He shook his head in helpless perplexity, then turned and looked at Bill Oliver as if to say: 'What the hell has happened here?'

Although shaken and appalled by the tableaux of devastation before them, the two officers and had no illusions about the seriousness of the situation. Ashen-faced, they exchanged stricken looks but on realising there were scores of trapped and injured passengers in desperate need of help, their training and discipline took control. Neither said a word, and neither doubted what to do next. Tentatively, they edged forward crunching over a welter of rubble towards the wreck. With shredded and sparking electrical cables and flames emanating from the damaged sub station along with the overpowering stench of volatile aviation fuel, they knew that a serious fire and explosion was imminent; every second mattered if they were to save lives. John Heath continues:

As Bill and I approached the wreckage, a man in his fifties, visibly shocked, staggered towards us from the direction of the aircraft; his clothing was torn and blood flowed freely from a vicious head wound. Bill, fearing the aircraft could explode at any moment, showed his authority and bellowed at him in no uncertain terms to get clear; he stumbled past us and was helped away by local shopkeeper Brian Donohoe.

It was only on entering the cabin that the true scale of the disaster became clear – it was a scene of indescribable horror. I vividly recall the almost overpowering heady scent of perfume and aviation fuel, which, with other smells, created a distinct peculiar odour. Nearly all the seats had broken away from the floor anchorages and had shot forward in a confused heap piling passengers on top of each other, many of the dead hiding survivors underneath. The majority of those still conscious were very distressed, screaming and pleading to be rescued, whilst a few others appeared relatively calm – one man politely asked me to help him get his seat belt off.

An unidentified female passenger dragged from the wreckage with devastating leg injuries. Behind, standing on the cockpit roof PC John Heath reaches out for a fireman's axe to hack his way into the flight deck to rescue the trapped pilots (Philip Dunn/Rex Features).

Bill and I quickly set about to try and extricate those who showed signs of life. Sometimes we worked together, sometimes separately, freeing the survivors and handing them down and out of the fuselage to willing civilian helpers – at this point, we were on our own, as none of the emergency services had yet arrived on the scene. I had never been in an aeroplane before and certainly had no training in air crash drill. I remember both Bill and I experienced great difficulty in releasing the seat belt catches which seemed to have jammed. Another difficulty was that many of the casualties were hopelessly trapped by their legs in the broken and twisted frames of the seats in front.

Bill Oliver, in his statement of events typed up the following day, reported:

When I entered the cabin, it was deathly quiet. All the passengers appeared to be still strapped into their seats which had broken away from the floor and violently concertinaed forward in a confused heap at the front end of the fuselage. There did not appear to be any gangway between the seats but were roughly in disrupted rows all across the cabin floor. In the chaos of the cabin interior, I immediately saw that some of the passengers were alive, many with broken legs, lacerated faces and other serious injuries. On the right-hand side of the cabin near the front, I noticed a blond-haired girl

26

had started to move and was screaming out for our help. With colleague John Heath, we forced our way through the chaotic clutter to get her out.

The girl was 20-year-old dental nurse Vivienne Thornber from the Lancashire mill town of Nelson. With her blond hair almost bleached white from ten days in the scorching Spanish sun, she easily stood out amongst the confusion of passengers and seats. Although seriously injured, she was very much alive. The urgency of her screams brought an immediate response from the two policemen. She told me:

I came round soon after the impact and when clear thinking became possible again, I became aware of the cockpit door swinging on its hinges and flames creeping towards me. I thought: *Come on Vivienne, do something, or else you're going to be burnt alive here.* I knew then I had to get out of there and made a huge effort to scream – or tried to. I thought to myself there's nothing coming out – like in a dream when you try so hard to make a noise and nothing comes. Bill Oliver told me later that it was because I made such a hell of a commotion shrieking that he made his way to me first. My next recollection was hearing a voice close by – who I now know was John Heath – shouting, "Oh my god Bill, watch her legs." Then someone was on my right-hand side with their hands under my arms trying to pull me out and I screamed in agony because my legs were trapped in the metalwork of the seat in front.

Bill Oliver leaned over and saw horrific fractures to her left leg which was twisted back on itself quite out of position. Sensing her excruciating pain, he put a hand on her shoulder and whispered encouragingly, "Don't worry, we'll soon have you out." With considerable pain to herself, they gently as they could disentangled her legs from the distorted metal. She was then was unceremoniously half dragged, half carried out of the wreck across the debris field and bungled into the back of a waiting police car which immediately roared off in the direction of the nearby infirmary with sirens screaming. Vivienne continues:

My next memory is coming round to find myself on a trolley in hospital where doctors and nurses were cutting away my clothing. I don't know why but I said to someone standing close by, "You do know I'm Rhesus negative blood group, don't you?" I then must have passed out again because when I regained consciousness, sometime later I found myself lying in a hospital bed asking for my mum. On fully opening my eyes, I saw a lovely lady from the Salvation Army sitting beside me holding my hand. She leaned over and quietly said, "Look, I'm not your mum but I'm here for you," and she never moved until my uncle Melvin turned up and he sat with me until Mum and Dad arrived from the airport.

Vivienne's holiday companion, Susan Howarth, suffered retrograde amnesia in the crash – a not unusual occurrence in shocking and violent situations – leaving her unable to clearly recall events. She told me her hazy recollections of the final part of the flight: "I really don't remember very much, but I do clearly recall the Fasten Your Seat Belts sign coming on and the aircraft turning onto the approach. Soon after the pilot banked to the right and flew away from the airport, which I thought was very strange, as we were given no information that anything was wrong. A few minutes later, I remember leaning over Vivienne and looking out of the cabin window to see what was happening and was astonished to see how close we were to the ground; we seemed to be surrounded by tower blocks, factories and houses. I have absolutely no memory of crashing, only a vague recollection of being dragged from the wreckage and put down on the ground. Lying there, I could hear the crackle of fire, smelling smoke and hearing people rushing about. Thankfully, that's about all I remember until waking up later in a hospital bed next to Vivienne."

After pulling the two girls to safety, Bill Oliver and John Heath scrambled back into the smouldering cabin to effect further rescues before a serious fire took hold. Bill Oliver said: "The operation of removing people from the wreckage was made more difficult by their broken lower limbs being trapped under their own seats and the seat frames in front. I remember, at one point in the rescue operation, carrying a small boy in my arms who I think was dead. Throughout this time, I did not consciously remember going away from the plane, but passed survivors as they were freed to others who took them away behind me; it was about this time that other police officers and civilians arrived in considerable numbers to assist."

Struggling in the confines of cabin searching for further survivors, John Heath came upon 42-year-old Mary Green sprawled in her collapsed seat beside her holiday companion Linda Parry. Both women were best friends and seasoned flyers and had flown abroad on holidays together many times before. Both worked as administrative clerks at the Lancashire Fire Brigade Headquarters in Preston – which, ironically, was one of the brigades later called out to assist the Stockport and Manchester services. Mary Green describes the final moments leading up the crash and the immediate aftermath:

As we were passing over Stockport, I glanced out of the window to my right and was staggered to see a giant gas cylinder and cooling tower in the town centre sail by at our level – we were that low! I suddenly had an overwhelming feeling of foreboding and instinctively knew we were not going to make it. All of a sudden, the aircraft began to pitch and vibrate and then I was aware we were diving towards the ground. Panic seized me and I gripped the arms rests in fear. Then came the dreadful noise as we smashed into the ground. I could see seats and passengers being flung forward and debris flying everywhere – then darkness closed in and I fell unconscious.

I came round a few minutes later feeling a bit woozy with my ears ringing and became conscious that we had come to a stop. On opening my eyes, I saw my friend, Linda, sprawled on the floor beside me. She looked up and said quite calmly: "Mary, you're burning, unfasten your lap strap." I looked down and was horrified to see my upper clothing was on fire. I thought, *I'm going to be burnt alive here because I couldn't use either arm to release my seat belt.* Then, seemingly out of nowhere, a policeman was leaning over me; he released my belt, dragged me from my seat and carried me out of the aircraft stepping over bodies as he went. I remember little else after that point other than a vague memory of being put into the back of a police car.

Linda Parry, speaking to a reporter from her hospital bed the following day, said:

Both Mary and I had seen the airport runway lights at one point and for some inexplicable reason, we turned away. As the minutes passed by, I became a little concerned that we were a long time getting back to the airport when all of a sudden, the aircraft began to shudder and rock from side to side. I stretched over Mary to look out of the cabin window to see what was going on and was staggered to see the rooftops rushing past just a few feet below us. Then, without warning, we lurched sharply to the right and felt my stomach leap as we plunged towards the ground. I closed my eyes and reached out and gripped the seat in front to brace myself. I thought, *We're going to crash.* Everything happened so fast I didn't have time to panic. Then there was a sickening bang as the left wing struck a building and I had the sensation of being hurled out of my seat.

I regained consciousness a moment later to find myself lying spread-eagled on the floor and seeing Mary slumped in her crumpled seat with her clothes on fire. On looking around, I saw a jumble of seats and passengers and the front left-hand side of the cabin ripped wide open and beyond that open air. At which point I must have passed out because my next memory was waking up in the hospital ward and, even then, not fully realising what had happened.

Bill Oliver's frantic radio alert to police headquarters was received at first with disbelieving consternation. When it became clear that they had a major disaster on their hands, the quiet Sunday morning routine in the station suddenly burst into life. Fortuitously, a shift change was just taking place so there was no shortage of manpower to assist. Within seconds, scores of police officers poured down the station steps and sprinted with frantic urgency down the labyrinth of narrow side streets towards the billowing pall of black smoke. By coincidence, a high-level meeting between senior police officers had just got underway in the building, including the Chief Constable, Leonard Massey and his deputy Tom Walker. On being alerted to the news, Massey immediately abandoned the meeting and took overall charge of the unfolding drama.

Local baker, Brian Donohoe, a hardworking, unpretentious, down to earth family man was a well-known and popular figure in the local community. That morning, like any other Sunday morning, he was sitting at the kitchen table above his shop on Middle Hillgate having a leisurely breakfast with his wife Florence and their 11-year-old daughter, Margaret. Engrossed in reading an account in the newspaper about the Air Ferry DC-4 crash in the Pyrenees the previous evening, he gave scant attention to the distant heavy drone of an approaching aircraft. His bakery was located directly under the busy approach path for the airport, so he was more than accustomed to the sound of airliners passing over; it was just a familiar background noise that over the years he hardly noticed. But on this occasion, instead of noise receding, it increased alarmingly. He had just drawn the last sip of his tea when the sound of the roaring engines abruptly ceased, followed seconds later by the heart stopping sound of the concussive thump of impact that rattled the casement windows. He banged his cup down, threw the newspaper aside, shot to his feet and peered through the rain flecked kitchen window.

I looked out in the direction of Hopes Carr and saw a cloud of black smoke billowing above the rooftops. My immediate thought was that the electricity sub station or garage down there had blown up. I shot downstairs, dashed out into the back yard and on opening the gate saw half-a-dozen Bobbies I knew sprinting down the alleyway. I shouted after them: "What's up lads…what's happened?" One of them turned and yelled back over his shoulder: "THERE'S BEEN A PLANE CRASH BRIAN… DOWN IN HOPES CARR!" I could hardly believe his words.

I was already dressed and wearing slippers so I raced down after them. When I got to the bottom, I saw this chap in a blue pin stripe suit covered in dust with a camera dangling around his neck staggering across the road. He was very shocked and incoherent with blood pouring from a gash on the side of his head. He appeared to have survived the impact and had crawled out of the wreckage unaided. We later found out that his name was Albert Owen from the Wirral and that his wife had died in the crash. In his confusion, he kept wandering away. One of the policemen shouted over: "Grab him, Brian…bring him back." I went after him, grasped him by the arm and led him back to the garage forecourt. All the time, he was tugging at my shirt, his voice choked with sobs asking: "My wife, my wife…where's my wife?" He kept pulling away from me, so for his own safety and to free me up, I tethered him to a petrol pump with his camera strap – which I suppose looking back was not the best idea at the time.

The first thing I saw on looking around was the badly crushed nose of the airliner tilted at an angle against the burning sub station. Looking through the crazed windows, I could make out the white-shirted pilots slumped forward up against the smashed instrument panel. The one thing I always remember about that sight was the reams and reams of electrical wiring, cables and instruments spilling out of the cockpit onto the garage forecourt. Then just behind the nose, I saw the passenger cabin split wide-open and inside a jumble of blooded passengers slumped in their seats.

Brian had no real-life experience or training to prepare him for a disaster of this magnitude, but felt he couldn't just stand aside and do nothing. With an overwhelming burden of self-imposed responsibility, he sprinted into action. Scrambling over the demolished remains of the garage, he hauled himself through the gaping hole in the side of the cabin. Pushing past Bill Oliver and John Heath, he made his way inch by tortuous inch through a confusion of disrupted seats and bodies searching for anyone who showed signs of life. He stopped momentarily and stared at an arc of blood splatter on the cabin wall, then close by he came upon 15-year-old local schoolgirl Fiona Child hanging upside down in her upturned seat. With great difficulty, he released her seat belt and disentangled her legs from the wreckage and scooping her up in his arms, he stumbled out of the wreckage all the time reassuring her that she was going to be all right. Emerging from the jagged rent into the light, he carried her over the rubble-strewn forecourt and carefully put her in the back of a waiting police car.

Like the majority of the passengers on board, it was Fiona's first flight, and ironically, the crash site was barely two miles from her home in Bramhall. She had gone on the holiday to Majorca with her school friend, Christine Benton, and her parents. Sadly, Fiona was the only survivor of the party of four. Her mother, who was employed as a records clerk at the infirmary where all the survivors were taken, was at that very moment waiting to meet her at the airport.'

An aerial view of the crash site (author's archive).

Fiona's recollections of the crash are obscure and fragmented at best. From her hospital bed, she told a friend the little she could remember. "I was sleeping during the final part of the flight and woke up just minutes before we crashed. I remember looking out of the cabin window and realised we were flying very low over the town. We were given no warning by the pilots that anything was wrong – it just happened. The plane started to shudder and we were thrown around the cabin. My next recollection was coming round and finding myself hanging upside down suspended by my seatbelt and seeing flames." She remembers nothing more until being wheeled into the infirmary where she regained consciousness just long enough to whisper her name to a hospital porter and tell him her parents were waiting for her at the airport and to let them know she was all right. Her injuries, none of them serious in themselves, were enough to keep her in hospital for a month and under specialist care for many months more.

Seated two rows behind Vivienne and Susan were schoolboys, 15-year-old Harold Wood and his 13-year-old brother Billy. They had gone on the ten-day holiday to Majorca with their father, William. Their mother Gill had no choice but to stay at home to run the family pub – split holidays were pretty much the norm for licensee couples in those days. Harold told me about the final part of the flight:

The flight home was pretty much uneventful until the usual landing procedure began. On the approach to the airport, I vividly recall a strong smell of perfume wafting down the cabin, then suddenly, we were banking quite steeply to the right. I thought at this point, *We aren't going to make this*, then the perfume got me again and feeling a little bit nauseous, I reached for the sick bag. From this point, I can't remember a thing about the crash other than waking up in the chaos and darkness of the wrecked cabin. It took me a few confused seconds to realise that we had actually crashed. Apart from being shocked and disorientated with some minor cuts and bruises, I was otherwise OK.

On seeing smoke and flames, I felt a sudden rush of fear and the instinct for survival kicked in. My immediate thought was to get out of the aircraft, so I unbuckled my seat belt and pushed aside a pile of debris that had rained down on impact and struggled to my feet. Somehow, I had lost my shoes in the crash and I don't know why but I started to look for them. Then I made my way around the back of my seat and leaned over Billy to release his seat belt but I couldn't pull him clear because his legs were pinned by the seats in front which had come back on him. Seeing flames and smoke seeping into the cabin, I knew I had to get out of there and get help for my brother.

Unseeing Harold stumbled instinctively towards the light streaming in from the gash in the side of the fuselage and emerged into daylight. "I saw a policeman picking his way over the rubble towards the aircraft and on seeing me he shouted: 'Are you all right lad?' I yelled back: 'MY BROTHER'S IN THERE, GET HIM OUT.'"

"Then I must have passed out, because my next memory is coming round in the front passenger seat of a police car. Lying across the back seat was Fiona Child who was sitting behind us in the aircraft; to me she looked in a bad way. The next time I saw Billy, he was on a trolley in the casualty department. He was badly knocked about with lacerations to his head and legs and was bleeding a lot. There was no sign of Dad who was seated at the front of the aircraft. It was over a week before we were told that he had been killed – but to be honest, I think we already knew."

Outside the Salvation Army Citadel on Middle Hillgate, the twenty strong brass band were tuning up in readiness to set off when they were alerted to the crash. Bandsman and Corps secretary, Arthur Thorniley, told me how they reacted on being alerted to the shocking news:

We were just about to march off, to go and play at an open-air bandstand, which we did almost every Sunday. Because of the wet weather, we decided at the last minute to go and play at one of the old-folks' homes in the area. Then, just as we were about to move off, a terrified white-face youngster came chasing round the corner of Waterloo Road towards us, waving his arms above his head. He stopped at the front door of our building and breathlessly blurted out: "MISTER, THERE'S A PLANE CRASHED DOWN IN WATERLOO!"

Those were his exact words, and we could hardly believe it, because we hadn't heard a sound of a crash or anything of that nature even though we were only a few hundred yards from the scene. Our bandsmen immediately downed their instruments and we dashed around the corner to see what assistance we could offer.

On turning into Waterloo Road, I saw an incredulous sight, it was a scene I can only describe as utter desolation and chaos. I saw what I thought was the main body of the airliner settled down on the rubble of the collapsed garage and the wing tipped up. There was smoke and dust all around the scene and the air was thick with the stench of aviation fuel. The only police officer I saw was Bill Oliver with a few local residents; they must have been on the scene within seconds of the plane coming down. Within what I would think was about ten minutes, all sorts of emergency services began to arrive; the fire brigade, ambulances and the police in force. Ten or twelve of our bandsmen waded in helping to do what they could to rescue people from the wrecked plane.

Ernie Taylor, like everyone else involved in the frantic rescue attempts, never gave a thought to the possible dangers. With his head swimming and heart pounding, he followed close behind Bill Oliver and John Heath over a melee of crumbled masonry and debris and hauled himself up into the cabin. Inside, his eyes darted around the dark interior taking in an unrecognisable heap of passengers, seats and debris. The dreadful sight of injury that met his eyes was gruesome and unnerving, but he did his utmost to stay focused and in control. Ernie recalls:

Inside, it looked as if a bomb had exploded. All the seats had broken away from the floor and been thrown forward along with the passengers. We spent a short time just looking around thinking how the hell are we were going to extricate all those who were still alive. We couldn't just pull them clear because the majority were still strapped in with their broken legs trapped in the twisted seat frames.

The only people who seemed to be alive and moving were on the front right-hand side of the cabin. With Bill Oliver, I pulled out a young fair-haired girl about the same age as me – perhaps 23 – she was conscious and was pleading with us to help her. She was in a terrible state, all her upper clothing had been ripped away in the crash so she was quite exposed. With some difficulty, we managed to release her seat belt, disentangle her legs and pull her clear. Bill picked her up under the arms and I took her by the legs. As we manhandled out of the wreckage, I felt something warm and wet oozing down my side. I glanced down and was shocked to see her foot had been severed and blood was pumping freely from her leg. We laid her down carefully on the garage forecourt next to a petrol pump. Bill then stood up, turned to me and said: "She's gone." She had died in that short time from picking her up and carrying her out of the wreckage.

With no time to dwell on the shock, we scrambled back into the aircraft with a number of civilians and police officers, who had now appeared, to try and get more survivors out. As more rescuers piled into the cabin, the space inside seemed to shrink and we were all working shoulder to shoulder.

Stockport resident, Ron Needham, chanced upon the scene within minutes of impact and was to witness the first dramatic rescue attempts before the aircraft exploded and the fire took hold. However, it took him some time to comprehend the true reality of what was happening.

On that Sunday morning, I had taken my seven-year-old daughter to an early swimming session at Stockport baths. I was driving home down Middle Hillgate when I saw a column of thick, black smoke rising from the rear of, what was then, Shaw's furniture shop on Middle Hillgate. Naturally curious as to what had happened, I turned into the car park in front of the police station. Outside, I noticed a policeman and policewoman frenziedly throwing bandages and dressings into the boot of a patrol car, which then sped off towards the traffic lights at the junction of Middle Hillgate and Waterloo Road.

Leaving the car, I crossed over Hillgate, hand-in-hand with my daughter and made my way down a narrow passageway between the rows of shops which brought us out onto some high banking directly overlooking Hopes Carr. On looking down, I saw the electricity substation was partly demolished and burning fiercely. My attention was then drawn to the left of the building from where two men suddenly appeared struggling through the undergrowth carrying a man by his arms and legs. My first impression was that he was dead. I had of course no idea at this point that an airliner had crashed. I thought the poor devil must have been involved in a workshop accident, but I did think it odd that he was casually and smartly dressed – I vividly remember he was wearing a light blue sweater. As I was taking all this in, another man came into view carrying a small child in front of him, his arms around his waist with the child doubled forward, again there was no sign of life. Again, I thought it strange that a child should be in the building.

I walked further along the banking in the direction of Waterloo Road to where two men were standing – there was hardly anyone about at this time. They told me that a plane had crashed, but on looking down at this point, there was little to be seen apart from the burning sub station and a considerable amount of black smoke. I assumed it was a light aircraft that had come down. The shock came as I continued to walk further along the banking when the astonishing sight of a large airliner lying on the ground suddenly confronted me. My abiding memory is of an endless row of cabin windows on a pristine clean fuselage. There was a surreal stillness around it. As I stood and watched, two muffled explosions came from inside the front section of the fuselage; apart from some smoke, there was little sign of fire.

I could not have reached the aircraft from where I was standing and, having my young daughter with me and the fire being imminent, I hurriedly returned to my car and headed for home. If I had left any later, I would have had great difficulty getting away due to the large amount of traffic that quickly poured into the area.

That sight has haunted me over the years, but I find it almost impossible to equate what I witnessed to what the scene must have been like during and after the fire. It was only later that I heard of the exploits of one of the rescuers – PC Bill Oliver. I went to school with Billy – as we all knew him – and I remember that as a lad, he was up for 'up for anything', so it came as no surprise to read of his bravery that day. Billy of course was not the only one, but he was the one I personally knew.

Chapter Three
Faces at the Windows

"What I will never forget was the agony on the faces of the passengers who screamed at us from behind the cabin windows."

Anonymous Stockport Police Officer

Having caught his breath from his exertions, Brian Donohoe, in an adrenaline-fuelled rush, braved the dangers of explosions and fire and re-entered the smouldering wreck in a determined search for anyone who was too badly injured and disorientated to help themselves.

I came across an unconscious woman still strapped in her seat; both her ankles were dreadfully shattered and deeply embedded in the metal framework of the seat in front. I eventually managed to free them, release her seat belt and then began to drag her towards the break in the cabin wall. She was a large heavy woman and I was really struggling to manoeuvre her around and over the mass of seats and bodies. Eventually, I managed to prop her across the remains of two seats near the breach in the cabin wall. I climbed out of the wreckage and was just about to pull her clear when Charlie Holt, one of the local policemen I knew, began tugging at my shirttails demanding that I get out. He screamed: "Brian, for Christ's sake get the fuck out, it's going to blow up." I looked out of a window on the far side of the cabin and saw small explosions coming along the starboard wing – BANG… BANG… BANG. Charlie, who saw the aircraft was now being engulfed in flames, pulled me so hard that I lost my grip on the woman and both Charlie and I fell to the ground hugging each other.

Lying on his back gasping at the fresh air with his adrenaline pumping, his urge to save the woman was overwhelming and he was determined not to give up without a fight; to do nothing went against all his instincts. His inborn stubbornness gave him the strength to make another attempt to pull her clear – she was tantalisingly close. Charged with urgency, he refocused.

I immediately got to my feet and was about to climb back in to pull the woman out but, before I could reach her, Charlie grabbed me, pulled me back and punched me hard on the nose to stop me. It was as well he did because there was a massive explosion which violently shook the cabin showering everyone around with shards of metal, glass and burning debris. As the fire rapidly engulfed the cabin, I caught a glimpse through the cabin window, and in the flickering glow of the flames, I saw the woman was beginning to revive, her eyes filled with terror, but there was nothing I could do; within seconds, she disappeared from view behind the flames. I knew then she was beyond my help.

John Heath, still frantically struggling to extricate further survivors, recalled the final moments before the aircraft exploded and burst into flames:

As I continued to work away trying to free the hopelessly trapped passengers, there were a number of small explosions coming from underneath the cabin floor and I could feel the heat increasing. Suddenly, there was a flash of orange flame followed by a tremendous blast which shook the whole fuselage almost knocking me off my feet. Flames suddenly began to appear in the cabin setting fire to the overhead storage racks and roof panels. Bill Oliver bellowed: "OUT, OUT, OUT… EVERYONE GET OUT." Bill and I half jumped, half scrambled out of the fuselage with the others. Once outside, I looked back and saw the cabin was now fiercely ablaze. I could hear the muffled screams of the passengers above the roar of the inferno. Somewhere deep in the darkness, a voice screamed out in agonised panic: "FIRE!" Another voice pleaded: "PLEASE HELP ME I'M BURNING!" Others, as if prompted, joined in a beseeching chorus, all screaming for us to help them; it was heart-breaking to hear. I estimate that we were only in the aircraft for no more than five minutes before the fire drove us out.

When the fire took hold, there was a lot of screaming and panic as the remainder of the passengers despaired of escape or rescue and faced the impending horrors that were beyond speech. Confronted with an unyielding reality that they were soon going to die horribly, their screams of terror rose in intensity as the flames surged down the cabin like some grotesque monster hell bent on death. Everyone standing around the scene could plainly hear their horrendous cries as they were horridly consumed. At this point, many of the survivors must have given up the struggle for self-preservation and accepted the inevitable – their final thoughts no doubt filled with absolute terror.

During his frantic rescue efforts, Ernie Taylor was unaware that he had lost his slippers and his feet were now lacerated and bleeding profusely from the broken seat mountings that protruded upwards like daggers from the shattered floor. Like the others, he too found the situation inside the fuselage was becoming desperate and impossible to tolerate. Ernie explains:

There was no fire at all in the cabin when we first went in, it was only as the minutes progressed that it got too hot. Two explosions close together came from below the aircraft from the detonation of the fuel tanks of the crushed vehicles in the demolished remains of the garage below. Then without warning, there was one almighty explosion which literately bounced and shook the cabin. That really put the frighteners on me, all I wanted to do then was to get the hell out of there and go home to Kath. Jets of flame were now shooting up through the floor and snaking up to the top of the cabin setting the overhead panelling and luggage racks alight from which globules of molten material dripped down on us. Everyone had to manoeuvre around these to try and get to the survivors. It was now getting really scary in there, the build-up of heat was breath-taking and the smoke and fumes worsened by the second. There was an atmosphere of panic and hysteria amongst those passengers still trapped in the rear of the cabin. Then came sounds: Groans, coughs, the crackle of fire and the tortured screams of passengers pleading with us: "I'M HERE… I'M HERE, PLEASE HELP ME" – first one voice then another, then more.

I clearly remember the last person we tried to get out, who I now know was David Ralphs. He was in absolute agony because the whole of his seat was ablaze and he was screaming and swearing at us to get him out. I grabbed hold of his hand and literally tried to physically pull him out of his seat with brute force. Bill Oliver was behind me pulling on my arm and a group of others behind him – all pulling together like a human chain but try as I might, I just couldn't pull him free, and because of the vicious heat I couldn't get close enough to release his seat belt. The heat was now searing and I too was burning. Half my hair had already burnt away and my arms were red raw where the skin had blistered and peeled away. I was also choking and struggling to breathe because of the thick, black, acrid smoke that was now rapidly filling the cabin. I knew then it was time to get out otherwise it was life or death for us as well. All the time I was in there, I was thinking of Kath at home who was pregnant with our first child. In the end, I had no choice but to let go of David's hand and scramble out of the aircraft before I succumbed. I just couldn't stay in there any longer wearing nothing more for protection but a T-shirt and jeans. I am almost certain that it was Bill Oliver, protected somewhat by his motorcycle gear, who went in behind me, released David's seat belt and dragged him clear with just seconds to spare.

As I scrambled out of the cabin, I shot a glance down the length of the cabin and for a split second, I glimpsed dozens of terrified faces surrounded by flames staring at me. I literately fell out of the blazing wreck and stood on the forecourt doubled up retching and choking; my lungs labouring as I gasped at the air. There was nothing more I could do but watch the raging inferno destroy the aircraft and hear the haunting agonised screams of terror from the passengers being burnt alive in their seats. Then the screaming chorus of death was drowned out by the deafening howl of the flames, quickly followed by the horrific stomach-wrenching stench of burning flesh. It was a smell that will stay with me for the rest of my life.

Everywhere around the blazing wreck, pandemonium ensued with people frantically running about in all directions trying to find another way in; but it was impossible. It was then that I saw a young man in the crowd pick up a brick from the pile of rubble, run across Hopes Carr to the garage opposite, smash the window and snatch an emergency fire axe off the wall. Perhaps that was the same axe that others used to hack their way into the cockpit to rescue the pilots.

As I forced my way through the mass of people that had now gathered around the scene, a bystander, seeing my burnt and bloodied clothing and bleeding feet thought I was a survivor and asked if I needed any help. I said nothing, pushed my way through the crowd, crossed over Waterloo Road and in a daze made my way home where I found Kath sitting on the front doorstep with her head in her hands crying. She knew I had gone to the crash; heard all the explosions; saw the smoke and flames; she didn't know whether I was alive or dead.

To this day, I cannot honestly tell you what was going through my mind. Looking back, I wouldn't have done it but, at the time, like everyone else involved, we just went straight in without thinking of the dangers and started to pull the passengers clear. I didn't sleep well for months afterwards. The events of that day seemed to continually haunt me. Even today in vivid dreams and nightmares, I always see David Ralphs trapped in his seat surrounded by flames and I can never quite get him out. I'm glad he was rescued and I have spoken to him since.

Another local man who witnessed the crash and its hideous aftermath was Brian Taylor (no relation to Ernie). On that morning, he was driving his Bedford Dormobile towards the town centre with his brother, Roy, beside him in the passenger seat. Nothing could have prepared him for the awfulness he was about to encounter. Brian takes up the story:

As we turned into Waterloo Road, the airliner flew right over us and belly flopped hard down on the garage. I slammed the brakes on and came to a screeching stop alongside the metal railings overlooking the scene. My brother, who was a bit panic stricken looked helplessly at me and said, "What should we do?" I looked at his ashen face and told him: "You go for help… I'm going over." I leapt from the vehicle and vaulted over the railings landing feet first in the sodden undergrowth. On my hands and knees, I began to scramble up the embankment towards the burning tail. As I made my up, I saw a young woman with dark brown hair (the stewardess) scrambling down the slope away from the wreckage in the general direction I'd just come from; she seemed not badly injured, so I left her and continued on.

When I reached the wreckage, there must have been a handful of policemen and civilians doing what they could to rescue the passengers. I climbed though the gash into the cabin. Inside it was utter chaos and devastation; twisted and ripped seats; bodies and all sorts of debris littering the cabin. Those passengers still alive were in a terrible state and screaming for our help. There was a heavy smell of aviation fuel everywhere and with small fires here and there, I realised there was the very real possibility that it could go up at any moment so a bit of panic set in. We looked around the cabin and tried to make a judgement – which ones do we help at that moment, and who do we leave; it wasn't easy to decide. So we went straight for the passengers who were nearest to us. Between us, we managed to get a few people out and carry them over to the garage forecourt – I don't know if those we pulled out were alive or dead. I was wearing my best checked jacket with it being a Sunday and remember putting it around the shoulders of a young woman whose hair had burnt away, I dragged her away behind me then someone else took over.

At this time, there was no real fire just choking black smoke. Then without warning and to everyone's horror, came the fire – it was not so much an explosion but more like a whoosh – like throwing petrol on a fire. The flames spread with frightening rapidity down the cabin. At that point, it was time for everyone to get out. Standing outside on the forecourt, I could see the agony on the faces of the passengers screaming and beating on the cabin windows for our help. We exchanged beats with them until the fire overcame them. I will never forget the horrific sight of their hair burning away in an instant and then disappearing from view behind the flames that surged down the cabin. Then came the sickening smell of burning flesh, that is one vivid memory I will always remember about that day; it was horrible. During the fire, I tried to pick a spot that didn't look as hot, but it was impossible because of the searing heat and hot choking black smoke; it was like acid burning my throat and lungs.

Then the fire brigade and ambulances arrived who brought in stretchers, before that we had to improvise, using anything to hand, corrugated iron sheeting, plywood and boarding to use as makeshift stretchers to move the dead and injured.

One of the 72 victims being stretched away to the nearby temporary mortuary (Stockport Express).

I stayed on the scene for most of the day helping out; sifting through the remains, assisting the firemen with their hoses and that sort of thing. I was black as coal when I left the scene in the late afternoon. On arriving home, I went straight up to my bedroom, sat on the bed, put my head in my hands and had a bit of a weep. For the next few days, I kept out of the way whilst I tried to get to grips with it all.

Looking back, it was one of those dreadful situations where everyone was so helpful and, disregarding their own safety, bravely went in to try and save the passengers. I can only describe it as the most wonderful act of humanity. There was some incredible heroism shown that day, not just on my part but by all the people who came to help. It wasn't me being brave; it just seemed the natural thing to do at the time.

For Arthur O'Neill what should have been a joyful Sunday suddenly dissolved when news of the disaster came. Arthur, a Salvation Army Major at the nearby Citadel, described the dreadful scene that greeted him when he rounded the corner with the rest of his bandsmen.

My first reaction was one of bewilderment; it was a frightening and shocking sight. The whole area was humming with activity, people were swarming about in every direction, many willing to help and many with no clear idea of what to do. Within a minute of my arrival, the aircraft exploded and caught fire. It was an absolute hell, an inferno, just a wall of flames. It was sheer horror, because the whole fuselage from behind the cockpit had split wide open and I could clearly see all the passengers down the length of the cabin; they just sat there all arms and legs in a jumble of seats enveloped in flames staring at us in a shocked stupor. Some were half-naked because their clothes had been burned or ripped away; others with their clothes alight waved their arms at the rescuers frantically appealing for help.

Suddenly, I was aware of our own bandsmen moving in with others to try and rescue people. They were tremendous as they climbed into the wreckage, because all the time, there were explosions and flames coming from underneath the cabin. Then through the swirling smoke, I saw a lovely little girl of seven or eight being carried out in a rescuer's arms – she was really pretty – I hoped and prayed she was alive. She brought home to all of us that this was a family plane.

Then there was a middle-aged man in a blue suit and bloodied shirt aimlessly wandering about the garage forecourt in great distress, he said to me: "My feet are burning – please will you take my shoes off." He pleaded with me to help his wife who he said was trapped in the burning plane. There was nothing I could say or do to help him, so I held his hand. Then there was a teenage lad, he was very much shaken and in a state of deep shock; he couldn't speak except with his eyes, so I held his hand too. I just stood there stunned holding both their hands.

The injured and dying were lying all over the forecourt unable to talk, they just blindly stared at the obscene writhing orange flames totally consume the aircraft and its human cargo. I couldn't help but think of the rescuers. There were factory workers, men in blue overalls from the nearby garage, young policemen, our bandsmen and local folk. Suddenly, they had forgotten themselves and everything to face that inferno.

The grim scene inside the garage now put to use as a mortuary (author's archive).

When the cannonade of explosions ripped along the starboard wing, it marked the end of those surviving passengers still trapped in their seats. It started an intense fire that engulfed the forward section of the fuselage which rapidly intensified and swept down the cabin with a cruel determination to incinerate everything in its path. Seats, roof panels the overhead luggage racks dripped fire and collapsed adding to the conflagration devouring oxygen at a prodigious rate. The burning cabin furnishings not only consumed the breathable air but emitted deadly hydrogen cyanide gas. It would have taken just a few breaths in that toxic atmosphere to incapacitate and suffocate all those still alive.

Within a few minutes, the whole of the fuselage was burning with a staggering intensity that began to devour the cabin structure at a phenomenal rate – it was as if all hell had opened up. Then suddenly, without warning, there was a flashover – a phenomena that occurs when the concentration of highly toxic gases and smoke become so concentrated and confined that it suddenly erupts in a colossal fireball.

The fire had taken hold so quickly that those rescuers still inside the fuselage, although reluctant to abandon their rescue attempts, had no option but to save themselves and evacuate leaving the remaining survivors to their fate. Any attempts to go back in were unthinkable. For the remaining trapped passengers – and there were many – their fate was now sealed. Their initial anxiety in the minutes after impact waiting to be rescued quickly turned to horror and helpless despair and finally resignation as the ferocious vortex of flames surged down the cabin towards them. They knew then that in the next few minutes, they were going to die in excruciating agony. There seemed to be faces at every window, their eyes filled with terror and despair. In sheer desperation, they hammered their fists on the blackening windows, thrashed about in their seats and tore at their burning clothes as they played out the last agonising seconds of their lives. Their muffled agonised primal screams could be clearly heard above the roar of the flames; a dreadful collective haunting sound of humanity being incinerated alive.

A police sergeant said: "What I will never forget for as long as I live was the masks of pure agony and terror on their faces as they screamed at us from behind the windows. We were impudent to do anything; all we could do was stare back in horror as they disappeared from our view behind the flames to perish in one of the most terrifying ways imaginable – it was heart-breaking to witness."

It takes little imagination to sense the sheer horror and mental turmoil experienced by those passengers who saw the flames rapidly creeping down that claustrophobic tube seeking them out. The dreadful irony for them was knowing they had survived a major air crash and were now going to die horribly in full view of their would-be rescuers.

The physical and mental torture on the rescuers who bore witness to these horrors was palpable. All were overwhelmed by the sheer enormity of the human holocaust they had just witnessed. With all hope gone, they wandered away from the blazing funeral pyre feeling hopeless in mind and spirit trying to gather their tortured thoughts. Some, including experienced, hardened police officers, not easily put off their stride, simply sat down dejectedly at the roadside and openly wept as the sustained, awesome roar of the firestorm consumed the aircraft and its humanity. Others, deeply shocked and moved by what they had witnessed, stood around in stunned and silent groups, all lost in their own thoughts; their grim haunted expressions epitomised the sheer horror of the situation.

One of the scores of police officers involved in those desperate rescue attempts was John Lomas, who has since passed away. His wife, Joan, speaking on his behalf, told me how her husband was tortured in the aftermath by what he witnessed first-hand.

John had always been passionate about all things to do with aviation. At the age of 15, he joined the Air Training Corps and was never happier when he was flying and allowed to join the pilot at the controls. That summer, he was eagerly looking forward to the time we, as a family, would be flying abroad for our holiday. That day never came because of the traumatic experiences he went through on that awful day, after which he never wanted anything to do with flying ever again.

John set out from home on that Sunday morning to go on duty at ten o'clock – he should have finished at six that evening but, because of the dreadful air crash, he came home very late that day. At the scene, he joined his police colleagues and others frantically trying to rescue the trapped passengers, many of whom he told me, were still strapped in their seats with broken legs and unable to escape the inferno.

Having seen people being burnt alive and being helpless to do anything to save them, he walked away from the blazing aircraft, sat down on the ground and cried bitterly. It was then someone handed him a cup of tea and that was when the memorable photograph of him – with his faraway haunted eyes – was taken that appeared in the newspaper the following day, with the caption: 'Tea break for a weary rescuer.'

P. C. John Lomas. After seeing passengers burn to death and being powerless to save them, sat down at the kerbside and wept (Phillip Dunn/Rex Features).

He arrived home late from duty, physically and emotionally exhausted. We had to dispose of his uniform – even his boots – all were saturated with aviation fuel and oil. John didn't work from the police station for almost a month afterwards; he was allocated to work at the pathology department at Stepping Hill Hospital to assist with the post mortems and the identification of the unfortunate victims. I think this was the most traumatic time for him piecing together everything that was retrieved from the wreckage.

This was a very sad time for him feeling too sick to eat and not wanting to go away from the house which became his sanctuary. At the time, we had a young family, so it was very hard for all of us to cope with the situation. John was ill for some time in the aftermath – when I say ill, I don't mean physically – he went to work and came home in a robotic sort of way. Had there been counselling available in those days, he would have been a sure candidate for it. It also affected the children too who could not understand why their rather silent father sat at the dining table each evening picking at his food saying little. Normally, he was such a jolly chap full of fun. The only time he could unwind and open up a little and talk to me about things was when the children were in bed.

Over the coming weeks and months, life gradually eased and got back to some sort of normality and we started to talk about going on holiday and having fun together with the children. Later that summer, we all went down to Devon where we all learned to relax and enjoy ourselves and get back to some semblance of regularity.

I know John would not wish for any sense of glory for what he and the others did on that dreadful day. He was just a good, sensitive man doing his best throughout this traumatic time and I am very proud of him for that.

Refusing to be contained, the fire quickly penetrated the aluminium alloy of the fuselage skin and began to consume the cabin at a phenomenal rate. Once the temperature reached a certain point, the magnesium content of the alloy caused such an intense fire that once it had a hold was going to be almost impossible to extinguish. The cabin windows quickly surrendered to the intense heat, blackened, melted and, because of the sheer pressure of the internal heat, blasted outwards from their apertures from which thick, black, twisting coils of greasy smoke pumped skyward. Within minutes the tail section, weakened by the sheer ferocity of the inferno broke away from what was left of the fuselage and slowly subsided down the scrub-covered slope of the ravine.

At 10:22, the shrill ringing of the emergency telephone shattered the Sunday morning peace in the Stockport ambulance station control room in the Heaton Norris district of the town. The duty shift leader, Mr Goodwin, snatched up the receiver and was given the shocking news that an airliner, with the possibility of a hundred passengers on board, had crashed in the vicinity of Waterloo Road. He immediately contacted the Ambulance Superintendent who in turn initiated the well-rehearsed emergency procedure for dealing with a major incident.

At the time of the crash, ten ambulance personnel were on duty at the Stockport station manning five vehicles, which was the normal Sunday compliment. Neighbouring Cheshire and the Manchester ambulance services were notified and requested to send all available vehicles and crews to the scene. All the local hospitals were also alerted informing them to expect multiple casualties. Extra staff was sent for and all routine work was suspended temporality. Three ambulances that were already out on the road were redirected, and within minutes, the scream of sirens could be heard around the town centre as they weaved their way through the now thickening traffic. As the minutes passed, more sirens could be heard – first one, then another, then more than you could count. In all 22 ambulances were in operation – nine from Manchester, six from Cheshire County and seven from Stockport. On hearing the news, thirteen off-duty drivers and attendants along with two shift leaders immediately volunteered for duty. Apart from the Cheshire and Manchester services, offers of help were received from as far away as New Mills, Rochdale, Blackburn and Oldham. Stockport Infirmary, because of its close proximity to the accident scene, was designated to receive casualties and the ambulance service diverted routine surgical emergencies to the nearby Stepping Hill Hospital.

Within minutes of the alert being sounded, ambulances arrived and lined up in Hopes Carr, their doors open in hopeful readiness. Regrettably, because of the small number of survivors rescued, their work changed almost immediately from one of rescue to one of recovery.

There were dramatic scenes at Stockport Infirmary when they were notified of the accident by a telephone call from the police at 10:14: 'AEROPLANE CRASH, STAND BY FOR CASUALTIES.' From the moment the alert was received, the staff had everything under control. Immediately, the building was cleared of all outpatients and non-urgent cases as the major accident and emergency department swung into operation. The unit was headed by the senior orthopaedic surgeon, who, by an amazing coincidence, was on his way to the infirmary and passed by the scene, so was able to make an immediate assessment of the situation.

As they had no idea at that point about the number of casualties to expect, the Out-Patient Hall was immediately cleared and twelve beds were set up with drip stands, suction apparatus and other emergency equipment. Consultation Clinics and other rooms were also put to use, making a total 22 beds immediately available to admit casualties. As an extra precaution, Stepping Hill Hospital was put on emergency standby in case further beds were required.

By 10:45, off-duty staff responded positively on hearing the news, additional staff began to arrive; doctors and nurses from other hospitals offered their services, as well as members of the public who descended on the infirmary to donate blood. Surgeons from other hospitals were called in and even local GPs telephoned to volunteer their services. Both operating theatres were immediately put to full use, where nine of the survivors underwent emergency operations. Julia Partleton, the stewardess, who suffered extensive burns, underwent a major operation before being transferred later to the burns unit at Wythenshawe Hospital for specialist care.

The usual protocol regarding the reception of accident victims was for them to be received through the casualty department. But on this occasion, it was decided to admit survivors directly to Holden Ward and for the first time in the Infirmary's history, men and women shared the same ward. It would prove to be group therapy at its most basic, each taking comfort in each other and the nursing staff which went someway to ease the ordeal that they had been through.

By lunchtime, a separate room was designated for use as a relative's reception area. Refreshments were provided for members of the police, ambulance personnel and relatives. Overnight accommodation was made available in a waiting room where chairs, tables and camp beds were provided; in all some forty relatives and friends were catered for.

Members of Stockport Salvation Army dished out refreshments to rescue and recovery workers (author's archive).

Susan Butcher started her career as a cadet nurse in 1961, qualifying as a State Registered Nurse in June 1965 at which point she became a Staff Nurse at Stockport Infirmary. In April 1967, at a relatively young age, she was promoted to Junior Ward Sister. She had no knowledge of the air crash when she arrived for duty in the early afternoon. On entering Holden Ward, she describes the scene that greeted her as like a 'battle zone'.

On the morning of the air crash, I had gone to Norbury Church with my future husband to hear the banns read for my forthcoming marriage. I was due on duty at one o'clock so, after the church service, I went home, quickly changed into my uniform and we set off by car down the A6 towards the Infirmary. At a set of traffic lights, there was a diversion in place, a policeman peered through the window, saw my uniform and just waved us through. Then further down the road, we came to another diversion and again the same thing happened. I thought this was strange; it must be because I've got my uniform on that they were letting us through because I hadn't a clue then what had happened. Eventually, we turned into the ambulance yard at the Infirmary.

When I walked through the doors of A & E, there was a student nurse standing there, but there were also lots and lots of people in there. I said to her, "What's going on, why are all these people here?"

She said, "Haven't you heard? There has been an air crash and all the casualties are on your ward." I was astounded.

"What! My ward. Why have they all been taken there?" I immediately felt as though I'd gone through a lump of jelly because I ran a very quiet ward.

I rushed up the stairs to Holden Ward and opened the doors to a quite horrific scene; it was nothing like the ward I recognised. There were piles of blankets everywhere, drip stands, trolleys, lots of staff who had come up from A & E along with lots of others who had come in voluntarily to help out – it was like a battle zone. In the beds, I could see the survivors, and what struck me was they all had brown luggage labels on them giving their identity. I then went into the office where one of the staff from A & E explained to me what had happened and what was going on. I was bit nervous initially because I'd only done orthopaedics as a student so I knew the situation I was faced with was going to be very challenging.

Most of the patients had more or less every bone in their body x-rayed. The only two casualties who were relatively unscathed were teenage brothers Harold and Billy Wood; they were typical of their age and took everything in their stride. They did have injuries, of course, but they were fully conscious and discharged within a week. I also remember 15-year-old local schoolgirl Fiona Child, she was a lovely girl and I recall she was very much traumatised by the disaster. On the other hand, Vivienne – who was in the bed next to Mary Green – was a lively personality with a great sense of humour so there was quite a bit of laughter on the ward as the days progressed. I didn't see a great deal of the stewardess who – because of her serious injuries – was later transferred to the burns unit at Wythenshawe Hospital. Captain Marlow was put in a side ward so I didn't actually see him.

Chapter Four
An Appalling Vista

"It was like a carnival, a carnival with human misery as the main attraction."
Television Reporter – David Hamilton

As the aircraft blazed completely out of control, PC John Heath, now separated in the mayhem from his colleague Bill Oliver, turned his attention to the cockpit where the two injured pilots were imprisoned. Apart from a few strips of metal, it had virtually broken clear from the fuselage. As this was not seriously affected by fire, attempts to rescue the crew now got underway. John Heath recalls:

I heard muffled shouting from the cockpit area and a civilian told me he could see movement inside. Local baker, Brian Donohoe, was already hitting the cockpit windows with an iron bar, but this made little impact against the armoured glass. There was no possibility of getting into the cockpit from the rear because of the searing heat from the blazing fuselage immediately behind. Then someone in the crowd passed me a fireman's axe and with the pointed end of the head, I swung the axe hard to try to break through the windows, but frustratingly, they just crazed making no impression at all. With the help of others, I climbed on the cockpit roof and started to pound at the aluminium skin just above the windows. This too was extremely difficult to penetrate because the whole area was congested with flying controls, instruments and other equipment. After a great deal of effort, I eventually managed to break through and as I hacked away others began to prise back the aluminium skin with their hands to make the hole larger. After some five or ten minutes, we managed to make the hole large enough for me to lean through and reach Captain Marlow, and with some difficulty and pain to himself, I managed to manoeuvre him towards a hole that firemen had cut in the rear of the cockpit. His only concern was about his passengers. His agonised words to us were: "How many have got out…how many have got out?" As soon as he was pulled clear, I turned my attention to Chris Pollard, the co-pilot, who was alive but seriously injured. I asked him was he all right but he didn't respond to any of the questions I asked. Leaning through the hole, I released his seat harness and manoeuvred him between the two crew seats and over towards the break in the cockpit where a fireman pulled him out by his clothing.

As the two pilots were put onto stretchers, Inspector Marsland instructed me to accompany them to the infirmary in case I needed to witness any statements. Both stretchers were put on runners in the ambulance and I climbed in. There was no ambulance attendant so I knelt between the two casualties facing the driver's cab. Unfortunately, the stretcher on my left carrying the co-pilot had not locked properly on its runners and consequently every time the ambulance lurched forward in the traffic, the stretcher shot towards the rear and I struggled to keep it steady.

The co-pilot was breathing but very loudly and Captain Marlow was very quiet and I feared the worst for him. When we pulled up outside the infirmary, we were met by doctors, nurses and porters with trolleys awaiting the two casualties. I was saddened to learn later that the co-pilot had died on arrival without recovering consciousness but encouraged to hear that Captain Marlow was not critically injured and was expected to survive. Leaving both casualties in the care of the infirmary staff, the ambulance turned around and returned me to the scene.

John Heath was just one of hundreds of Stockport police officers mobilised to assist that day. Those out on the beat, on motor patrol, on inquiries and even those off duty, were immediately summoned to go directly to the crash site or report to police headquarters. Chris Knowles, a new recruit to the force, will never forget the dizzying speed of events of that Sunday morning. It was to be a real test of his recent training.

It was my very first shift as a trained – albeit still probationary – police constable, PC236, Stockport Borough Police Force. I'd absorbed thirteen weeks of instruction at the Police Training College, followed by five weeks of night shifts back in Stockport. This was the standard induction process, accompanying an experienced bobby around all the beats in the town and surrounding areas, taking in as much local knowledge as possible and also getting to know the local characters both inside and outside the force.

Now I was joining the rota on the 10:00 a.m. to 6:00 p.m. day shift on a dull, wet Sunday morning ready to patrol a beat on my own for the very first time. Being young and keen – I was just 20 – I arrived at Police Headquarters twenty minutes early, and was immediately called over by the desk sergeant. He told me: "There's a stake-out following a robbery at a carpet warehouse overnight. We're expecting them to move the stuff soon. Go with the car to assist." Exciting! The five weeks of nights had been largely uneventful. This was more like it.

We drove up a side street in the Heaton Moor district of the town and parked where we could see a van owned by one of the alleged thieves. Our job was to follow discreetly when the time came. The police car driver was a long-serving officer and he quickly levelled my expectations by saying we could be there all day with nothing happening – patience is a necessary quality for a PC.

This though was to be a day unlike any other. At eleven minutes past ten, the radio crackled and burst into life: 'ALL MOBILES… PLANE DOWN HOPES CARR. REPEAT, PLANE DOWN HOPES CARR!' We looked at each other in utter disbelief. "Hold tight," the driver exclaimed, and we sped off towards to the centre of town with sirens screaming.

We were early on the scene before the fire brigade had arrived and were faced with the shocking sight of the crashed Argonaut which exploded, with flames engulfing the main fuselage, ending the lives of many still trapped inside.

Time and presumably natural defensive mechanisms dim most of the memories of the horrors of that day; trying to break into the shell of the cockpit to free the pilots using anything to hand such as iron bars from a broken fence; sifting through the wreckage after the fires had been extinguished and subsequently moved to less onerous duties for a new recruit by a senior officer to help control the vast crowds of onlookers who had descended on the scene.

The initial alert to the fire service came with an emergency 222 call from Stockport Police Headquarters at 10:12. The Brigade controller immediately dispatched two appliances, one from the Whitehill Street Station under the command of Station Officer Fred Matkin, and a water tender from King Street, which was first to arrive on scene at 10:17 and found the fuselage and surrounding buildings burning fiercely. They immediately got two jets positioned to cover and protect rescue workers who were still attempting to enter the burning cabin. Within minutes, the appliance from Whitehill Street arrived and Station Officer Fred Matkin took overall command, ordering two more jets on the burning aircraft.

On arrival, the Brigade frustratingly found that the water supply from the mains supplying the hydrants was limited due to a weekend pressure reduction. Brigade Control immediately contacted the water company for an increased supply. In the meantime, an alternative supply was urgently required and in desperation, it became necessary to run a snaking relay of hoses from the scene to hydrants on Wellington Road South a quarter of a mile away.

Meanwhile, the buildings on Waterloo Road damaged when the aircraft crashed, were now burning ferociously and steps were taken to try and bring these fires under control. One jet was positioned ready for use outside the burning sub station until the incoming power supply was cut off. Additional foam and water jets were kept in reserve, in anticipation of a serious fire developing in the two 500-gallon petrol storage tanks under the garage forecourt which were almost full to capacity. Thankfully, as a result of these precautions, the storage tanks were not involved.

Appliances were now arriving from the Cheshire and Manchester Brigades and the airport fire service reported two foam tenders were on the way. As the operation to control and contain the fires was underway, a number of explosions took place caused by the detonation of fuel tanks of the wrecked cars in the demolished garage directly under the fuselage. It says much for the bravery of the firefighters and all the rescue workers involved that this danger was totally ignored.

One young fireman, who turned out from the Whitehill station with Fred Matkin, was 21-year-old Mike Phillips. He was still considered at the time as a 'rookie'. He had all the training and knew the drill, but he was totally unaware when he reported for duty that morning that he was about to face the most horrific and gruelling experience of his career.

Fire Officer Mike Phillips (author's archive).

Now retired from the service, he still retains vivid images of that tragic day:

At the time of the disaster, I had been in Fire Service for just two-years; first joining the Lancashire County Brigade in July 1965 aged 19, then transferring to Stockport at Mersey Square in February 1967 before moving to the newly opened station at Whitehill Street in the April. I had never seen a dead body before the air disaster and, with 72 people losing their lives tragically in one incident, it was for me an absolutely horrendous experience. All the training in the world cannot prepare you for the job that faced us on that dreadful day.

As I recall, the day started as normal. I reported for duty at 09:00 hours and was detailed on parade to ride the water tender JDB 393. My other crewmembers were Sub Officer Gregory, Alf Gee, Pete Clucas and myself in the back with Station Officer Fred Matkin who was in overall charge. I was down as station orderly that day – kitchen duties – and there were quite a few people to cater for. I remember the Sunday joint was actually burning and smoke pouring out of the oven – I was no cook – when the klaxon which turned us out went off. The voice of the firewoman in the control room came over the tannoy: "PLANE CRASH... HOPES CARR... PLANE CRASH... HOPES CARR!" We all looked at each other in utter astonishment, jumped on our appliances and set off with sirens blaring. As we sped to the scene, the adrenalin was pumping and my mind was working overtime as to what we were going to be faced with on arrival. My first thoughts were that it was more than likely going to be a false alarm – a 'joker' as we called them – but when we reached the top of Lancashire Hill which gave an uninterrupted view over the town centre, we could plainly see a huge pall of solid black smoke rising skyward. I knew then, without any doubt, that this was going to be my first major incident.

When we turned into Hopes Carr, the water tender from the King Street Station was already there parked up facing us. I jumped down from the cab and took a terrified look around. The scene that met my eyes was truly horrifying. I remember a handful of men standing around smartly dressed in suits as if they were on their way to church. They pointed frantically at the blazing aircraft and screamed at us: "THERE ARE PEOPLE IN THERE!" I saw a number of bodies that must have been ejected on impact strewn across the garage forecourt area. There was a small boy lying amongst them without a mark on him and nearby was the shocking sight of a woman whose legs had been severed – both were dead. It was a truly hideous sight to witness.

I didn't have time to dwell on the carnage as I was immediately ordered to get a jet to work on the burning aircraft. When the hose had been run out and a branch inserted, we got water on and Sub Officer Gregory and myself moved forward towards the blazing fuselage stumbling over bodies and debris as we went. At the time, I think I was surviving on a mixture of shock, adrenalin, fear and a sense of duty. In the back of my mind – and I'm sure in the minds of my colleagues – I had the overriding thought that I was a fire fighter and rescuer with a job to do and I just had to get on with it no matter how unpleasant it was.

It seemed that when we first arrived at the scene and got to work, there were only a handful of spectators scattered around the area watching us. Perhaps I was too engrossed to notice, but I remember sometime later looking up – it was like an amphitheatre – there were now hundreds, hundreds of people all around, TV cameras, reporters and even ice cream vans had arrived to cash in on the tragedy.

Later, when the fire was brought under control and the recovery of the casualties was underway, I had the job of getting canvas salvage sheets off the appliance to cover some of the badly burned and mutilated bodies. To see them lined on the ground was heart-breaking. I chanced to look across at Mick Hurst, a fireman from the King Street Station, he was considered by all of us in the service as a 'hard nut' and known never to be fazed – he was as pale and shocked as I was. Besides the human carnage I witnessed, my abiding memory of that day is of the huge pile of fuel and oil sodden clothing, luggage and personal items that had been thrown out or salvaged. One solitary image that struck me cold and brought home to me the tragedy in sheer human terms was of a scorched and fuel sodden child's teddy bear lying amongst the twisted metal.

At the time of this dreadful accident, I was a young 21-year-old with little experience of life. I had been in the Royal Marine Band from the age of 15, and then took a couple of factory jobs until I joined the service. I was young, naïve and innocent and suddenly out of the blue, all this was happening to me.

It must have been around 16:00 hours when we were stood down and returned to Whitehill Street. I remember scrubbing down with the rest of the lads in the washroom. The atmosphere was strained to say the least and nobody said much, but, one thing that was said, and we were all in agreement at the time, was that none of us would ever fly; of course, I suppose we all have since.

I went off duty at 18:00 hours and had previously arranged that evening to go bowling at Belle Vue in Manchester with my mate, Derek, and our girlfriends. We did go, but it was a dour outing because of the state of my mind – I'm afraid I wasn't very good company that night and probably for most of the following days and weeks.

Over the next 12 months, I suffered from torturous nightmares and flashbacks – you must bear in mind that there was no counselling in those days, it hadn't even been heard of; you were expected to deal with it on your own. There is no doubt that those events made a deep imprint on my mind, and I was only a rescuer who arrived after the fire had started. The people early on the scene, who saw the faces of those desperate trapped passengers appealing for help from behind the cabin windows as they burnt to death, must have suffered far more than I did. I have tried hard over the subsequent years to blot out much of the work I did that day and to erase those horrific images seared in my memory – but realistically, I suppose I never will.

Another young fireman thrown in at the deep end was Mike Conroy from the nearby Manchester Brigade that had been called out to assist: Fifty years later, he recalled his involvement with vivid lucidity:

On that morning, I got up, got dressed and walked to work at the Philips Park station. With it being a Sunday morning, I most likely had a hangover. Arrived at work as normal at about 8:20. Same routine; got changed and went on parade. Did the normal checks on the machine, tested hose reels, tested escape then a bit of drill ready to knock off at ten.

I remember standing idly in the yard when Taffy Jones popped his head out of the side door and shouted over that we could be turning out to a plane crash – a few mumbled words from the lads – then Station Officer Wilf McLaughan appeared. The bells went down and over the tannoy came the words: 'PLANE CRASH... PLANE CRASH, STOCKPORT!'

I remember sitting in the back of the pump escape thinking: *Plane crash...what type of plane?* and, *planes don't crash in town centres.* The journey seemed to take ages. I remember looking at Taffy who was staring blankly out of the window saying nothing, he was usually always talkative, but not this time. My main memory of the journey was Station Officer Mac screaming: "FUCKING HELL ALAN, SLOW DOWN!" Alan Gaunt was our driver and I later learnt that we were going flat out down Lancashire Hill in Stockport and on a bend was a Burtons shop – Mac thought we were going right through the bloody window.

On arrival, the Station Officer said: "Right young Conroy, clench your teeth and breathe through your nose." I climbed over a wall to a sight I have never seen before or since – mutilated bodies all over the place. I looked down at my feet and found I was standing on the body of a young boy; he was badly disfigured from the waist down. In the papers a few days later, they published photographs of all the people who had been killed and straight away I recognised this young lad.

Our first job was to try and cover as many of the casualties as possible. We then moved into the burnt out remains of the fuselage to help free the badly burnt bodies still trapped in their seats; we put them on stretchers and moved them away from the crash site. I don't remember for how long we worked – time just flew by in a blur that day.

We got back to the station late in the afternoon and cleaned off all our gear. The only counselling we got was Station Officer Mac saying that 'control have been on and you can all go down to Ancoats Hospital and have a tetanus injection in your arse' – I don't think anyone bothered. After parade, I had a shower, walked home, got changed and went on the piss.

The first press reporter to arrive on the scene was local man and larger than life character Jim Lovelock. He got his first job on the *Stockport Express* by sitting on the doorstep of the printing office in St Peter's Square. Each day the editor, Joseph Walley, had to step over him and each day Jim handed him something new he had written. At last, an exasperated Walley said to him one morning: "Come in you bloody idiot – at least you are the only one who didn't put an 'aitch' in my surname." Jim started work as a cub reporter on All Fools Day 1940 and quickly rose through the ranks to become the editor in 1949 at the exceptionally young age of 28. By this time, he was as notorious for his socialising, as he was famous for his writing.

Despite the fact of suffering polio as a child that left him with a limp and the loss of one eye, he became a legendary caver and mountaineer. He was later to be part of a team that made the first successful attempt of Everest's nearby neighbour, Nuptse, and another which set the world caving depth record in France's Gouffre Berger cave. When it came to climbing, he was up for anything, whilst working as a reporter for the *Daily Mail,* he once, for a bet, scaled the south face of the building and clambered in through the editor's office window whilst he was on the telephone!

Friend and colleague, Alistair MacDonald said: "Jim was a journalist of the old school; hard-working and famous for churning out prodigious quantities of copy, hard drinking and perennially short of cash as caving and climbing trips often interrupted his working life. He was an entertaining raconteur too, often fulfilling the old journalistic maxim of never letting the facts get in the way of a good story. In short, he was truly a brilliant bloke."

The air crash was not the first time he had reported on a local disaster. One late afternoon in November 1948, a choking yellow smog descended on the town, so dense that pedestrians literately had to grope their way along the walls of the Public Library and the shops in Princess Street to find their way. Jim, then the chief reporter, was just about to call it a day and put the paper to bed when the phone rang. He told Peter Clowes, the only other reporter in the office: "There's been a train crash on the viaduct!"

They immediately grabbed their coats and notebooks and left the office. Outside, they picked their way cautiously through the silent fog shrouded streets towards the railway station where, on arrival, they were greeted by a police inspector carrying a blazing torch. He led them down onto the track towards the crash scene – which was about half way along the viaduct. A train had run into the back of another that had stopped at a signal on the viaduct waiting for a platform. Five people lost their lives and there were 27 serious casualties in the accident that was caused by a catalogue of human errors. Late that night, Jim was back in the Express office writing up the tragic story. It was well passed 4 a.m. when he eventually arrived home and crawled into bed.

Before his death in 2007 aged 86, Jim told me, from his retirement home in Spain, his graphic memories of the most unforgettable day in his long journalistic career.

I could never forget that weekend in the early summer of 1967 when I actually reported on two air disasters within twelve hours of each other. On Saturday 3 June, I was working a night shift on the *Sunday Mirror* in Manchester, when a press flash came over the wires that an Air Ferry DC-4 airliner, flying British holidaymakers from Manston in Kent to Perpignan, had crashed in the Pyrenees killing all 88 passengers and crew on board. My colleague Bill Barton – a staffer on the *Daily Telegraph –* worked with me over the phone on the developing story with agency copy and what we could pick up on telephone calls. Due to the importance of the story, the editor decided to keep back the print run on the last edition well beyond the usual time, so Bill and I didn't leave the Withy Grove office until after six in the morning. We heard that the Green Door Club – a favourite haunt of journalists at the time – was still serving, so we wandered over there and spent a couple of hours relaxing over a drink or two from the stresses of what had been a long and arduous night.

In those days, I lived on Dialstone Lane in Stockport with my first wife June. I was awakened shortly after ten o'clock, after only a couple of hours sleep by the telephone ringing. It was Isobel Slater, the wife of my good friend Arthur, licensee of the Red Bull pub, my local watering hole in Middle Hillgate. I heard her say: "Jimmy, I think the garage in Hopes Carr is on fire as I've heard some explosions." I thought, after spending all night reporting on an air crash in France, I certainly didn't fancy getting dressed and going out to report on a garage fire in downtown Stockport. I was just thinking of going back to my warm bed when the phone rang again. This time it was Don Smith who was manning the news desk of the *Daily Mirror*. "All right Don," I told him wearily, "I'm going out to the garage fire." I heard silence; then: "GARAGE FIRE BE BUGGERED… IT'S A PLANE LOAD OF HOLIDAYMAKERS!"

I immediately knew this was a scoop of a lifetime and within two minutes, I was dressed and in my car racing towards the centre of Stockport. Five minutes later, I skidded into Waterloo Road, narrowly missing two cars that had collided head-on as their owners had taken their eyes off the road to take a terrified look at the appalling vista. I stopped the car short of Hopes Carr and my pounding heart almost stopped at the horrifying sight of the wrecked and burning airliner filling the little bit of greenery. From then onwards, it was a kaleidoscope of horror, with friends from the fire brigade, police and ambulance service, who I'd known all my journalistic life, impinging bright images on my mind. I won't dwell on the horrific details of that day, they still come back to haunt me even now. I well recall being shouted at by one of my oldest friends, Station Officer Fred Matkin – known to all of us in the press as 'Fearless Fireman Fred'. Standing on part of the burning wing, he yelled and gestured at me to get away: "JIM," he bellowed, "FUCK OFF… THE THING'S GOING TO EXPLODE!"

Just standing there, I was a useless impediment and I staggered away seeking a telephone. It was the biggest story of my life and I hadn't even filed a line. This was superbly taken care of by my colleague, Peter Blake, at our freelance office in Millgate from where we filed stories from all over the world. Later, I was to feel great pride as I recollected the efforts of the emergency services and the way ordinary Stockport folk rose to the challenge of that tragic occasion. There was disgust also at how the tragedy was turned into a Roman carnival by thousands of sightseers who had arrived on the scene. Arthur Slater, landlord of the Red Bull, was so incensed by the gawping masses that he refused to open his pub, as did a few others around the Hillgate area.

I felt a twinge of pride the next day when I saw, amongst the national daily contents boards outside newsagents, my own local paper the *Stockport Express*. Harry Evans, the editor, had quickly rounded up a successful team of reporters, photographers and compositors to work overnight and produce a special edition that found an honoured place amongst the national dailies. The *Stockport Advertiser*, sister paper of the *Express,* but in direct editorial competition was left standing. One of their reporters, with notebook and pencil in hand, arrived at the scene late on in the day and did a quick walk-around-and-look, shook his head and said: "There'll be no one local in this." And promptly disappeared!

Air disasters by their sensational nature, have always inspired a morbid fascination on members of the public, and the Stockport crash would be no exception. Within minutes of the crash, the normally tranquil streets around the town centre soon began to scream and bubble with activity as the wail of emergency vehicles cut the Sunday morning peace.

At first, there were just a handful of spectators that lined the pavements to watch the unfolding drama but, as news of the disaster was broadcast over the radio and TV, thousands more were drawn irresistibly to the town from the outlying suburbs. Like jackals to the kill, with a shiver of excitement, they made their way *en masse* through the tangle of narrow streets and damp alleyways with a ghoulish determination to view the scene of death and destruction. Their cars were parked indiscriminately, many three abreast, and soon all the roads leading to the site were choked with pedestrians and motorists. Traffic jams quickly surpassed that of a weekday rush hour and a large number of police officers, which could have been used more effectively elsewhere, were diverted to control them. Within an hour, swarms of people travelling on all kinds of transport – bicycles, motorbikes, scooters, cars, even mothers pushing prams – were all asking: "Which way to the crash?" They gathered in their thousands, as close as they could get, standing shoulder to shoulder taking up every possible square inch of space. Groups of youths shinned up lampposts with apparent suicidal intent, climbed on walls and rooftops to get an advantage over others. Many tried to force their way through the police cordon, and at one time twenty people were standing on the sagging roof of a derelict building with complete unconcern for their own safety – for them, the danger only added to the excitement. For others, it was somewhere to go for a Sunday afternoon drive, something to talk about with authority at the office or in the shops the next day.

In festive mood, they clustered round as if they were spectators at a Stockport County football game, watching the endless flow of the hapless victims being dragged from the wreckage and stretchered away. They craned their necks to marvel at the scene of death and devastation whilst parents held up small children above the crowd for a better look. Then there were heated arguments with the police because they refused to let them get closer to view the grim carnage. Added to all this chaos were baying packs of teenagers who freely roamed the area with their portable transistor radios – a novelty at the time – from which the hits of the day blared out at full volume. One pop song heard reverberating around the amphitheatre of death – belted out with a macabre mocking irony was, *Let the Heartaches Begin.* Police tempers became evermore frayed as they toured the area with loud-hailers pleading with people to keep off the streets, but to no avail. For most, the disaster was nothing more than a grotesque carnival to be seen in mute wonder. Not one of those who gravitated to the scene had any concern or tears of pity for the unfortunate victims; their voyeurism had a sickening revulsion that turned the stomach. It seemed that air disasters had become a new spectator sport.

Police sergeant, Ken Sloan, also remembers the carnivalesque atmosphere and appalling behaviour he witnessed first hand. "Unbelievably," he said, "an official complaint was actually made against me by one woman because I refused to allow her ten-year-old son to view the bodies!"

Stephen Clegg, another local police officer, engaged in trying to control the masses told me:

I was meant to commence duty at 2:00 p.m. that day, but arrived early after hearing the news of the crash on the radio. It was normal practice to parade at police headquarters before going out on patrol but, that day, we were ushered out to the scene straightaway. The fire had been extinguished by the time I arrived and most of the casualties had been extricated and taken to the nearby Salvation Army Citadel. Everywhere was in absolute chaos and the police, fire and ambulance services were all being hampered by the sheer volume of people gawking at the scene. Nobody had cordoned anywhere off and I remember police officers yelling at the public, physically pushing them and trying to back them away, but it was like pushing a field of tall grass. Whilst those in front backed away, more closed in behind; it was an impossible task. I was grabbed by the shoulders by an angry duty inspector who ordered me and two other officers to instruct, and if necessary eject, some callously profiteering jerks that had arrived with mobile hot dog stands within the crowd. In the end, I recall two being pushed over before they eventually departed. Having done that, I pushed my way through the masses and attempted to go down to the crash site to assist, but was stopped by a police inspector, who looked at me, said I was too young and told me to go over to the Citadel to help out. That turned out to be the scene of my most harrowing memories of that day.

Brian Donohoe too has never forgotten the shocking scenes of the mindless sensation seekers that greeted him when he returned home to his bake house after his involvement in the rescue and recovery had finished. His first reaction was one of astonishment which quickly turned to disgust and anger. "All of Stockport was a bottleneck," he told me, "but around Waterloo Road and the Hillgate area there were literally thousands of people milling around. It was like coming out of Wembley Stadium on Cup Final day. I even saw the disgusting sight of a couple with a picnic table and chairs set up on the pavement with a Thermos flask casually munching sandwiches and drinking tea as if they were on a day out."

It is estimated that in excess of 10,000 people turned out to view the crash scene within the first few hours. These appalling scenes were no doubt due to the sheer perverseness of human nature, the news reports broadcast over the radio and TV, the sheer novelty of air crashes and the fact that Sunday, for most, was a workless day. One disgruntled senior police officer said that he had never witnessed such irrational and irresponsible behaviour from the public in the whole of his service. Even eight hours after the disaster, the streets within half a mile of Hopes Carr were still thronged with cars and pedestrians, and this situation, to a somewhat lesser degree, persisted for several days.

Six miles to the west, at Manchester's Ringway Airport, death intruded suddenly. In the busy arrivals lounge, thronged with holidaymakers, some fifty expectant friends and relatives were waiting to greet parents, grandparents, brothers and sisters off the Palma flight. For them, the first inkling that something was not quite right came with a matter-of-fact announcement over the airport tannoy, that the British Midland Airways flight BD542, due to land at 9:20, would be forty-minutes late. Ten o'clock came and went with no further news. As time passed, those waiting began to have feelings of concern and apprehension, but they were totally unaware of the real reason for the delay. Through the rain-streaked panoramic windows that gave an uninterrupted view over the vast expanse of the airfield, they saw and heard the airport fire service turn out with blue lights flashing and sirens blaring and wait at the runway intersections in readiness for what they believed was an imminent emergency landing – an emergency landing that never came.

Shortly afterwards, another announcement requested that they should go immediately to a designated private lounge. Once assembled in the suite of rooms, the airport director, George Harvey, who had been urgently summoned from his home, entered and painfully broke the news that the aircraft they had been waiting for had crashed in the centre of Stockport on its approach to the airport.

The news was greeted with shock and incredulity. A deathly silence fell over the assembled as they slowly tried to absorb the devastating news. Then suddenly, like a shockwave reverberating through the group, disbelief quickly turned to grief. Pandemonium broke out, women fainted and others openly wept, whilst airport staff, near to tears themselves, tried to comfort the inconsolable. Nurses that had been ferried in from a local hospital, took care of those in a state of deep shock, brandy was freely dispensed and blankets wrapped around the shoulders of shivering and sobbing women whilst bewildered children with puzzled looks in their eyes asked unanswerable questions. It was an impossible task. Now began the long anxious wait until the casualty list could confirm who, if any, had survived.

Relatives leaving the airport after being given the devastating news that the aircraft they were awaiting had crashed in Stockport town centre (author's archive).

Three long hours later, the British Midland station manager, Michael Bishop, who all morning had shuttled between the airport and Stockport gathering as much information as he could, entered the room now thick with cigarette smoke. A sudden hush fell upon those assembled. Everyone slowly rose from their seats and stiffened with tense expectancy. Bishop quietly closed the door behind him, walked towards them, stopped and uncomfortably faced the group. He looked down at his clipboard and with a tremble in his voice read out a list of ten names – the names of those passengers pulled from the wreckage alive. For a handful, the news came with sobbing sighs of relief, but for the majority, it snuffed out the last spark of hope.

Just outside the lounge door, the bustle and clamour of airport life went on uninterrupted; the whine of aircraft engines; the flight announcements over the tannoy and the happy chatter of holidaymakers. Life went merrily on and that, for all those united in grief, was probably the hardest thing of all to bear.

Having taken the two pilots to the infirmary, the ambulance returned John Heath to the crash scene, by which time delayed shock had started to kick in. He told me:

By now, the events had started to catch up with me. I began to feel upset and was shaking uncontrollably. Inspector Marsland, who saw my condition, told me to leave the scene immediately and return to Police Headquarters. As I was walking away, I was pounced on by a group of reporters pressing for interviews. One of those I recognised was David Hamilton – a well-known and respected television personality here in the northwest. Clearly seeing how shocked and shaken I was, he led me across the road to the Waterloo Hotel – which was diagonally opposite the crash site – and bought me a stiff drink to settle my nerves, despite the fact that I was still on duty. I recall I answered a few questions before leaving to return to the Police Station where, on arrival, I was told to go home to rest and recover. I drove home in a daze and was met by my wife who, by that time, had heard the news on the radio but didn't know I had been directly involved. As I explained to her what had happened, I became quite upset and broke down. What I experienced that day made me ill afterwards. I never want to be involved with anything like it again.

David Hamilton is best known today as a television personality and presenter but, it was as a disc jockey – first with Radio One and later Radio Two – that he achieved his greatest popularity as the 'housewives choice'. In fact, such is the effect of his smooth voice on female listeners that a woman once turned up at Broadcasting House saying she wanted to devote the rest of her life to him – having abandoned her husband and children along the way – whilst another fan claimed that he was sending her telepathic messages of an erotic nature over the airways! However, back in the summer of 1967, David was still on the threshold of his TV career working as an in-vision continuity announcer for the now long defunct ABC Weekend Television company in Didsbury, Manchester. Living a few miles from the town, he was hurriedly called out to report on the tragedy for ITN.

Disasters of any kind, especially air disasters, are notoriously one of the hardest stories to cover and a challenge for any reporter. That morning, David, for the first time in his career, had to suppress his trademark cheerful banter, be tactful and sensitive. Standing amongst the snaking fire hoses in the middle of Hopes Carr, he buttoned his suit jacket, adjusted his tie, faced the camera and reported his unscripted piece live to air. Like so many others, it was the disturbing element of the morbidly curious that were his abiding memory of that day.

Most people remember me as 'Diddy' David Hamilton, disc jockey and life and soul of the party but there was a moment in my life when tears replaced laughter. On that Sunday morning in the early summer of 1967, the peace at our Marple bungalow was shattered by a telephone call from Dougie Fairbairn, the duty transmission controller at the ABC Weekend Television studios in Manchester. He told me to get dressed and get myself to the centre of Stockport immediately. "An airliner has crashed in the town. We're sending an outside broadcast unit to the scene and we want you to report on it for ITN."

At first, I didn't believe him. It took Dougie – a man with a huge reputation as a practical joker – a lot of persuasion before I realised he was deadly serious. I quickly shaved, dressed and roared off to Stockport. When I arrived at the scene, the chaos and devastation were unbelievable. The pilot had somehow managed to miss every house and the plane had crumpled up on a patch of open land. A few yards in any direction and the outcome would have been even more devastating. Pieces of aircraft were strewn all around and as the rescue workers sorted the injured from the dead and carried them away on stretchers, I fed the news to ITN in London for their lunchtime bulletin.

To someone like myself, who had never before come close to any sort of disaster, the scene was shattering but it became even more sickening as news of the tragedy spread. Thousands of people poured into the town centre to gape at the appalling destruction and loss of life. It was like a carnival, a carnival with human misery as the main attraction.

Having to report on it was an example of the sort of versatility that television called for in those pioneering days. Royston Mayo, who directed that outside broadcast, had been in the TV studio the night before directing the talent show *Opportunity Knocks,* and the last time I'd been seen on national television was in a knockabout sketch with comedian Ken Dodd. Both Royston and I had to forget about our entertainment backgrounds for that tragic and harrowing day. It's a day which still lives with me now and always will.

Another local reporter caught up in the thick of it was the late Bob Greaves who went on to become the patriarch of regional television and Granada TVs perennial news anchor, fronting over 12,000 live shows. He told the author how a quiet and relaxing Sunday morning at home leafing through the newspapers and drinking coffee suddenly turned into one of immense proportions.

There are some days you are never likely to forget, and the day of the Stockport air disaster is for me one of them. I was at my home in Sale – at the time I was Granada's news editor and fledgling newsreader – when I received a telephone call from a contact in the Manchester police force telling me there had been an air crash in Stockport. It was within minutes of the event, and the message was a touch garbled and lacked detail. I made a few quick calls myself to try to access the strength of the story which, may sound callous, but has to be done by journalists. I soon realised that it was indeed a major disaster, so I immediately called my departmental boss, David Plowright, at his home in Cheshire.

Once I had convinced him of the seriousness of the crash, he and I started to 'round up' technicians and journalists, who of course were not in the office or studios. In those days, there were no scheduled weekend news bulletins and Granada did not really exist at weekends. Its licence was to transmit programmes throughout the North West and Yorkshire, because ABC Television based in Didsbury were the weekend company. They did not have a full news desk in operation, so it was really down to us, plus some of their staff, to get on with what proved to be a harrowing day's work.

As soon as I finished my organising people from home, others and I joined our teams in Stockport. We all played our part in the operation, finding out background and doing interviews with witnesses and the emergency services. ITN in London did not have a regional office or staff in the north in those days, so we fed a whole lot of live and recorded material to them for transmission throughout the UK.

One particular memory I do have is, that within an hour or so of the crash, the police were desperately asking us to put out an appeal on air trying to persuade people not to go into the town centre. As the accident had happened in such an accessible area, ice cream vans and various food vendors had made their way there, as well as thousands trying to catch glimpses of the crash site and the activity going on. Human nature I suppose – rather like the modern-day equivalent of motorists slowing down on motorways when accidents happen to 'rubberneck' what is going on.

Looking back, I like to think that our day's work was done without intrusion and with the humanity that good journalists can demonstrate in what can be very difficult and trying conditions.

The Reverend Arthur Connop had the unique distinction of being chaplain to the Stockport police force, fire and ambulance services as well as the Infirmary, where he was an almost daily visitor on the wards. A Yorkshire man by birth and ordained in 1947 he began his pastoral work in Stockport in the early 1950s and in 1963, he became the minister of Tiviot Dale Methodist Church in the town centre. Displaying his legendary dry sense of humour with a fund of one-liners, he once joked that he was only on this side of the Pennines on missionary work and would return home when his work was done – he never left.

He first came to the attention of the police one dark dank December evening in 1961, when he witnessed a fracas outside a public house as he was driving past. He helped the lone police officer trying to deal with the incident by leaping out of his car in full ministerial garb and sitting on one of the louts. As the police officer called for back up, Arthur was overheard telling the man: "Now listen son. The police can't hit you but I can – and who would believe it?" With that, the man gave up the struggle.

From that time on, Arthur was adopted as police chaplain – believed to be the first in the country and, as it turned out, the longest serving. There were countless occasions when families suffered bereavement, under tragic circumstances, desperately needing caring support and the first place everyone would think to turn was to send for Arthur.

On that Sunday morning, just like any other, he was to be found in his vestry getting ready to go into the pulpit to take the morning service but the shrill ringing of the telephone abruptly interrupted his preparations. It was a call that would hurl him into a maelstrom of unimaginable horror and grief and gave him a unique insight into the disaster's impact in personal human terms.

"The call was from the police," recalled Arthur, "telling me there had been a serious accident and would I attend. I immediately abandoned the service, apologised to the congregation and left them to it. At the time, I had no idea what had happened. I initially thought I was on my way to a road traffic accident."

Arriving at the crash site, he was shocked by the enormity of death and destruction that met his eyes. 'Horror – a kind of cold feeling' was how he described it as he wandered aimlessly around the burning wreckage trying, like so many others, to help those who were beyond help.

When I arrived at the crash scene, there was just smoking debris – that was all. The site of devastation was both pitiful and shocking. Everywhere people were rushing to help and the fire crews were fighting the blaze. I found it incredible how everyone just pulled together and became a team. At first, the whole thing was disjointed and chaotic but it was amazing how quickly things got in order. I realised from the start there was little I could do on the scene; the others could do this kind of thing far better that me. As I recall, a senior police officer approached me and asked if I would go over to the nearby infirmary to make arrangements for meeting the relatives and friends as they arrived in the town.

We had expected that they would all rush to Stockport when they heard the news. We didn't know then that the radio had told them to go straight to the airport. This gave us some breathing space to make preparations. Eventually, of course, the relatives began to arrive here. By that time, we had prepared a room to receive them. I do remember the first couple to arrive was a young man and woman. The man was asking about his mother, father and sister and the young lady was asking about her sister who was travelling with them.

People of course were terribly upset. One minute they were waiting, in happy anticipation, to welcome home from holiday their relatives and friends and the next minute their loved ones were dead and gone. I did what I could but, to be perfectly honest, it isn't an easy task to comfort people in that situation. How can you comfort them? I think here is a mother, a father, a child, a somebody. I can't think in terms of multiple casualties; there is little to say, religious or any other kind of talk. All you can do is be kind and compassionate and try your utmost to feel what they feel.

It was a frenetic time for Arthur who spent his time shuttling between the infirmary and the police station. It was his grim and unenviable duty to inform the majority of the relatives of the loss of their loved ones. It was, however, a more pleasing task to comfort the handful of survivors and their families who had come through the ordeal alive. The following days passed in a flurry of activity. His home became 'open house' where he and his wife, Alice, provided hospitality, compassion and support for relatives and helpers and, indeed anyone else involved – and there were many – who just needed to drop by for a cup of tea and talk.

Arthur was annoyed at the time of how the press portrayed him as some sort of local hero without even talking to him. It was a term that made him feel uncomfortable. "I wasn't heroic," he told me, "few people involved were. It fell to us at the time to do what we could, and we all did our very best in what were very trying and tragic circumstances."

When the inferno was brought under control and the fire fighters began to damp down the smouldering wreckage, rescue workers moved back into the blackened skeletal remains of the passenger cabin with the blind hope of finding further survivors. It was a futile hope. All that they could to do now was disgorge Hotel Golf's ghastly cargo of the dead. There were poignant scenes as stretcher after stretcher meandered through the melee of spectators carrying away the blanket shrouded remains of the unfortunate victims, their blackened disfigured limbs locked in grotesque poses. They were taken the short distance over the cobbles of Hopes Carr and laid out in regimented rows on the oil-stained garage workshop floor. Bill Oliver, who took part in this harrowing work, like so many others, was now suffering from not only shock but a deep sense of frustration at being unable to rescue more passengers. He described this part of the recovery operation as 'futile and useless and too horrible to talk about'.

When the recovery work was concentrated on the rear of the aircraft, it revealed a terrifying sight; a pile of charred and mutilated bodies huddled together that were barely recognisable as human. What little remained of their clothing was fused to their blackened burnt flesh by the intense heat of the fire. The sight was truly repellent and many of those engaged in extricating the remains were unable to conceal their feelings and indeed their stomach contents. It was a surreal sight of human tragedy on a massive scale that would be seared into their memory for the rest of their lives.

The sombre and stomach wrenching recovery work continued for over an hour, until it was certain that the whole of the wreckage was completely cleared of human remains. For all those involved first hand in this distressing and unenviable task, it was difficult for them to believe, that these carbonised blackened shapes were human, each one a person, who just a few short hours ago could talk with you, share a joke; each one with hopes, dreams and aspirations. Whether they were young or old, life held out so much. Now their shrouded, grisly remains lay row upon row, on the cold, undignified, concrete floor of a garage workshop.

The destruction of the fuselage was total. All that part from aft of the cockpit to within ten feet of the rear pressure bulkhead in the tail had been severely gutted by fire. Indeed, such was the ferocity and extreme temperatures of the inferno that much of the fuselage had melted down into pools of unidentifiable metal alloy. Remarkably, despite the violence of the crash and the all-consuming fire, a grim miscellany of half burnt and charred personal possessions somehow miraculously managed to survive amongst the blackened heaps of fragmented metal. All were poignant reminders of happy carefree family holidays in the sun: A child's flip flop; a broken snorkel; a bottle of sun tan lotion; handbags; a straw hat worn in the sun; wallets, purses, a packet of duty-free cigarettes and a scorched passport for five-year-old twins. Sodden with oil and aviation fuel, they were all carefully gathered together on canvas salvage sheets and taken away.

It was highly unlikely that the owners of this macabre miscellany would come forward and claim ownership.

In addition, nearly a ton of sodden unidentified clothing was recovered and subsequently incinerated with the permission of the airline in order to prevent it getting into the possession of ghoulish souvenir hunters and looters, of which there were aplenty milling around the scene like jackals patiently waiting their opportunity.

When the Fire Brigade was finally stood down in the late afternoon, Whitehill Street Station Officer, Fred Matkin, his eyes red-rimmed with fatigue, told gathered reporters: "All those working at close quarters had to bear up in the face of terrible sights of death and injury as they tried to get into the blazing fuselage. I saw the burnt lifeless bodies of about fifty men, women and children pulled out – nobody could have survived in the rear of the cabin. In the fire service, I have attended three air crashes, but I have never seen one as bad as this; the death and destruction was truly horrendous."

David Hamilton and the author seen here at the memorial in 2002 (author's archive).

Chapter Five
The Bitter Taste of Death

"I found it almost impossible to sleep that night. I kept seeing all those bodies covered in white sheets."

Cadet Nurse – Jacqueline Collins

Peter Eyre, British Midland's Duty Operations Manager at East Midlands Airport has an unforgettable tale to tell. The tragic loss of one of the company's aircraft affected him deeply and in the ensuing years has never wanted to talk about it. Forty-years later, he found the courage to break his self-imposed silence to speak for the first time about the tragedy. He told me:

It was the most stressful twenty-four hours of my life. I had been up all Saturday night as my wife was in Belper Hospital due to give birth to our first son David but, owing to complications, she was later transferred to the Derby City Hospital. I followed behind the ambulance on my motorbike and stayed with her throughout the night until I had no choice but to leave as I was due on duty at East Midlands Airport at six o'clock.

As I started my shift, the outgoing controller, Adrian Nettleship, passed on to me the dreadful news – that anyone associated with aviation dreads – that a DC-4 belonging to the British independent operator, Air Ferry, flying a holiday charter from Manston to Perpignan had crashed in the Pyrenees with the loss of all 88 passengers and crew. This was certainly shocking news, but little did I know then what was soon to follow.

As the morning progressed, I was keeping tabs with the situation at the hospital and flight watching, which included radio calls to and from our aircraft that were airborne at the time including Hotel Golf. Later in the morning, Roger Wise, flying one of our Viscounts back from Palma with a full passenger load, called up on the company frequency to give me his flight details and his estimated time of arrival at East Midlands. Soon after, Harry Marlow – who took off from Palma 45 minutes before Roger – called up to give me his ETA at Manchester, number of passengers and aircraft serviceability. I chatted over the radio for a few minutes in good spirit and humour as the aircraft passed by on its final leg to Ringway. Harry gave me the impression that there were no problems and that the aircraft, although delayed somewhat, was fully serviceable and would be able to leave Manchester for its next flight to Barcelona more or less on time. Then over the radio chatter, I overheard Roger – who had overtaken the much slower Argonaut en-route – call up Harry and say: "What kept you, mate?"

Harry laughed and quipped back: "You know what these bloody old lumbering Argonauts are like Roger, chug, chug, chug chug…"

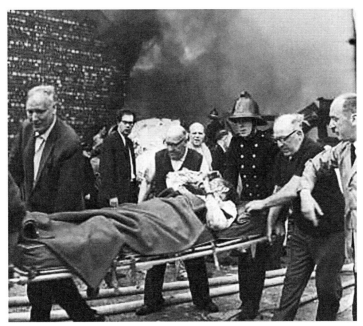

Captain Harry Marlow being stretched away after been freed from the wreckage to an awaiting ambulance (Philip Dunn/Rex Features).

Sometime later, the phone rang and my world fell apart. It was from our Manchester station manager, Mike Bishop, who gave me the devastating news that Hotel Golf had crashed in the middle of Stockport on the approach to Manchester. I remember the phone literately shook in my hand as I stared at the handset trying to take in the enormity of the news. I asked Mike to repeat what he had just told me, because I found it almost impossible to believe, having spoken to Harry Marlow earlier that morning. When I recovered enough from the initial shock, I told Mike to get out to the scene immediately and get as much information as he could back to me. From that point on, what had been a very ordinary routine Sunday morning, took on a surreal quality.

By this time, Roger Wise had touched down and arrived with his crew in the operations room to complete his paper work. Roger took one look at me and knew that something was seriously amiss and he asked me what the problem was. I gave him the terrible news and the girls in his crew broke down, which made it extremely difficult for me to focus on the task in hand. I asked Roger if he would take his crew out of the room so that I could get on with what was now an extremely heavy workload.

My first task was to get another aircraft and flight crew up to Manchester ASAP to continue the flights that Hotel Golf could not now operate. It was in these early stages that I reflected on the crew who I knew so well, especially dear Chris Pollard, the First Officer, who was so young, talented, cheerful and full of life. In the operational sense, I also became concerned if the aircraft's library was up to date with their navigational charts and documentation that I had previously dealt with.

During the morning, I had to break off from the distressing work and call the hospital to find out how my wife was going on. I was told she had given birth to our son, David, an hour after the crash. Under the circumstances, it was impossible for me to get away, so I left a message with the ward sister to tell my wife that I was unable to visit her for some considerable time because I was dealing with an accident to one of our aircraft.

As the day wore on, the workload intensified as I attended to the many FAX messages and frantic telephone calls that came streaming in regarding passengers and crew not accounted for. I remember Chris Pollard and the flight engineer were amongst this list and that someone had given me the wrong name for the engineer, and again this caused terrible pain.

Again, I thought of my involvement with the crew and, more importantly, that Harry Marlow the day before had asked me to cancel his hotel room near the airport as he loved a game of golf and preferred to rest at home before a night flight. Such minor things become major issues when the investigators look at the crew experience; rest periods, hours on duty etc., which play such an important part in the build-up to an accident.

The Stockport air disaster made a huge impact on my life and the memory of that day has stayed with me ever since. Many years later, whilst working at Coventry Airport, I was taking a visiting party on a tour of Air Atlantique's historic aircraft. As we approached a DC-6 – which from certain angles looks very much like an Argonaut – this aircraft suddenly became Hotel Golf in my mind and I became extremely emotional, tears flooded down my cheeks and I was unable to talk with my guests. For as long as I live, I will never be able to forget that traumatic and harrowing day. I have good reason to, as each and every year my son's birthday is a constant reminder.

PC Roger Gaskell was the Coroner's Officer with Stockport police. Normally, he would deal with one or two fatalities at the most in any one week. But in the coming days, he would deal with violent death on an unprecedented scale. He told me:

On that Sunday morning, I was at my mother's house paying her a visit when I received a phone call from my wife. She told me that Sergeant Jones had just called and informed her that an airliner had crashed in the town centre and that I was to go there immediately. With that shocking news, I put on my coat and rushed off. I reached the end of the drive and, as luck would have it, one of our lads, Walter Caldwell, was passing in a CID car. He stopped and asked me if I wanted a lift. I climbed in and passed on the dreadful news that a holiday airliner had come down at Hopes Carr. He was absolutely staggered. He turned to me and said: "You're joking. That's where I am going now. We're doing a surveillance job there on a carpet warehouse, we've had a tip-off that there is going to be a break in."

We sped to the scene down Hall Street and turned left into Upper Brook Street. On reaching the end, at its junction with Waterloo Road, we could go no further because by this time, it was packed with spectators. Walter told me to jump out whilst he tried to find somewhere to park. I went over to the edge of the crowd, looked over and saw Sergeant Bill Gathercole and two constables trying to keep the over excited crowds under control. Bill spotted me and told me to go over to the garage immediately and help out.

When I arrived, the rescue and recovery workers were just bringing in the first of the bodies. Sergeant Jones, who was inside supervising the operation gave me a pile of plastic bags and told me to search each body for any identification and property, put it in the bags and then tie the bags to the wrists of the casualties. We went about these tasks as unperturbed as it was possible in such circumstances.

As the bodies began to be stretchered in a nursing sister appeared at the door – where she had come from I had no idea – she asked me if there was anything she could do to help. I told her exactly what Sergeant Jones had told me and handed her a pile of

64

bags and ties. Then two of our lads from the Regional Crime Squad arrived to start the preliminary work of trying to identify the victims.

The sheer number of casualties now being recovered from the wreckage threatened to overwhelm the established protocols for dealing with the dead. There had been no talk about numbers yet but some were speculating that it could be up to one hundred. Roger Gaskell continues:

It soon became apparent that we were not going to have enough room in the garage to accommodate all the victims. Sergeant Jones told me they were thinking of taking some, if not all the bodies over to the Salvation Army Citadel on Hillgate.

We brought in a few more, searched them for anything in the way of property and belongings. With that, we finished off, tidied up as best we could, put a uniformed police officer on the door and then forced our way through the thickening crowds over to the Citadel to see what we could do there.

Brian Donohoe, caught up in tumult of the mornings events, found himself in the garage workshop with half a dozen others helping to deal with the casualties as they were brought in. The sweet smell of burnt flesh caught their throats and turned their stomachs. When the last of the victims were stretchered in, the garage doors were slammed shut and a senior police officer asked those present if they would volunteer to stay behind and wrap the bodies with blankets pending their removal to the temporary mortuary now being set up at the Citadel. It was whilst Brian was undertaking this sombre and gut-wrenching assignment that he was suddenly profoundly shocked and saddened to be confronted with the badly burnt body of the woman he had been so desperate to rescue, but had to stand helplessly by and watch her burn to death – seeing her burnt lifeless body shook him to the core.

Immediately after the crash, one section of the town worked with unstinting devotion, they were the members of the Salvation Army, who laboured with relentless energy throughout the day. They maintained contact with the rescuers, ran messages and gave personal comfort to all those affected by the tragedy. In addition to all this, they organised the time-honoured British solution to every calamity and the universal panacea for all ills – endless mugs of hot, steaming, restorative tea dished out in liberal quantities to the rescuers and recovery teams.

Anxious faces outside the garage on the Hopes Carr, set up as a temporary mortuary as they awaited further casualties (author's archive).

Because of the lack of mortuary facilities available, the Salvation Army came to the aid of the police by offering the use of the nearby Citadel as a temporary mortuary. Bandsman and Corps secretary, Arthur Thorniley, explains how it came about:

I spoke to a senior police officer at the scene, who informed me that, as far as he knew, there were no mortuary facilities available to accommodate all the victims – which at that stage we thought could possibly amount up to a hundred or more. So I told him I would go and open the Sunday school room in the Citadel and clear out all the benches with a view to using that as a base.

Probably an hour later – which I would estimate was getting on for 11:30 – the first of the casualties started to arrive at the Citadel. The crowds gathering outside were now so vast that we had to put benches outside to keep the road clear for the ambulances bringing the victims to the hall. I remained there for the remainder of the day dealing with documentation and, to place as circumstances made it available, identification adjacent the bodies.

The day went on and before we knew it was early afternoon, by which time the rain had stopped and the sun had come out. It seemed like a normal summer Sunday,

66

except within the confines of our building which was sombre and depressing to say the least. By this time, the crowds were becoming immense outside – it was as if we were giving something away. There were literally thousands of people jostling around and, before long vendors arrived to cash in on the tragedy selling burgers, hot dogs, ice cream, you name it – it was like the entrance to a football ground on match day. I'm afraid it rather took us by storm.

As the victims were brought into the building and laid out on the floor, I, along with the police and others, started to list the bodies as far as we could with a view to identification. This was almost impossible in the majority of cases because they were so badly burnt and mutilated that it was extremely difficult even to tell what sex they were. One of the most awful experiences I had with regard to the casualties was a whole family – a father, a mother and their two young children. To me, it seemed so tragic that they were just six miles from home and yet this disaster had befallen them.

I had a further shock later in the day when parents with their young children in tow came banging on the door of our building, asking matter-of-factly: "Can we bring the children in to have a look at the bodies?" I was, as you can imagine, astounded and angry by this callous behaviour; we turned them away of course, obviously. This shocking disaster was nothing more than a peep show as far as some were concerned. I could hardly believe what I witnessed that day.

During the following week, I was given time off from Stockport College – where I was employed as an engineering lecturer – to help with the counselling of relatives who came to Stockport; the police in this instance were very helpful. Senior Salvation Army officers from Manchester also arrived in the town and one stayed with us all week, giving what help and support he could.

To my mind, it was the worst weekend that we had experienced in the Salvation Army in all the years I had been in attendance and that dates back all my life. I personally had seen battle. I was a commander of a Crusader tank and landed in Normandy on D-Day and went all the way through the campaign to Lubeck on the Baltic. Prior to that, I had been called as a witness to the hideous Nazi concentration camp at Belsen where, of course, 50,000 emaciated bodies had been found. I was there on the second day the camp had been discovered and to my mind the horrors of this tragedy, on our own doorstep, was something akin to what I had seen over there in action.

Arthur's wife, Bertha, told me how the sheer magnitude of brutal death she witnessed that day anaesthetised her emotions and totally dislocated her mind from reality. For the remainder of that day, she operated on autopilot.

I arrived at the Citadel a short time after the crash. The first I heard about it was when a gentleman on Hillgate, with a child on his shoulders, said to me, "There's a plane come down in Waterloo." The news came as a terrible shock. When I entered the building, I realised there were young children about who had come to attend Sunday school. We quickly gathered them together and moved them into another part of the building and settled them down because, by this time, news had filtered through as to what exactly had happened and what our bandsmen were doing.

Someone said we are going to need some food and other provisions, so I volunteered and set off for home and eventually got in touch with my local grocer who opened his shop and gave us what supplies he could. When I was driving home, the roads were fairly clear but on the return journey I had an awful job to get through because of the thousands of sightseers that had flocked to the scene clogging all the roads.

I don't know what I was prepared for really when I entered the Citadel. I just realised we had things to do. The building was buzzing with people but the only ones I can remember being there were Arthur and my sister-in-law. The sight of row upon row of burnt and mutilated bodies defied imagination. I just looked at them and realised there were various parts missing because, at this time, they hadn't been covered up. They were lying exposed on the floor because we were still in the process of trying to identify them. We just tried to piece people together. It was amazing really. We carried on throughout that day doing what we had to do, we didn't stop to eat or drink, it didn't cross our minds, besides our appetites were quelled by the horrendous sight and smell of what we were dealing with. At the end of the room, on the raised platform, there were what I can only describe as blackened 'tree trunks', these were bodies that were burnt beyond the remotest possibility of identification. Even then, I had no feeling whatsoever; it just didn't seem to register with me. I was in a state of numb shock, it was the strangest of feelings – it was as if this wasn't really happening. There were a small number of bodies that were whole and unmarked, I assumed they had been thrown out of the aircraft and killed on impact. I will always remember one little boy who had no visible injuries at all, just some dust on his face as if nothing had happened, he gave me the impression of simply being asleep – there were several like that.

Stockport PC Stephen Clegg, ordered by a senior officer to go and assist at the Citadel, told me about the horrific sight that met his eyes on entering the building:

When I arrived at the Citadel, most of the bodies had been laid out on the floor on what looked like field stretchers and covered from top-to-toe with blankets. Others could not be placed so because of the contortion in how they'd died. You only have to imagine that most had met their end in their seats and, as such, were shaped thus, with arched backs and legs bent. Others had been clinging on to loved ones and had become fused together in death. These poor individuals presented a particular daunting image even under cover. The injuries were horrific in the extreme   I will spare you the most graphic details – suffice to say that legs had been burnt off to the knee, arms to the elbow and everybody who had been extricated from the aircraft – save one small boy who had died on impact – had been charred black.

Then there was the smell. Not what you would expect and, to me, as gross as it may sound, it was like a huge Sunday roast. Indeed, every one of the days I worked in that awful place, my stomach rumbled as it would before partaking of a cooked meal. I am sorry if readers find this offensive, but it was a fact.

When Roger Gaskell entered the Citadel, he found the whole floor area had been cleared and the bodies, and remains of bodies, were reverently placed in rows. By this time, they had been wrapped in white plastic sheeting obtained from a local undertaker in order to provide some semblance of dignity in death. The unmistakeable odour of burnt flesh was overpowering in the confines of the room and assaulted the senses of all those who entered. Roger Gaskell continues:

By this time, all the casualties had been recovered from the aircraft and everyone involved was now at the Citadel. The Chief Constable, Leonard Massey, his deputy Tom Walker and a lot of the town's dignitaries put their heads together and realised that this was not a satisfactory situation. I don't know who it was who made the decision but it was decided to move some of the bodies to the Centenary Hall, which was the old Sunday school building near the police station.

Later in the afternoon, an emergency meeting got underway in the Chief Constable's office at police headquarters. The chief was there, his deputy, detective superintendent Aspinal, other senior officers and some local dignitaries. Half way through the meeting, there was a knock at the door, which I answered to see a young police constable standing there who said: "There are two gentlemen from the RAF here, who would like to speak to the chief." And in walked Group Captain Mason and Squadron Leader Tarleton. They presented their credentials and told us that they were now in charge of all the casualties and would undertake the post mortems – it was bloody amazing, the speed of events that day.

Later, I escorted them the short distance down to the crash scene by which time the whole area was like Blackpool Prom on a Bank Holiday – parents with children on their shoulders, it was an unbelievable sight to witness. After they had briefly examined the site and taken some notes, we went back to police headquarters where some representatives from British Midland Airways, including Michael Bishop, had now arrived. I remember the Chief couldn't conceal his rage and went absolutely ballistic with them because they hadn't got a passenger list. Apparently, they were waiting for one to be telexed over from Palma. When the Chief eventually calmed down, we all sat down and discussed what the plan of campaign would be on the Monday.

In the early afternoon, the drizzle and grey overcast gave way to clearing blue skies and warm bright sunshine – a typical English summer's day to be enjoyed, apart from the townsfolk of Stockport. As salvage work continued at the site, a light aircraft wheeled noisily overhead at 500 feet. Inside the cramped cabin, half a dozen press photographers, clutching their cameras, jostled in media frenzy for the best position to aim their lenses at the pitiful scene of devastation below, all hoping for that special shot that would adorn the front pages of Monday's newspapers. Higher still, at 1,800 feet, airliners continued flying over the scene on their approach and let down to the airport and those who cared to crane their necks skyward would notice a Boeing 707 jetliner dipping its wings in salute to the stricken remains of the airliner below.

In order to ensure a complete search for any further casualties, two mobile cranes were commandeered from a local contactor to move the twisted burnt out sections of wreckage to more convenient positions. Local man Gordon Smith recalls his involvement:

On that Sunday morning, I was working on the British Home Stores building on the Merseyway Shopping Precinct which was then under construction. I actually saw the aircraft and remarked to everyone that it was flying very low. A few seconds later, there was an almighty bang which echoed over the Precinct followed by a huge column of black smoke. No one realised just what had happened until later, when a police officer came onto the site and requested the use of our mobile crane. The crane driver dismantled enough of the jib to allow transit and six of us jumped on the back with our tool kits just in case. On approaching Hopes Carr, we were sickened by the sheer volume of people who were standing around watching. This made our progress rather difficult until the police came to our aid and guided us to the site.

Several things still vividly remain in my mind fifty-years later; the smell of aviation fuel, warm oil and acrid smoke. I was amazed to see the cockpit 'parked' neatly alongside the sub station wall and thought what an incredible thing to do in such dire circumstances. A hasty mortuary had been set up in the nearby garage and one could clearly see blood on the floor and numerous St John's Ambulance personnel trying to hide it from public view.

As our crane lifted the tail section clear of the main wreckage, we could see items of clothing – I hope it was – spilling out onto the grassy bank. I personally did not witness any dead or injured but helped search the wreckage where I found a pair of flip-flops, a child's doll, some photographs and a miscellany of other personal items which I handed in to the rescue people.

Later, we returned to the Precinct where the site foreman, Jim Ackers, told us that under the circumstances to leave work and get off home. Upon arriving home, covered in oil and foam, I spotted a copy of the *News of the World* and on the front page was a picture of an air disaster in France. When my wife asked where I had been to get into such a state, I pointed to the picture and said in my confusion that I had been there. Neither she nor I had any idea that two crashes had occurred that weekend.

Back at the police headquarters, an emergency incident room had now been set up to deal with the situation. The building's designers had woefully failed to anticipate the heavy demands on the telephone system in the aftermath of a major disaster such as this. By lunchtime, additional phone lines were provided by the GPO in order to cope with the massive influx of calls now being received.

The incident room was put under the supervision of a senior officer with a mixed staff of police and civilians. Their duty was to log and deal with all messages connected with the accident. In the early stages, every telephone line was fully occupied by a flood of calls from anxious relatives and friends, many of whom had been waiting at the airport to meet relatives off the flight. To prevent repeated press enquiries, it was announced that two press conferences would be held at 4 and 10 p.m., and would be addressed by the Chief Constable. The incident room dealt not only with the Accident Investigation Branch (AIB), relatives and witnesses, but with a wide range of other services and organisations heavily involved with the disaster and its aftermath. The early establishment of the incident room prevented what otherwise would have been an impossible overloading of the normal communications system.

It quickly became evident that a special procedure was necessary to deal with the problems of relatives and friends now arriving at police headquarters in considerable numbers. It was decided to set up a separate room on the first floor, where charts showing the disposition and details of all the victims, the correlation of the property to the passengers, a progress chart, that as the days went on would show how far visual, dental, medical and pathological methods of identification had progressed and other miscellaneous information relative to each individual casualty. This room also housed dedicated experienced police officers to interview relatives and friends. Arthur Connop, the police chaplain, with other ministers assisted, refreshments were provided and everything possible was done to comfort and support the bereaved.

Almost without exception, due to the sheer ferocity of the post-crash fire, hand luggage, passports and other miscellaneous documentation were totally destroyed, although a few passports and other means of identity were recovered from bodies and clothing. Where possible, jewellery and other personal effects were recorded, bagged and left on the body until pathological examination was carried out.

A policeman examining a burnt passport in the hope that it may lead to the identification of one of the 72 badly burnt victims lying in the nearby mortuary (author's archive).

In each of the two temporary mortuaries, a senior police officer was put in charge. Anterooms were prepared for identification purposes and chaplains were made available to comfort the next of kin. Visual identification by relatives was delayed as long as possible in order to clean and arrange bodies – many of which were so badly burned and mutilated, they presented a frightening spectacle – and make them as dignified as was possible before relatives had the harrowing ordeal of viewing and identifying their loved ones. To ensure corroborative evidence from dental and medical sources, a casualty officer from the hospital with nurses to assist was attached to each mortuary and in every case – according to strict legal protocol – life was pronounced extinct on each of the victims. Bodies were divided into groups for identification – males, females and children, so as to prevent inspection of unnecessary large numbers by the relatives

A considerable number of police officers, who were officially off-duty, either went straight to the scene or reported to their headquarters where their offers of help were readily accepted. Some of those who were alerted at home by telephone first thought that their Sunday morning was being disturbed by a civil defence exercise; only to find that what was normally a routine practice drill had become tragic reality.

Police Sergeant Charles Hunt, an experienced officer with nearly twenty years of service under his belt, was mobilised to take charge of one of the hastily setup mortuaries. He explains how it came about:

On the day of the air disaster, I was off duty at home when my eldest son – who was upstairs studying for his A Levels – rushed down stairs and said he'd heard the sound of aircraft engines that had suddenly stopped followed by a noise like faraway thunder. I had a rather tatty garden shed in those days; the door wasn't hinged and was leaning up against it. I looked out of the window and saw it was lying on the ground. I said: "Well, that's what you heard." And thought nothing more about it. Soon after, I heard on the radio the shocking news that an airliner had crashed in the centre of the town.

Without hesitation, I changed into my uniform, jumped in the car and roared off. Driving down Hillgate, the crowds that had converged on the scene were so immense that I had to drive one handed holding my helmet out of the driver's window and operating the horn at the same time, but in fairness, they parted to let me through. I arrived at police headquarters and parked in my usual spot – I was in such a rush that I left the door and window open!

On entering the building, I was asked to take charge of the second mortuary at the nearby Sunday school at the Centenary Hall where a number of bodies had already been taken. I was allocated a small team of constables to lay out the victims and a doctor and a handful of nurses came over from the infirmary to assist. At first, we tried to separate the victims into males and females, but because of their fragile burnt state, it wasn't always possible. There was certainly no possibility of recognising anyone facially – apart from one aircrew member and a girl aged about six who didn't have a mark on her.

We were half anticipating that there would be more dead coming from the infirmary because the situation was still fluid then. We knew we had 32 bodies but we didn't know how many were at the Salvation Army Citadel and if there were more bodies to come they would be coming to us. So we had to keep the road clear for arriving ambulances. It was at this point that a man drove up with his children to view the crash site and was looking for somewhere to park. I told him he could not leave his car outside because we were waiting for ambulances. His attitude was belligerent to say the least; he said to me: "I don't care. I want to park my car here. It's a street so I can legally park here if I want to."

The ground opposite was a bit rough in those days and hadn't been developed and there was a 10-foot drop. I was in no mood to argue with him, so I told him in no uncertain terms: "Leave your car there and it will be down that ditch when you get back." He took great exception to this and stormed off to the police station to complain. From my position, I watched him bound up the station steps and thirty seconds later, he was ejected at a rate of knots with a policeman's boot behind him.

It was things like that, that stick in my mind, but what I will always remember, more than anything else about that dreadful day, was the help ordinary people gave. That's the primary thing that will always stay with me. If you're a uniformed organisation, you've got to help, no question about it – but there were those ordinary Stockport folk who didn't have to assist but voluntary got stuck in without being asked. It is that, above all else, that I will always remember about that day.

I arrived home at about six o'clock that evening, went upstairs to wash and change then flopped on the bed and burst into tears.

Everybody in the local community it seemed was, in some way, involved in the tragic events of that day, even the very young, including Salvation Army youngsters and nursing students who shouldn't have had to witness such hideous sights. One of the youngest involved was 16-year-old cadet nurse Jacqueline Collins. She was utterly unprepared for what she was about to face when she awoke on that Sunday morning.

I was just about to set off with my mum to visit the cemetery when Mrs Marsden, our next-door neighbour, told us the news that there had been a plane crash at Hopes Carr. I ran back into the house, put on my uniform and went down with Mum to see if I could help. On arrival, I was escorted down to the crash site – it was a truly awful thing to see. We were then taken over to the nearby Covent Garden flats where a lot of old people lived and we went door to door to tell them what had happened and that they were safe and in no danger. From there, I went to the police station and was given a notebook and asked to take down names and details of those people arriving at the station seeking news of friends and loved ones. That's where I met John Benton – I will always remember him because he was so young; tragically, he lost both parents and his sister in the accident. I remember there was a lot of crying – it was all so sad. I was starting to get upset too when I felt a hand on my shoulder. I looked up and saw the Reverend Arthur Connop standing beside me. He just smiled and nodded; it was he that gave me the reassurance that I needed to carry on.

When I had finished at the police station, I went back down to the crash site and was given what I thought at first was a pile of charred wood – they were in fact body parts – but you would never have known. I carried them over to the second mortuary at the Centenary Hall, where just a few months earlier, I had been made a Sunday school teacher. But when I entered the building that day, it looked very different to the one I knew. I found myself in the hall with a handful of men and women helping to piece the bodies together. It was a terrible sight – something you can't imagine. I saw and did things that day that no one should ever have to do – let alone a 16-year-old girl.

Later, I was thanked for my help and told to go home and rest. It was late when I arrived home to be greeted by my concerned mum and dad. Also waiting for me was my friend, Sheila, who I had arranged to go with to the Tabernacle Club that evening. I just had time for a quick wash and change of clothes and left the house like a robot. When I arrived at the club, all my friends wanted to go and see the crash site which was close by. When we got down there, it suddenly hit me what I'd been doing all day and I was so overcome I rushed home in floods of tears. I found it almost impossible to sleep that night – I kept seeing all those bodies covered in white sheets.

The next morning, as I made my way to work at Stepping Hill Hospital, a car pulled up to ask me if I knew where the survivors had been taken – they were a pilot and a stewardess from the airline looking for their friends. When I told them what I had been doing the previous day, they got out of the car, shook my hand and thanked me. On arrival at work, I got into terrible trouble from the Matron – who was a tyrant – for turning up in a dirty uniform and from crying.

Tony Miller, the divisional director of the Cheshire Red Cross, was away from home that morning attending a charity event in Stratford. When news of the disaster on his patch broke, he was naturally anxious to help out. He said, "I knew from telephone calls that our members were already on the scene assisting but, nevertheless, I needed to be there. I made my apologies and immediately drove back up to Stockport."

On arrival, he organised 20 Red Cross nurses to help console grieving families identify loved ones. He couldn't help but notice that the two halls put to use as mortuaries – besides the unpleasant nauseating odour – were cold, stark and impersonal, so he paid a visit to a nearby florist and asked if they could donate some flowers to put around the make-shift morgues to give the rooms a touch of humanity. "They told us to take the lot and actually came with us to dress the rooms – it made all the difference – at the very least it provided a splash of cheerful colour in the stark mourning gloom."

Chris McNeill was one of the local Red Cross volunteers mobilised. Within an hour of the crash, she received a telephone call at home from her Commandant, informing her of the disaster and instructing her to go to the temporary mortuary at the Salvation Army Citadel to help out. She told me:

All the roads into Stockport were blocked with cars and people who had come to stare and gawp at the scene. Eventually, I broke through the crowds – my uniform helped – and reached the Citadel. When I entered, the whole of the floor area was filled with blackened, burnt corpses covered with plastic sheeting; that sight certainly brought home the appalling reality of the situation. Some of the bodies had their intestines exposed, others their brains and everywhere the terrible noxious odour of aviation fuel and burnt flesh filled the air. It was truly an appalling and shocking sight and one that I will never forget.

My role there was to comfort the relatives and friends of the victims who came to identify their loved ones. All the personal effects, such as jewellery, wallets, handbags, purses and other documentation which had been recovered from the scene, had been brought over to help with their identification, as most of the bodies were completely unrecognisable.

Whilst I went about this task, I caught the sickening smell from the horribly burnt and mutilated bodies that pervaded the whole room, you could actually taste it – I can only describe it as the bitter taste of death. We sprayed cans and cans of 'Haze' air freshener all around the room to try and combat the terrible odour – with little effect. From that day on, I have never bought that particular brand as I am sure that certain smells provoke certain memories, and for me that is one memory I want to forget. But like everyone involved on that awful day, I probably never will.

No official action was taken to secure and mobilise the services of the local Civil Defence Corps who were well trained in rudimentary rescue and first aid. The Corps were at the time a prominent civilian volunteer organisation established in 1949 to prepare and take control in the aftermath of a Soviet nuclear attack – a threat which was taken very seriously at the height of the cold war. However, the devastation likely to be caused by thermonuclear weapons would be so great that it is hard to envisage what the Corps could possibly have done. Their well-trained members had in the past assisted in other national catastrophic events, like the severe flooding at Linton and Lynmouth in 1952; serious train crashes at Sutton Coldfield in 1955 and Lewisham in 1957 and not forgetting the mudslide at Aberfan in 1966. Their expertise in these national disasters cannot be underestimated; it was their involvement in these major incidents that did much to enhance the prestige of the organisation. The same was true at Stockport where its members were able to play a crucial role in supporting the rescue and other services.

When the full-time rescue officer heard the news, he immediately contacted the police to offer their services. Amazingly, considering the scale of the disaster, his offer of assistance was declined. Nevertheless, on his own initiative, he contacted Corps members by phone then immediately reported to Civil Defence headquarters where 47 field stretchers – that had not seen the light of day since the Second World War – were put to use along with other specialised rescue equipment. In addition, the Corps supplied a number of metal dustbins for, what was described as, 'the more unpleasant material' which in the main consisted of unidentifiable lumps of human flesh and other body parts that were recovered from the wreckage.

Part time Civil Defence worker, Joan Lally, was one of some 30 volunteers from Stockport and surrounding districts called out to assist. She had previously undertaken rudimentary air crash training at the nearby United States Air Force base at Burtonwood. However, despite her basic training, nothing could have prepared her for the magnitude of the disaster she faced. She told me:

On arrival, we were told to take as many blankets as possible over to the temporary mortuary set up at the Citadel. I remember the dreadful trouble we had forcing our way through the vast crowds of spectators. On entering the building, I was absolutely shocked to see row upon row of horribly charred bodies – some very small, obviously children. Being a paediatric nurse, I was used to seeing death, but never on such a tragic scale as this – it was a sight that has always stayed with me. Another onerous and upsetting task we had to undertake was to sift through all the burnt and fuel-soaked debris looking for any personal belongings of the unfortunate victims. Some of which were teddies, dolls and other trinkets belonging to children – I found that part of the operation really heart-breaking.

As Vivienne Thornber was being stretchered into Stockport Infirmary, her uncle, Melvyn Scorer, was settling down to what he hoped was a restful and relaxing Sunday at his home in the Lancashire town of Clitheroe some 25 miles to the north of Manchester. But in reality, it turned out to be a day unlike any other. He told me:

Apart from some early morning rain, I remember it being quite a pleasant morning. Whilst my wife, Joan, was upstairs getting ready for church, I went out into the garden with my coffee and Sunday papers. I had hardly sat down when the telephone rang and I dashed back in and snatched up the receiver. It was Arthur, Vivienne's dad – my brother-in-law – he was calling from the airport to say there had been an air crash. They were, as I understood it, 'locked' in a VIP lounge and not allowed to go out, because at that early stage, they didn't know about survivors or anything. I think in shock and panic, he had called to ask me if I would go over to the airport to see if I could help.

I told my wife, Joan, and we climbed into the car and immediately set out for the airport. In those days, there were no motorways as such and the airport was a nightmare to get to. Basically, it involved travelling south through all the towns and villages between Clitheroe and Manchester for a start, and from that point out towards the airport southeast of the city.

On the way, we had the car radio on picking up what information we could, not really knowing what we could do when we got there, apart from giving them help and support, because understandably, they were going to be terribly upset. Then as we were going through Manchester city centre and I was looking to strike out towards the airport, a news report came over the radio – which has always stuck in my mind because it changed the course of our direction that day. The reporter said he had just walked away from the crash site and all that could be seen was smoking wreckage and the relatives being led away. We put two and two together and came to the conclusion that Vivienne's parents were no longer at the airport; they must have been taken to Stockport. Without thinking how we were going to find them, we immediately changed course and headed for the town centre.

Along the way, we were stopped a couple of times at police roadblocks, which were diverting traffic away from the town. We just gave them the information that we had a relative on the aircraft and they flagged us through. Coming into Stockport, we spotted signs for the police station and headed there, again we were stopped by the police who directed us into the car park.

We entered the building and were escorted upstairs. The whole area was set up as an emergency incident room with desks, tables and chairs, information boards, people rushing about and the incessant ringing of telephones. We were immediately taken on one side and interviewed as to whom we were and whom we had on board the aircraft, which obviously was my niece, Vivienne, and her friend, Susan Howarth. We were informed that there were a few survivors but, at that early stage, they had no names. That's about all the information they could give us, but we were asked to leave a telephone number where we could be contacted with any further news. My parents lived in Nelson in those days, so I gave the police their number knowing that there would be someone there to receive messages.

With that, we came out of the police station not knowing what to do for the best. I turned to Joan and said, "Let's go and see if we can get nearer the scene, there might be an incident van there that can give us a bit more information." We walked the short distance down to the crash site and we were taken aback by the sheer volume of people clustered around. I managed with some difficulty to push my way through and get near enough – my wife wouldn't come further than the particular corner she was standing on. I went closer and standing on tiptoe looked over the heads of people. All I could see was this gigantic scorched tail fin stuck up in the air and little else. Everywhere around was charred smoking wreckage and the fire brigade damping down. I just walked away in dismay and said to Joan: "There's nobody come out of that alive." At that point, we felt so desperately low and, again not knowing what to do, we wandered aimlessly down the road amongst the crowds with no purpose in mind just trying to collect our thoughts.

By sheer chance, we came across the Salvation Army Citadel, and I wondered if they had any information. I spoke to a lady standing in the doorway. She took down all my details, as did the police, again with the telephone number for Nelson. She apologised, saying that they hadn't enough details at that time to release any names.

With that, we wandered away discussing things as we walked along. We had now twice given my parents number and I suggested that we should find a call box, phone home and let them know of the possibility of someone contacting them with news. In the distance I spotted a telephone box. I went in, snatched up the receiver and called my parents. It was my brother who answered. He said, "Have you heard anything?"

I said, "No, that's why I am calling."

He said, "Before you go any further, the Salvation Army have just called, Vivienne's alive and so is her friend Susan. They're both in Stockport Infirmary." At which point, I broke down.

My wife carried on speaking on the phone and I stepped out of the box. I saw a man walking towards me and as he passed, I asked him where Stockport Infirmary was – in fact, we were by the very door! The telephone box was virtually set up against the wall of the building. Joan joined me and we went through the entrance doors into a large, dimly lit, waiting room with rows of hard wooden bench seats. What was strange and eerie – considering the enormity of what had occurred only a few hundred yards away – it was totally empty. There wasn't a soul about, only a woman sitting at the reception desk. After I explained to her who we were, she told us to take a seat and she then disappeared. About five minutes later, a gentleman appeared – who I found out later was the Police Chaplin, Arthur Connop. He sat down with us and calmly went through all the details of who we were and what relatives we had on board – we also explained about Susan as well. He then turned to consult his clipboard and a few seconds later, he looked up and said: "Yes, they are both alive. Would you like to see them?"

We were escorted upstairs to a ward where all the survivors were being treated. I think we were the first of the relatives to arrive. I found that was quite a moving experience. The sheer emotion of that time I have always found difficult to explain. Within about an hour, we had gone through hell, come back out and gone back in again, and now finally we were face to face with the fact that she had survived – albeit seriously injured.

We sat at Vivienne's bedside for some time as she drifted in and out of consciousness, I think she was a little sedated at the time, but she was able to tell us bits about the crash before drifting off again. It was whilst I was sitting beside her that I noticed a small piece of metal from the aircraft stuck in her ear which I carefully removed. We then walked over to the next bed and sat with Susan for a while. Within twenty minutes of our arrival, the rest of the relatives began to arrive from the airport, including Vivienne's parents Joan and Arthur. It was a tearful reunion for all of us.

The Infirmary Staff allocated a private room for the relatives, across from the ward, which we could use as a lounge. They also warned us not to go outside the hospital by the main entrance as the press were there in numbers waiting to pounce on us for interviews.

Late in the afternoon, the surgeon came to see us to discuss what he hoped to do with Vivienne's badly smashed leg. Due to the serious nature of her injuries, he had grave doubts at that stage whether he could save it. Later that evening, we were all standing by the ward entrance when she was wheeled back from the operating theatre. Her mother, Joan – not to be confused with Joan, my wife – turned to me and said: "Melvyn, I can't go near. Will you go and see if they have saved her leg?" I followed the trolley slowly down the ward and waited until they had put her in bed. I pulled the screens away and gently lifted the sheets and saw two legs! It was quite comical in a way. That day had a huge impact on me, the memories of which will stay with me for the rest of my life.

Considering the enormity of the death and destruction that had occurred, there were certain bureaucratic and trivial formalities of officialdom that had to take its ordered course. In the late afternoon, two uniformed men from H M Customs and Excise with clipboards in hand arrived in the town. It was their dutiful task to account for the alcohol and tobacco carried on the aircraft as duty free. Of course, none of it had survived the intensity of the post-crash fire, but nevertheless, they still spent a considerable amount of time on site, painstakingly sifting through the charred debris counting the blackened and distorted tops from the exploded and melted spirit bottles. Their final report simply stated: 'cargo destroyed'.

The securing of an accurate passenger list was vital before relatives could be contacted. The usual practice at the time was for one copy to be carried on the aircraft – which in this case had been destroyed in the fire – and one copy to be retained at the point of departure. As this was in Palma – where in the 1960s, communications were notoriously bad – it wasn't until midnight before a complete list was telexed through to Stockport Police Headquarters. There was a passenger manifest available of those who flew out at the start of the holiday but this could not be relied on as correct for the return journey.

Holiday rep, Jackie Martinez, who managed Arrowsmith's Palma office, was given the unenviable task of compiling the list of her happy sun-tanned clients who she had been chatting and laughing with only hours earlier. She recalls:

My job with the company was to arrange accommodation, excursions and airport transfers. From time to time, I was asked to do the odd weekend transfer, which is exactly what I did in the early hours of Sunday 4 June. At the time, I was based at the Tahiti Hotel in Palma Nova, so I got to know most the clients quite well. Some of the groups we looked after were bloody awful, some OK and some very nice. As I recall, the group involved in the Stockport disaster was one of the better ones. In particular, I remember two smashing lads in their early twenties, one of them played the piano in the hotel bar for a singsong most nights – he was great. Another couple had a daughter, aged about eight, who sang Sandie Shaw's Eurovision hit, *Puppet on a String* over the coach microphone coming back from a barbecue; she was a real entertainer. Then there was another couple I recall with two teenage children, and they were late for the transfer coach to the airport. We waited as long as we could and, just as we were about to leave without them, they just came strolling along without a care in the world. I think all of the above perished in the accident.

I had planned to fly home that weekend as my grandmother was ill and it was also my mum's birthday. We had just two flights to Manchester available – the British Midland Argonaut and a Caledonian Airways DC-7. My boss's wife had just given birth in the UK so naturally, he was anxious to return home at the earliest opportunity. He grabbed the only remaining seat which, fortunately for him, was on the Caledonian flight. Disappointed, I fired off a telegram to Mum to tell her I couldn't make it home and to wish her a happy birthday for Sunday 4 June. She had heard the news on the radio about the crash and when the telegram boy knocked on the door sometime later, she immediately thought it was to inform her that I was onboard the aircraft.

If I remember correctly, the flight was late in taking off but I cannot remember why or for how long. I did the coach transfer from the Palma – Magaluf side and one of the other reps did the Arenal – C'an Pastilla. Dawn had long since broken by the time I got back to the hotel, very tired and in much need of sleep.

It must have been around lunchtime on the Sunday when the receptionist from the Tahiti Hotel came banging on my door to tell me that Arrowsmith's were holding on the phone and that I had to go immediately. I was given the terrible news and then I contacted the head rep, Mel Rossello. I clearly remember going with Mel to see the parents of Susan Howarth – one of the survivors. They were still on holiday and staying at the Hotel El Cid in C'an Pastilla. We gave them the news that their daughter had survived the accident and arranged to fly them back to the UK the same day.

On the Monday morning, when I went to open the office, there were about twenty of our clients waiting impatiently outside. They, of course, had heard the news by this time and in what I can only describe as a highly charged atmosphere, they were refusing point blank to fly home on the Argonaut. Some of them were quite nasty and threatening. In the end, Arrowsmith's never used the Argonaut again and, for the remainder of that season, we chartered Laker Airways BAC One-Eleven jets for all our inclusive tour flights.

Jackie's fellow holiday rep, Susan Maddocks, remembers the collective shock within the travel industry when the news of the disaster broke on the island.

I had worked for Arrowsmith Holidays for the previous two seasons and had just transferred to Gay Tours – another northern-based tour operator. When I arrived at the Hotel Riviera, near C'an Pastilla, one of the receptionists told me there had been a holiday air crash. I first thought she was referring to the one at Perpignan the previous evening, which I already knew about but was shocked to discover it was another one near Manchester Airport. My parents lived close to the airport at the time, so I was desperately worried about them and obviously, I wanted to make contact with home to see if everything was all right. That was easier said than done, as we were really isolated from the outside world in those days. There were only a handful of telephones on the island and, if you wanted to make an international call, you had to book a line days in advance and then wait for a couple of hours for it to be free – there was no television or international news either. Eventually, we discovered it was an Arrowsmith chartered British Midland Argonaut – in fact, the very same one I had flown home in the year before. A group of us immediately dashed off to the airport for any further news and found out it had come down in Stockport town centre, which naturally greatly eased my concerns about my parents.

The next day, I had to go to the Arrowsmith office in Palma to ask about various clients who had been staying in some of my hotels and had left friends and family behind on the island. Jackie was in the office with the passenger manifest and it really brought it home to me the sheer magnitude of the disaster when I read 'deceased' written next to so many names.

In the sombre chill of the temporary mortuary within the Citadel, the lights were switched off and the door closed and locked against the overpowering repugnant odour. The tags on the charred gruesome remains wrapped in white plastic sheeting said in the majority of cases – 'unidentified'.

In the hallway, a single bulb provided a pool of pale, yellow light where a 14-year-old, dirty-faced and dishevelled schoolboy with a faraway look in his eyes put on his coat in readiness to go home. "He's one of us," explained the Sunday School Superintendent to a querying reporter. "He was helping at the crash with the rest of them…he grew old today."

The sun, as if having seen enough of this terrible and surreal day began to sink behind the rooftops splashing the sky pink. Down at the crash site, as the dusk intensified the gloom, the streetlights gradually began to illuminate the roads surrounding the scene where voyeuristic sightseers still roamed in pathetic little groups. The scorched and blackened tail fin, silhouetted against the darkening sky gave the impression of a huge gravestone that had been erected in commemoration for the dead that now lay in the nearby mortuaries. It bore testimony to a summer's day that began so peacefully and ended in abject horror.

It was just passed midnight when the telex machine at police headquarters suddenly clattered into life as the keys hammered out a list of 84 names on a long sheet of pink paper – it was the long-awaited official crew and passenger manifest from Palma. The grim cold statistics it contained, confirmed the magnitude of the disaster in human terms; of the 84 souls on board a total of 72 men, women and children had perished. By luck or miracle, ten passengers and two crewmembers emerged from the devastation and now lay in the nearby infirmary – grievously injured but alive.

That night the town's stunned inhabitants slept fitfully but for those who were directly involved with the desperate rescue of passengers and the recovery of the dead found sleep difficult, if not impossible, to come by.

Chapter Six

Slaughter of the Innocents

"The sight of the four coffins side by side was almost too much to bear."
Relative – Pauline O'Sullivan

Monday dawned with crystal clear blue skies over most of the country, but in Stockport town centre and surrounding suburbs, there was an atmosphere of gloom and unreality as everyone tried to come to terms and make sense of the magnitude of the appalling tragedy that had upturned their ordered suburban lives. Despite the warm sunshine, a cold depression seemed to linger as the shocked and shaken townsfolk, with crumpled copies of the morning newspapers under their arms, wandered aimlessly around the immediate area, their faces blank with disbelief. Others gathered in huddled little groups ruminating on the tragic events, all unable to shake off a strange artificial sense of unreality. This feeling was to last for many days and weeks to come. Stockport was a town in pain.

At the disaster scene, the wreckage, which had been under police guard overnight to deter nocturnal looters, had been gathered into three major piles in some kind of distorted order. Two piles came from the aircraft itself and another made up from the burnt-out distorted shells of cars and vans destroyed in the garage. The huge charred tail fin, looking incongruous amongst the vibrant, green summer foliage, made up a fourth section.

There were few people in Britain who remained unmoved by the magnitude of the two disasters and the appalling loss of life. Naturally, all the national newspapers devoted acres of newsprint to both accidents and rightly declared that it was a 'black weekend' unprecedented in British commercial aviation history. They related harrowing and sensational eyewitness reports that were achingly familiar. This emotional response from the press no doubt helped to perpetuate a climate of fear amongst the travelling public, many of whom were about to take to the air on their summer holidays.

In their diagnostic post-mortems in the inside pages, journalists made much of the fact that both aircraft involved were elderly and were operated by charter airlines, making the strong implication that British independent airlines operated antiquated equipment on unscheduled operations flying into secondary airports, especially at night with poor navigational and landing aids.

Both accidents provoked typical press speculation: 'NO MORE OLD AEROPLANES ON HOLIDAY FLIGHTS' screamed the banner headline on one newspaper, whilst another speculated: 'ARE CHARTER AIRLINES MORE DANGEROUS THAN SCHEDULED OPERATORS?' The leader in the *Daily Telegraph,* entitled Disaster in the Air commented:

Air disasters have their own peculiar horror, because so often, those who are killed or maimed are cut off at moments which ought to be happy. Another element peculiar to such accidents is the high probability of complete loss of life; in all present generation aircraft with high cruising speeds, the sheer violence of the impact and fire risks immediately after leave only a small chance of getting out alive. All these factors tend to produce, in the public mind, disquiet about the present trends in civil aviation. As aircraft become, for economic reasons, even larger, must it inevitably follow that the toll taken by the air must rise? Need these eggs – all precious to someone – necessarily be put in one basket?

The leader in the *Daily Sketch* followed in similar vein.

Between 10:30 on Saturday night and 10:30 on Sunday morning, 160 men, women and children lost their lives in two air disasters. The heartrending irony of the moment is that people in search of some reviving sunshine should find death.

It is little comfort at such a time to be reminded that the statistical chance of being killed in the air is infinitesimal – a death rate of 0.6 per 100 million passenger miles flown. This year, five million British people will holiday overseas. Many will fly away from this squeezed and frozen land in search of a break. Many will, any day now, be zipping-up their bags for a charter flight on a package holiday. They will read the awful news of these disasters and will want reassurance.

How could it happen that two such terrible air tragedies could occur in seemingly perfect weather conditions? Are charter flights, by their economical nature, more accident prone than scheduled services – if so, why? How safe are 20-year-old planes – however well they are maintained? Why do airlines continue to fly their passengers into an airport like Perpignan, which, pilots say, is difficult and which already has a catalogue of crashes? These are urgent questions which swift and searching inquiries must answer.

The Perpignan and Stockport disasters with the grievous loss of 160 lives were the worst catastrophe that British civil aviation had experienced up to that point. The Stockport accident alone was the deadliest urban air disaster ever to occur in the United Kingdom, and the Air Ferry tragedy was the ninth to occur in the Perpignan region since 1951 and was the fourth involving British holidaymakers. It also held the dubious record of being the worst loss of life ever to occur in a DC-4 accident. What made the two disasters even more shocking is that they brought the number of accidents to British airlines in the previous twelve-year period to thirty-six with a total of 1,129 fatalities – an appalling record.

The two accidents naturally raised much disquiet amongst the travelling public about the safety of the independent operators, and with good reason – British airliners seemed to be dropping out of the sky with alarming regularity. There appeared to be widely held suspicion by many that because charter flights were much cheaper than scheduled services, the saving is affected by some lowering of safety standards which are applicable to the scheduled carriers. The truth is that the same exacting standards laid down by the then Board of Trade regarding maintenance and airworthiness applied equally to the independents and the country's two national flag carriers, BEA and BOAC.

However, because of the narrow profit margins of the charter operators, aircraft and flight crews had to be employed to the maximum, especially during the busy holiday season. Therefore, in order to show a profit, schedules had to be deliberately kept tight, turnarounds at airports short, and usually there was no back-up aircraft available to pick up the slack when delays and technical faults occurred – which was often. The 18-year-old Argonaut, Hotel Golf, which crashed in Stockport, amply illustrates the punishing schedule that the aircraft and its flight crews were worked. In the sixteen days leading up the accident, Hotel Golf spent more time flying than it did on the ground.

This heavy workload by the three Argonauts in the British Midland fleet was relentless and continued throughout the holiday season from April to October. This sort of punishing scheduling on aircraft and crews leaves little room for manoeuvre. In order to make a profit, the Argonauts had to be kept flying at all costs causing an inevitable strain not only on the aircraft, but its crews and maintenance personnel. The cumulative effect of all this is that pilots employed by the charter airlines were under a greater strain than their counterparts employed by the national flag carriers. Therefore, one would expect them to work shorter hours, but in fact, the opposite was true. It would be unfair to single out British Midland as an aggressive operator; they were typical of most of the independents airlines operating during that period.

The two accidents, without doubt, were an unprecedented blow for British civil aviation, not only did it shock the commercial aviation world; it sparked a major storm over British air safety. This led in turn to searching questions being raised by members on both sides in the House of Commons. In a statement made by the President of the Board of Trade, Douglas Jay, he told the House that he had given instructions for a 'special review' to be undertaken that would look into the performance of all British registered aircraft; examine the regulations and procedures carried out by the Board of Trade and the Air Registration Board, and the enforcement of those regulations. He also announced there would be a 'full-blooded' investigation and a public inquiry into the causes and circumstances of the Stockport accident, and the Perpignan disaster will, as required by international agreement, be investigated by the French authorities with British representatives and advisers from the Accident Investigation Branch. He resisted pressure from all sides of the House to order the grounding of all British registered DC-4s and Argonauts pending the results of the investigation. He said he was not convinced, on the evidence available, that such a drastic step was necessary.

Stockport Police Headquarters had been a hive of activity since dawn. At nine o'clock sharp, a conference was convened between all 'the interested parties'. This included the Stockport Chief Constable, Leonard Massey, his deputy Tom Walker, along with other senior police officers; also, in attendance were the East Cheshire Coroner, Herbert Sidebothan, the two RAF pathologists, inspectors from the Accident Investigation Branch and representatives from the airline. This was an important meeting and a debate immediately began as to how to proceed, because everyone needed to know what was going on and who was doing what, to ensure that no one was working in a vacuum.

The two pathologists, brought in by the Board of Trade were Group Captain Mason and Squadron Leader Tarlton. Mason was a consultant pathologist of international renown for both the RAF and the AIB. He had great experience and a long-standing reputation in the investigation of air transport accidents and in the field of forensic medicine and pathology. He had personally been involved in nearly 200 military and civil aircraft investigations.

In fatal aircraft accidents, the pathologist deals with the fragmented and burnt remains of passengers and crew – known in aviation pathological textbooks as 'the human wreckage'. The two pathologists would be able to reconstruct the accident, as far as was possible on the basis of the patterns of injuries sustained by the passengers and crew. Mason agreed to undertake a minimum of fifteen post mortems a day at the nearby Stepping Hill Hospital which was larger and better equipped than the police mortuary. For his part, the coroner said he would open the first of five inquests that day and hold inquests each day until all the evidence and identifications had been recorded on all the 72 victims so as not to delay the issuing of death certificates and prolong the suffering of relatives.

One of the most urgent tasks that were discussed at the meeting was the preservation of the bodies. It was clear that the post mortem examinations, identifications and disposal of the casualties would take a week at the very least, and in the prevailing hot weather decomposition and putrefaction would occur rapidly. If this situation went unchecked, it would quickly become a serious public health issue; therefore, it was of the utmost urgency to find some sort of refrigeration facilities. Stockport had suitable plants but they were either in use for food storage or had other limitations. Manchester had nothing that was ideally suitable for body preservation; although they had deep freezing units, the operating temperatures were too low for subsequent post-mortem work. In the end, it became necessary to obtain three large insulated containers from a Liverpool company, each capable of holding 24 bodies. These containers arrived by road later in the day and were located on spare ground next to the Centenary Hall in close proximity to police headquarters.

The important thing was to exclude as much oxygen as possible which would hasten decomposition. The method used was to pack the containers with blocks of dry ice; as this melted down, carbon dioxide was produced which substantially lowered the oxygen levels and accordingly, the rate of decomposition. PC Stephen Clegg describes the interior of these containers, 'like the worst cut-and-slash horror movie imaginable, and the smell of putrefaction pervaded everywhere'.

Inevitably, for those police officers faced with this unpleasant aspect of dealing with the bodies it was a stressful time. They tried to make light of the nightmarish work and naturally, some typical gallows humour crept in and they were soon cracking grim jokes between themselves. This flippancy was by no means disrespectful; in fact, it was a natural human reaction, part of a defence mechanism that arises in response to traumatic situations and served as a bonding and coping mechanism for all those closely involved in the operation. This black humour greatly eased the pressure and helped them do their job and still function as police officers. Many of the older policemen, who had seen action in the war, were somewhat desensitised to the horrific injuries the bodies bore which gave them some degree of resilience and were able to help some of the younger officers keep on an even keel.

Police officer Geoff Burgess, detailed to attend the Citadel that morning to help move the bodies, clearly remembers standing somewhat shocked and white-faced gawping at the rows of casualties when, an old 'seen it all before' sergeant bellowed: "Well PC 194, don't stand there with your mind in neutral and your finger up your arse! You're a police officer now, these bodies won't shift themselves, let's get on with it."

Even though the bodies had been kept refrigerated, decomposition still occurred in the warm weather. Geoff Burgess remembers the combined stench of burnt flesh and putrefaction that was absorbed by their uniforms. At the end of each working day, having ferried the casualties to and from Stepping Hill Hospital, he and his team had to spray themselves liberally with disinfectant before his fellow officers allowed them to enter the police station.

Also present at the conference were representatives of J H Kenyon, a London based company of undertakers, which specialised in major accidents involving mass fatalities. The company had had wide experience representing airlines in many previous air disasters. They had the experience of arranging mass burials and providing substantial zinc-lined coffins to accommodate unsightly human remains, embalming where necessary, and generally provide on the behalf of the airline free and liberal services to the relatives of the deceased. With the Air Ferry DC-4 crash in the Pyrenees on the Saturday evening, the company was stretched to the limit with many of their staff having earlier flown over to France to deal with the 88 casualties there.

Later that day, a train from London Euston eased its way into Stockport Railway Station from which 72 caskets where off loaded and stacked on the platform. For those passengers standing around patiently waiting for their trains, it was a poignant sight to witness, and brought home the true enormity of the disaster in human terms.

The first of the post mortems were undertaken that same day at Stepping Hill Hospital and continued throughout the coming week. After each post mortem examination had been completed and the identity of the victim was positively established, the body was placed in a numbered zinc-lined casket and a local plumber and his young apprentice were drafted into solder and seal the lids. By the end of the week, the majority of the post mortems had been completed and each of the casualties identified apart from four bodies, which because of their extreme carbonised condition remained unidentifiable. Mason, with the help of a dental expert drafted in from Guy's Hospital, London, were able by dental records to positively identify three of these. The fourth victim was made by a process of elimination and was identified as that of the air steward, Tony Taylor.

Later in the day, events in the Middle East took centre stage with the news of the outbreak of the Six Day War after Egypt moved against the UN peacekeeping force. Israel, without warning, attacked military airfields in Egypt, Jordan, Syria and Iraq and their ground forces made a spectacular push forward overland. Such was the international importance of these events; it effectively pushed the reporting of the Stockport and Perpignan disasters from the front pages of the national press as journalists covered not only the Middle East crisis but also other major stories that had been, because of the two accidents, largely neglected. The media went quiet and the Stockport disaster was not brought to the public's attention again until preparations began for the Public Inquiry in the autumn.

When Salvationist, Bertha Thorniley, returned to the Hillgate Citadel on the Monday morning, she was still in a state of shock and still unbelieving of what had occurred, but as the day progressed, the full extent of the catastrophe suddenly hit home as the distressed relatives and friends arrived in the town to try and identify their loved ones. She told me:

At the time, I worked at Stepping Hill Hospital as a nursing auxiliary. I went in early on the Monday morning and spoke to the Matron who gave me time off so I could go back to the Citadel and help out with the identification of the victims and meet the steady stream of grieving relatives now pouring into the town.

I remember this lady holding on to my arm, she said to me: "You will know my daughter; she was wearing a reversible coat." It hit me then that there had been this terrible disaster and what we had been attending were actual people not just bodies. That lady was so adamant that I would know her daughter because of this reversible coat. I knew I couldn't help her; there could be no reversible coat because everything – clothing and bodies – had been so totally destroyed in the fire.

As the day went on, other relatives began to arrive. One woman looked at me with tears in her eyes and said: "You know, they had everything to come back to." I had no answer to that either. But not one of those relatives who spoke to me that day asked why – which is the normal reaction, isn't it – to ask why has this tragedy happened to me? It was as if everybody was in a daze and it wasn't happening to them either, and I knew that as the days went on, they would get the same delayed reaction as I got on that second day when the full enormity of the disaster hit home. It was the strangest experience of dislocation I've ever had.

PC Stephen Clegg also recalls his involvement on the day following the disaster. Nearly half a century later, he told me how those awful memories still come back to haunt him.

On the first part of my shift on the Monday, I was detailed to search all of the foliage around the gulley into which the aircraft had plunged. This was to check for items that may have been thrown out upon impact. Most of what I discovered was wreck detritus, except for two items. One was an unopened pack of 200 Olivier cigarettes and the other was a plastic whistle on a white lanyard which, I have to admit, I kept and still have to this day – the cigarettes were 'disposed' of.

Over the next few days, we begged the relatives and friends to try to identify their loved ones by their artefacts, but they were pitifully sparse. Lots of the necklaces, rings, wristwatches, cigarette lighters and other things which looked much like the others on display and, therefore, few folks were positively identified by them. Worst of all, the relatives wanted to see the bodies. We did our utmost to deter them, but many persisted, and this led to my most awful memories of the disaster – the sounds; the long, loud, heartbroken howls, screams, wails and incessant anguished sobbing. Damn it, these are such simple words to write, but these vivid memories are the ones that still have the most appalling and upsetting effect on me. Every time I venture back there, I have to shut it down quickly to stop the upset overwhelming me.

As the day progressed, the true scale of the tragedy, in human personal terms, became shockingly clear when details began to emerge of those who had perished. As the reader can no doubt understand, there are so many individual stories regarding relatives and loved ones left behind to grieve that it would take a separate volume to record them all, but I describe here a few exceptional accounts from those who I have personally spoken with.

The 1960s was still a time of respect for authority and a stoical attitude to tragedy. Unlike today, there was none of the public outpouring of communal grief and those directly affected by the tragedy were expected to get on with it in typical British stiff upper lip fashion. It was also a time of no counselling – it hadn't been conceived of at the time – and there was little in the way of financial compensation for the victims and their families. The following poignant account stands out in its vividness and is typical of how family members, young and old, were expected to pick up the pieces and carry on.

For a ten-year-old schoolgirl, Susan Smart, her world ended when Hotel Golf plunged into the town centre with the loss of both parents. Some thirty years later, she spoke touchingly for the first time about that traumatic day and its consequences that profoundly changed the course of her life and that of her two younger brothers.

Just before waking up on that fateful morning, I actually dreamt that the aircraft my parents were travelling home in crashed. Was it a premonition, or just childish fears? I'll never know. But in reality, the drama unfolded exactly as I'd predicted.

My father's friend, Frank, drove my two brothers and me – Simon aged six and Justin aged three – to the airport that morning. I remember we were all bursting with excitement to see them because they had been away for ten long days; we had never been parted from them for so long. I can't help but think how excited they too must have been in anticipation of seeing us all again and how dreadful that they never made it home.

I had baked a special cake for them decorated with icing on top saying: 'Welcome Home Mummy and Daddy', which I proudly laid out in the centre of the dining room table. As we left to go to the airport, our grandma – who was looking after us while our parents were away – was busy in the kitchen preparing Sunday lunch for us all when we returned.

I clearly remember standing in the airport arrivals lounge waiting and waiting. I wasn't aware of much activity going on, but I am sure I heard my parents' name being called over the tannoy at one point and wondering why. I told Frank what I had heard, but he just ignored me and kept rushing off and leaving us, and then coming back to check if we were OK. I realise now he must have been desperate to find out any scrap of information he could, as the drama must just have been unfolding. The last time he came back he quickly shuffled us out of the airport terminal and back to his car – I couldn't understand why. Where were they? Why were we going without them? Frank stayed quite silent and didn't say a word. I found it all very strange.

On our way home to Dyserth in North Wales – which was a ninety-minute drive in those days – Frank kept stopping the car and rushing into the nearest telephone box. At one point in the journey, I remember shouting at him: "They're dead, aren't they? There's been a crash and they've been killed!" Goodness knows what was going through his mind at the time; what a terrible situation for him to be in. Of course, I had no idea what was going on, but I suppose at the time, I was just trying to shock him into telling me something.

When we finally arrived home, a very worried grandma met us at the door. She couldn't understand why our parents weren't with us. I learned later that relatives had been phoning her all morning, because they had heard the news on the radio that a plane inbound for Manchester Airport had crashed in Stockport town centre. But not for one moment did she contemplate that it could have been the one her daughter and son-in-law were on. She expected my parents to walk through the door at any moment.

From then on, the sequence of events became a kaleidoscopic blur. Sometime later – perhaps maybe an hour, I'm not sure exactly – the local vicar appeared at the front door and broke the news to my grandma that Jill and Geoff had been killed. She was very distraught and at first, I thought she was laughing really loudly – but it was real sobs. Then I started to tremble and laugh. I didn't know what to do or think – it all seemed so unreal.

Later that afternoon, my father's brother and sisters arrived and we all sat around our living room talking and drinking cups of tea. I didn't cry that Sunday, I just floated around in a kind of dream. It was the following day when the full enormity of the disaster suddenly hit me. I was with my brothers and cousins having tea, when some of my chips fell on the floor, and that was it – I broke down and burst into tears. My cousins started to laugh at me crying over my spilled chips and I remember my auntie taking them to one side and telling them the real reason why I was so upset.

My brothers and I weren't allowed to go to the funeral; in the late 1960s, it was still considered a taboo for children to have anything to do with death. In retrospect, I feel this was a mistake, for it continued in me that this was not really happening. The tragic loss of our parents affected all of us in different ways. My brother Simon made plastic model aeroplanes and over the following weeks, he and Justin went around smashing everyone in the house. Justin also suffered nightmares for over a year and once came downstairs in his sleep one night and threw a face flannel on the fire – the significance of this only became clear to me a few years ago when I discovered the true circumstances of the crash. He would also stand forlornly outside our cottage by the gate and ask passers-by: "Have you seen my mummy and daddy?"

Our grandmother courageously took over as our guardian and never moved out of the family home. Although it was hard for her at 62 to take on the full-time care of all three of us, a solution was found; I was sent away to boarding school in the autumn, where I knew not a soul and there was no teacher looking out for me. I was expected to cope and get on with it. For me, the abandonment was total.

I managed to deal with school life by living out a fantasy. I felt I was a character in a book – like 'Little Orphan Annie' – and since I had created my own special life story, I could live it. I cut off all my emotions, as the truth was too raw to contemplate. However, this method of coping is double-edged; it helps at the time but causes problems and pain later in life.

There is no doubt that the accident left a deep scar on all three of us and totally altered the course of our lives. It took its toll on my grandma too. She suffered from depression for the rest of her life and later developed Alzheimer's disease, passing away in 1988. My father's brother was also deeply traumatised by the tragedy and died prematurely; the shock of my father's death I feel being one of the contributory factors.

I often wonder how my life would have been if my parents hadn't died so young. Even now, after all these years, I miss them terribly and at times feel very sad. But I know life is too short to dwell on the past. I am fortunate to have a family of my own now and I cherish each and every day with them.

People think that things like this won't happen to their family – but they can and sometimes they do.

Another heart-breaking story is that personalised in the words of sisters Pauline O'Sullivan and Marilyn Bradley. Both are now married and settled with families of their own, but in the early summer of 1967, they stayed behind at the family home in Slaithwaite, Yorkshire whilst their parents, Arthur and Rachel Smith went on holiday to Majorca with their 14-year-old brother David and 16-year-old cousin Philip Cruse from Newcastle; all four were killed in the accident. Pauline told me how her close-knit family structure was suddenly shattered, and how her life and that of her sister changed irrevocably:

I remember getting out of bed, pulling back the curtains and looking up at the sky and thinking; they will be landing anytime now. I had just started preparing Sunday lunch when the phone rang – Mum said she would ring from the airport when they landed. But it wasn't Mum; it was John Barlow, a colleague of Dad's. He said he didn't want to alarm us, but there had been an air crash that morning near Manchester. I just couldn't believe what I was hearing. He told me not to panic and he would come over to the house straight away. Within minutes, the phone rang again – *Perhaps this is Mum,* I thought hopefully; it was my boyfriend Ted, just checking if everything was all right. He was convinced that there had been a mix-up as there had been a holiday air crash over France the previous night. Anyway, he said not to worry and he would come over straight away. Soon after putting the phone down, it rang again. By this time, I knew something was definitely wrong. It was Auntie Janet – Philip's mum – calling from Newcastle asking if they had all arrived home safely. I tried so hard to stay calm and just told her that they must have been delayed. As we chatted, I felt sick with worry and began to tremble, but I didn't tell her my fears at that stage.

My boyfriend, Ted, and John Barlow arrived at the house within minutes of each other and we all gathered around the television for the lunchtime news bulletin.

The house fell silent as the stark black and white distressing images from Stockport appeared on the screen. That's when the horror became real; the unbelievable had happened. Pauline continues:

I got the feeling then that they had been killed. In a way, I hoped they had all gone together. My sister, Marilyn, wanted to rush to Stockport, but everyone was advised to stay away. It all seemed like a nightmare and any minute, I would wake up and everything would be all right. This feeling lasted a long, long time – weeks and months. It wasn't until the following day that we finally got official confirmation from the police that they all had been killed.

The following week, the funerals took place. The little chapel in the Slaithwaite Cemetery was packed with mourners and the sight of the four coffins side by side was almost too much to bear. After returning home, we knew nothing would ever be the same again, but we were young and knew life had to go on. In those days, there was no counselling you just had to soldier on. But there was more heartache to come as our grandparents never recovered from the shock. Granddad Smith died six months later and Gran passed away the following May. We had now lost six of our loved ones within a year; before June 1967, I had never attended a funeral.

Ted and I married the following year. We have two children, Rachel and Tim, and we are a close loving family. Every year, I stay with Auntie Janet in Newcastle and we still talk of the happy times before that dreadful summer Sunday in 1967.

Pauline's sister, Marilyn, recalls the numbing shock and her personal reaction on hearing the news that all her family had been wiped out in an instant.

I stood at the top of the stairs in a daze staring blindly across the fields from the large window at home. I remember thinking that this can't be happening, these things only happen in films and books. I don't know how long I stood there thinking that it was all a dreadful mistake and everything would be all right – hadn't Mum and Dad always made everything all right?

I was seventeen, my sister Pauline was twenty and life for both of us was good – why should it be anything else my seventeen-year-old mind reasoned. I felt sure that there would be a telephone call any moment saying sorry about the mistake but Mum, Dad, brother David and cousin Philip were on their way home for Sunday lunch. But there was no mistake; their plane had crashed in Stockport just six miles from home and safety.

Time and the events that followed in the wake of the tragedy were a haze for a long, long time. We did, eventually, find out that they had enjoyed their holiday and brother David and Philip had had fun together. Thanks Mum and Dad for a wonderful childhood. I'll never forget your guidance and goodness, it was that that helped us to carry on. I'm sorry for being an awkward teenager, and David, I'm sorry for always fighting. I'll never forget Sunday the 4 June 1967, but I know and truly believe we will all meet again, 'above the bright blue skies', as the Sunday school song Dad taught us goes.

For Helen Cuthew, recently engaged to Hotel Golf's First Officer, Chris Pollard, her world fell apart on hearing the news of his tragic and untimely death. Three decades later, she told me how the disaster impacted her life.

I first met Chris when I was training to be a nurse at the Preliminary Training School for St Bartholomew's Hospital at Letchmore Heath, which was just down the road from the London School of Flying at Elstree Aerodrome where Chris was training. As you can imagine, there was some fairly lively traffic between the two places! I clearly remember our first date was doing aerobatics in a school owned de Havilland Chipmunk.

Chris was an exceptional pilot and I seem to remember that he was the youngest pilot in his group to pass his Instrument Rating. A good friend of his owned a Piper Tripacer, which he kept at Elstree and he got Chris to fly him around, in fact, we all flew down to Plymouth in it to have Sunday lunch with Chris's parents – the first time I'd ever met them. We spent a lot of time down there; in fact, we got engaged there and went into Plymouth to buy the ring in the spring of 1967; we planned to marry in June the following year.

I spoke to Chris on the phone the day before so I knew he was on flying duty that night. At the time, I was working at Gatwick Airport for British United Airways, and as I passed the Duty Officer on the stairs, he said to me: "Terrible news about the air crash." At first, I thought he was referring to the Air Ferry DC-4 that had crashed in the Pyrenees the previous evening, but when he said there had been another one near Manchester Airport I had a dreadful premonition. It took some considerable time for him to get through to British Midland at East Midlands Airport, and I remember anxiously sitting in his office staring down at the floor whilst he tried to discover if it was Chris's flight. Eventually, he received confirmation that it was, but there was no news at that time as to whether he had survived.

I was taken home and later another Duty Officer came to the house to tell me what I think I already knew that Chris had been killed. British United kindly provided a car to take me down to Cornwall to be with his mother and father during that dreadful time and I remained there until after the funeral.

I stayed very close to his parents over the coming years and continued to visit them regularly, eventually staying there with my husband and three children. They were probably the kindest people I have ever met.

It was nothing but miraculous, considering the location of the crash in the heart of the town, that there were no casualties on the ground. Patrick Finnigan and his son Martin had come close, when they chanced taking that short cut across the garage forecourt no more than a minute before the airliner plunged to the ground. Another extremely close call involved a group of ramblers about to set off for a day's walking in the Peak District. The organiser of that Sunday outing takes up the story.

I happened to be at Ringway Airport on the Saturday evening watching the ill-fated British Midland Argonaut being prepared for its outward journey to Palma. Next morning, I awoke to the news that a DC-4 airliner had crashed in the Pyrenees, not realising I was about to escape being involved in the Stockport disaster by a matter of feet and minutes.

At the time, I ran a hiking club and on that particular Sunday, we had booked a minibus to take our group to Kinder Scout in the Peak District. We picked up people at various locations around the town, the final pick up point being Hopes Carr at 10:05 where four of our party were patiently waiting. We then set off, turned left at Hillgate and then joined the A6 southbound. As we were approaching Stepping Hill Hospital, we were surprised to see no less than six ambulances with blue light flashing and sirens blaring rushing towards the town centre. We thought nothing of it until we reached our destination where someone in our party with a transistor radio heard the news of the Stockport crash – the exact location was unknown to us until we tried to drop off members of the party later that day.

I remember on our return Hopes Carr was literately swarming with thousands of spectators, at least two ice cream vans, a hot dog vendor, not to mention TV crews and the press – by this time, it was around 7:30. Amazingly, considering the circumstances, we were able to put our passengers down within 50 yards of the crash site. Later, it came as a terrible shock when we found out the exact time of the crash – linked to the ambulances we had seen and the time we arrived at Hopes Carr – we worked out that our minibus had stopped no more than 12 feet from where the tail of the Argonaut had come to rest and we had departed just three minutes before impact; a very lucky escape indeed.

Chapter Seven
The Infernal Machine

"Wise men learn by other's mistakes, fools learn by their own."

Proverb

The real tragedy of the Stockport disaster is the stark shocking fact that – like many aviation accidents of the period – it was totally preventable and need never have happened. Usually, after a serious accident, a whole history of previous incidents on the particular type of aircraft involved suddenly comes to light, and the Stockport crash was no exception.

Abnormalities found in the fuel log of Hotel Golf after the accident, and a potentially fatal fuel related incident that went unreported a week earlier when the aircraft was on its final approach to Palma Airport, should have sounded the warning bells, but British Midland pilots and engineering staff failed to recognise the true significance of this and other incidents. In fact, it took 18-years of Argonaut operations to reveal a deadly design flaw in the fuel system that was certainly known about by the original operator, BOAC, and the manufacturer Canadair, but both failed to fully understand the seriousness of the problem and it was never effectively communicated to British Midland or other operators of the type. If the airline had been forewarned, then the disastrous emergency that overtook Hotel Golf on that wet and overcast Sunday morning would in all probability never have occurred.

The events of 4 June 1967 was a long time in the making; to fully understand the complexities and circumstances of how the Stockport disaster came about we must rewind to the immediate post war years.

Britain showed a certain amount of complacency regarding the design and development of civil airliners after the end of the Second World War. Anxious to re-establish its civil aviation activities, it made do with ad hoc conversions of ex RAF bombers which were readily available. However, the Avro Company on its own initiative decided to design and produce an airliner using the wings and engines of the tried and tested Lancaster bomber married to a new pressurised fuselage; the resulting aircraft was christened the Tudor. In the end, it turned out to be an ill-fated luckless aircraft, an early example of which crashed on take off from Woodford aerodrome in 1947 killing its designer Roy Chadwick.

The British government, in support of its aircraft industry ordered the Tudor for the state run British Overseas Airways Corporation (BOAC) and gave them no say in the matter. The airline strongly protested at having this lack lustre airliner foisted upon them and made it abundantly clear that the aircraft was hopelessly uneconomic, totally unsuitable for the routes it operated and could never compete with the likes of the far superior American designed Lockheed Constellation and Douglas DC-6. In April 1947, BOAC wrote a strongly worded letter to the Minister of Civil Aviation stating: '*...there is no longer any justification for including the Tudor in the Corporation's future operating programme*'. Having lost all faith in any version of the Tudor – despite government cajoling, hostility and indeed bullying – they refused point blank to operate the aircraft and began to look around for an-up-to date economical and competitive airliner as a stopgap until the all-jet Comet and turbo-prop Bristol Britannia came on line.

At the time, there was a pro-American lobby within BOAC, which looked into a proposal put forward by the Bristol Aeroplane Company to build under licence the Lockheed Constellation. This modified version differed in that it would be powered by the British designed and manufactured Bristol Centaurus engines and incorporate many British components. This project was all a bit 'cloak and dagger' at the time that it was officially given the designation Project X. Although the idea was seriously considered in the latter part of 1946, it never came to anything, and it is believed that the proposal was scuppered by government intervention.

This was the period when the piston-engined airliner reigned supreme and in 1944, the newly incorporated Canadair aircraft company of Cartierville, Quebec, entered into an agreement with the Douglas aircraft company to initiate a reworking of their tried and proven Douglas DC-4 transport that gave such good service during the war. Throughout 1944, design work gathered speed on this unique DC-4 hybrid initially conceived to meet the requirements of Trans Canada Airlines and the Royal Canadian Air Force.

Like all Commonwealth countries in the austere post-war years, with the British economy struggling to get back on its feet after the privations of war, there was a very much a 'buy British' political agenda, and that was one of the reasons for Canadair's selection of the supercharged Rolls-Royce Merlin engine to power the aircraft. Another reason was simple economics, in that the Merlin, manufactured in the UK were available to the Canadians duty free, whereas the equivalent American Pratt and Whitney radial engines that powered the DC-4 had to be imported from just across the US border attracting huge duty charges. The Merlin also had the additional benefit of adding an extra 35 mph to its cruising speed and generally offered all round better performance and fuel economy.

This new variant emerged from the Canadair workshops as the DC-4M North Star, so named as a tribute to Polaris, friend of the traveller. But this new airliner was much more than just an engine swap. The North Star incorporated the DC-6 nose, landing gear and unlike the standard production line DC-4, it had a fully pressurised DC-6 fuselage shortened by two metres. The prototype made its maiden flight on 15 July 1946 and after extensive flight testing it was approved for transport use by the Canadian Department of Transport.

With their refusal to order the Tudor, BOAC was obliged to shop abroad and the new Canadair airliner looked as if it would fit the bill. Sir Miles Thomas, the then BOAC chairman said: "There was this nagging problem at the time of what aeroplane BOAC could mount to attract customers as against the other world airlines." The American aircraft available were faster, cheaper to operate and, above all else for the passenger, they were more comfortable to fly in. "With us," he commented, "it is always jam tomorrow. We were going to have the Comet jet quite soon and later the turboprop Britannia. In the meantime, we had to make the best of it."

It was an important purchasing decision and the immediate future of the Corporation depended on choosing the right aircraft; Sir Miles decided to fly over to Canada to evaluate the new airliner himself. In his autobiography, *Out on a Wing*, he wrote:

I well remember my visit to Canada and being given a very disappointing test flight on the prototype Canadair C-4. With an empty aeroplane and a light fuel load, we took off on a very cold day from the company's airstrip near Montreal. The pilot, wanting to show off the best paces of the aircraft, gave the engines plenty of throttle. We climbed rapidly and soon we could see what looked like an enormous area of the St Lawrence River, with the city of Montreal lying dwarfed amidst the great areas of forest and agricultural land.

I was being shown all the amenities of the airliner, how well the galley was equipped, how well the toilets were furnished with the latest space saving and comfort-making devices. If you have ever ridden in a coach or bus when the vehicle has suddenly changed speed whilst you are standing up, you will know with what intensified alarm I felt when the aeroplane almost moved backwards from under my feet as it sharply lost speed to the accompaniment of a complete change of sound.

The experienced test pilot quickly corrected the nose-dropping lurch. My guide and I, having recovered our balance by grabbing whatever was nearest, smiled wanly at each other and edged towards the windows on the side of the aeroplane to which she had momentarily lurched, and I was just in time to see a propeller jerk to a stop. Obviously there was one engine 'out' and, as always, I was beginning to wonder whether the cause of its failure was something unique to that particular engine of whether it was going to spread amongst the others.

There did not seem to be much more information coming from the engine itself, which was the starboard outer, until I saw considerable quantities of oil leaking back over the wing. We went up forward to the busy dial filled cockpit, where the pilot confirmed what we already knew. We flew around a bit more on three engines and once we were sure that there was no fire hazard, we landed safely. Apparently, what had happened was that an oil line had become blocked, probably during the transit of the Merlin engine from England to Canada, and had starved a train of gears of lubricant. Not unnaturally, they had seized solid, hence the jerk and the noise. Mentally, I balanced this failure against the established reliability figures of the Rolls-Royce Merlin engine, and very soon, I became a Canadair C-4 enthusiast.

Despite his alarming demonstration flight, Sir Miles returned to the UK, and after a meeting with the BOAC Board and the Air Ministry, he was given the go ahead by the airline's Whitehall paymasters to place an order for 22 of the type. The aircraft ordered were essentially the same as the DC-4M North Star version except for the choice of electronic equipment and other components which in most instances were of British manufacture. In addition, the cabin interior – seating and décor, of course, was designed to BOAC's own specification.

There was some urgency at the time that the Canadian export certificates of airworthiness for each aircraft should be validated as quickly as possible by the UK's Ministry of Civil Aviation so that BOAC could ferry the aircraft over to the UK and prepare them for service. In this matter, BOAC were invited by the Air Registration Board (ARB) to bring to its attention any matters in which the Canadair C-4, in its opinion, did not comply with British airworthiness requirements. As a result, the Corporation reported a number of features which did not comply with the British regulations. These were all considered minor and were either accepted as safe or could be rectified. The only relevant point that did not meet British standards was the fuel system – a design of questionable engineering. It was incredibly complicated and had the possibilities for future technical trouble. The actual ARB requirement regarding the fuel system specified that: *'The arrangement of the system and design of the fuel cocks shall be such that it is not possible for any pump to draw fuel from two or more tanks simultaneously unless means are provided to prevent the introduction of air into the system.'*

In the haste to get the aircraft into service as soon as possible, a meeting was convened between BOAC and the ARB. Rather than spend a great deal of time and expense to adapt the fuel system to meet with the British standards, it was agreed between both parties that the only practicable action to overcome this shortfall was to ensure that the fuel system diagram in the cockpit bears a placard, warning flight crews that: *'The supply lines from two fuel tanks must not be opened when they are connected by an open cross feed valve.'* This half-baked solution was ludicrous and a potential death trap. The warning placard only gave the illusion of safety; it was rather like stopping people from falling down an open lift shaft by putting a sign up! Aviation safety experts couldn't help but wonder what world the ARB was living in as this quick fix solution went entirely against standard ARB policy. Apart from the fuel system issue, the aircraft in all other respects met British airworthiness criteria. With no further questions asked, the Certificate of Airworthiness was validated and rubber-stamped by the Ministry of Civil Aviation for transport use on the recommendations of the ARB.

Another safety factor concerned the number of flight crewmembers that were needed to operate the aircraft safely and efficiently. Besides the Captain and First Officer, professional flight engineers were considered essential on complex four-engine propeller driven airliners of the era. However, many of the major airlines, including BOAC, had already begun to phase out the engineers position as they saw it as a chance to save a few pounds in operational costs.

Although the aircraft were officially designated as the Canadair C-4 North Star, BOAC chose the imaginative name Argonaut for their fleet, inspired by the Greek myth of Jason and his voyages in the Argo. Each aircraft was individually christened with names of classical Greek heroes, *Arcturus, Ajax, Argosy, Athena* etc. Hotel Golf, the Argonaut in our story was named *Aurora,* stencilled on the nose just below the cockpit windows.

Apart from the questionable fuel system, the excellence of the Argonaut is not superficially apparent at first glance. They held no speed records, had no unique attraction to offer the passenger and were not strikingly handsome in appearance. It may not have had the sleek and elegant lines of the bigger and faster Lockheed Constellation or the spaciousness of the lumbering Boeing Stratocruisers, but for BOAC the Argonaut was a tough-as-old-boots transport aeroplane and best of all it made money. Like any new aircraft there were a few teething problems in the early days, but BOAC soon established an unparalleled reputation for speed and dependability along with high utilisation, and the airliner became the mainstay of BOAC's Empire routes throughout the 1950s. This sturdy, reliable and economic airliner was of immeasurable value and at once began to change the fortunes of the airline.

Piston engined airliners of the '40s and '50s were renowned for the raucous din permeating their passenger cabins, but none were as notorious as the Argonaut. The four Merlin engines produced a thunderous, almost unbearable crescendo of noise that reputedly could still be heard long after the aircraft had disappeared from view. The eight stub exhausts from each side of the inboard Merlins beamed the engine noise directly towards the cabin wall and windows, and the fatigue factor, especially in the forward seats, which also suffered the battering of the slipstream from the propellers made for an ear-shattering intrusion. With only nominal cabin soundproofing, it was almost impossible to carry on a conversation with your fellow passenger. The decibel level in the cabin was considered so bad that before engine start-up the stewardess would stroll down the aisle with a tray handing out wads of cotton wool along with the customary complementary peanuts and barley sugar to protect their ears from the fearsome roar. The flight crew, somewhat forward of all this commotion did not suffer as badly, however, with just their flying caps between their ears and the racket from the engines, it is reputed that some long-standing Argonaut pilots suffered substantial hearing loss in later life – which no doubt boosted the sale of hearing aid sales in later years!

Such was the number of passenger complaints about the noise that BOAC consulted the design engineers at Rolls-Royce who came up with a new manifold system that took the inboard exhausts and diverted them over the top of the engine to the outboard manifold. This cross over arrangement reduced the noise in the cabin to a barely tolerable level, but right to the end of its service life, the Argonaut would retain the reputation as being the noisiest propliner of all.

In the early days of BOAC operation, there was no weather radar fitted to the aircraft – that would come later – but it was really needed on the stormy tropical routes the airliner operated on. For the passengers flying through these tropical storms, it was very much like riding a bucking bronco and forced them to hang on to the edge of their seats for dear life. For safety reasons, and to make the flight less uncomfortable, it was left entirely to the captain's judgement to fly around the worst of the storms encountered *en route*. One technique employed was for the co-pilot to put on sunglasses and stare straight ahead, then when he saw the pulsating glow of lightning flashes in the clouds ahead, he judged on which side of the aircraft it was brightest and advised the captain which way to steer. But even this low-tech method could be found wanting as the following account by one passenger who recalls being 'frightened rigid' on his first ever Argonaut flight.

In June 1953, somewhere over France, *en route* from London to Tripoli, eventual destination Accra, we entered cumulonimbus cloud for what seemed an eternity. We were flung around to the accompaniment of vivid lightning flashes and the clattering of ice coming off the propellers and hitting the fuselage. Eventually, we came out the other side unscathed, the cabin crew restored calm and the business of serving dinner got underway – for those who still had an appetite. No soothing words from the captain over the public address system – the Argonaut didn't even have one of those either in those days, presumably because of the competition from the din of the engines! Eventually, in time-honoured tradition, the white-faced captain with a magnificent handlebar moustache, emerged from the cockpit to pay a belated visit to the cabin and chat with his nervy passengers in typical British stiff upper lip fashion, resplendent in his four gold rings and medal ribbons. What a welcome to flying!

BOAC began scheduled Argonaut services in August 1949 with a flight to Hong Kong. The journey, including night stopovers at Karachi and Rangoon, was made in three days compared with five days by flying boat. Services later fanned out to the Middle East and South East Asia and later operated on the African routes. When British South American Airlines merged with BOAC in 1949, it was the Argonaut that carried on with their services to Latin America. Charters and special VIP flights carried the airliner's fame throughout the world, including the United States, Canada, throughout Europe and Scandinavia and even as far as Australia.

But it was the Royal flights that earned the Argonaut its greatest glory. Five aircraft in the fleet were converted to VIP interiors for the purpose and one was entrusted with taking the then Princess Elizabeth on the first leg of her Commonwealth tour on 31 January 1952; her seriously ill father, King George VI, braved the biting cold to travel to London Airport to wave her goodbye. The aircraft, G-ALHK, *Atalanta,* piloted by Captains R G Ballantine and R E Millichap flew from London to East Africa. It was during her stay in Kenya that news came through that her father had died and the same aircraft flew the now Queen Elizabeth back to the UK to step on to British soil for the first time as Monarch.

The airliner's service record for BOAC was not however without incident, losing two aircraft in fatal accidents. The first occurred on the night of 21 September 1955 when G-ALHL crashed on the approach to Tripoli-Idris Airport, Libya. The aircraft had taken off from London for a flight to Kano. Following a scheduled refuelling stop at Rome, the Argonaut continued on to Tripoli where on arrival at night, the visibility was poor with strong winds blowing as the aircraft approached the airfield. Captain Griffiths, with an immaculate record and almost 10,000 hours of flying experience, made the justifiable decision to land on runway 11 instead of runway 18, even though the latter had some advantages regarding length and landing aids. On the first attempt, not happy with his approach, decided to overshoot. On the second attempt, he had difficulty in lining up with the runway and once again was forced to overshoot. He had enough fuel on board to spend another thirty minutes above Idris before diverting with safety to Malta.

On his third approach, the Argonaut was better lined up but came in too high and too close to attempt a landing. This was the third attempt in within twelve minutes. During a fourth attempt, the aircraft came in too low, struck a line of trees and caught fire 1,200 yards short of the runway threshold. A stewardess, a steward and thirteen passengers were killed, five members of the crew and sixteen passengers were injured, only eleven escaped unscathed.

The cause of the accident was attributed to an error of judgement on the part of the commander of the aircraft, Captain R D E Griffiths, an Australian who joined BOAC in 1946 and had flown an impressive 9,417 hours. The report into the accident said that during the visual approach to the runway, he failed to make adequate reference to his flight instruments. In the restricted visibility, the runway lights gave him insufficient guidance as to height and angle of approach and unknowingly, he permitted the aircraft to descend below its correct approach path.

Less than a year later, another BOAC Argonaut came to grief soon after taking off from Kano, Northern Nigeria, causing multiple fatalities. The aircraft – Hotel Echo – in its seven years of operation had amassed 18,000 service hours without serious incident.

On the 24 June 1956, the aircraft, operating a scheduled service from Lagos to London, touched down at Kano Airport, Northern Nigeria, for refuelling and a change of crew who would fly the aircraft on to London via Tripoli.

Captain Tomlinson and First Officer Slatford – the relief crew – arrived at Kano Airport some forty minutes before the scheduled departure time. Both pilots had ample time during their briefing to study the onward weather forecast for the 1,400-mile leg to Tripoli. The met forecast was typical for the time of year in that part of the world – a moist south westerly air current surmounted by a dry easterly one, resulting in an unstable air mass. Captain Tomlinson, an ex-RAF pilot, had great experience of flying in all weather conditions, noticed as he walked out to the aircraft, the darkening clouds of a storm front near the edge of the airport. The commander of the incoming Argonaut informed him that on approaching the airport, he calculated that the front was some eight miles to the northeast. At the time, the British Ministry of Aviation advised pilots to plan their flights to avoid thunderstorms as much as it was possible to do so – especially in the vicinity of the operating airfield. The Ministry's advice concluded with: *'If there is any risk of the aircraft flying into the influence of an active thunderstorm cell during its initial climb, it will be advisable to delay the take off.'*

Anxious to be on his way, Captain Tomlinson told his First Officer and navigator that immediately after take off, they would track towards the west in an attempt to avoid the worst of the weather. As he started his engines, he noticed another Argonaut approaching the airport and make a perfect landing, despite passing much closer to the rolls of thunder and lightning flashes than he intended to do.

As Captain Tomlinson taxied out to the start of runway 25, it began to rain heavily which quickly turned into a tropical storm of exceptional intensity. Pushing the throttle levers forward, the four Merlins roared in unison as the aircraft barrelled down the runway in a sea of spray. At the 2,000-yard mark, Hotel Echo became airborne, the undercarriage was retracted and ground-based witnesses saw the aircraft quickly disappear into the murk.

On entering the black cloud at 250 feet, the aircraft encountered violent turbulence and the airspeed suddenly and unaccountably dropped. Full power was immediately applied but the aircraft was slow to respond and continued to lose height

Inside the cabin the lighting failed, there were lightning flashes, crashes from hand luggage being thrown from the overhead racks all to the accompaniment of crockery being smashed in the galley. As the frightened passengers clung onto their seats, the aircraft rapidly lost height until it struck a tree about a mile from the end of the runway. The Argonaut disintegrated and burst into flames. Despite rescue efforts, 29 of the 38 passengers perished.

The subsequent investigation naturally focused on the weather conditions prevailing at the time. The Board of Inquiry concluded that: 'The accident was the result of a loss of height and airspeed caused by the aircraft encountering, at approximately 250 feet after take off, an unpredictable thunderstorm cell which gave rise to a sudden reversal of wind direction, heavy rain and possibly downdraft conditions. The formation of the cell could not have been predicted by the meteorological forecaster and no blame can be attached to the pilot in command for attempting to take off.' It went on to recommend that further research was needed into the potential dangers of aircraft operating in the vicinity of thunderstorms.

An interesting footnote to the Kano accident is that told by BOAC stewardess Anne Fullager:

My strangest experience in my flying career was returning from Lagos to Kano, just a day's work. On landing in Kano, I was asked by the chief steward, who was taking the aircraft on to Tripoli, if I would carry on with the flight as the relief stewardess was not very well with sinus trouble. However, Kay Buckley, an Irish girl from County Cork, did not want to stay in Kano and despite feeling under the weather insisted she wanted to continue with the flight to London. She said to me: "I am not going to stay in this bloody hole any longer than I have to. I will do the flight." So she took over and about an hour later, I had a knock on my door at the Central Hotel. It was my First Officer with a grave face bringing me the news that the aircraft had crashed just after take off and the stewardess and second steward were among those killed. I could hardly believe it – it might well have been me. From that day on, I became a fatalist – my number was not yet up.

The next day we took the flight to London – another Argonaut had been flown out for this – and we had some of the surviving passengers on board, one of whom was a man whose wife had been killed and he was flying home to the UK to tell his children at boarding school that their mother was dead. It was a shocking experience, the whole thing!

BOAC's original plan was for the Argonauts to be replaced after just four-years of service, but when that period expired, they were far from being phased out. In fact, they soldiered on well beyond expectations and accepted the extra workload imposed by the grounding of the all jet Comet fleet after a series of fatal accidents, and again later, when the troublesome turboprop Bristol Britannia was several years late in coming into service – it was stalwart Argonaut that picked up the slack. Two-years later, there was more talk of retiring these aircraft and indeed, in 1957, three were sold off to BOAC's associate company, East African Airways Corporation. The Argonaut was hardly the aircraft East African wanted or needed, as it was totally unsuitable and uneconomic for their route network. At the time, they were seriously looking to re-equip with the American-built twin-engined Convair 440 which was much more profitable and better suited to its routes. But BOAC – a major shareholder with a controlling interest in the airline – were horrified that they were contemplating buying American equipment and firmly vetoed it, forcing it to take three of its surplus Argonauts which thereafter became a major source of trouble; two of which were later involved in accidents. Aden Airways, also a BOAC subsidiary, had two aircraft all but foisted upon them.

BOAC operated the Argonaut on the London to Singapore route right up to 1957 when the Bristol Britannia finally entered service. The remainder of the fleet continued in revenue earning service until the end of 1958 when sales were resumed with some of them parked out on the tarmac at Stansted Airport awaiting disposal.

When Hotel Golf, *Aurora* – piloted by Captain E N Wright, touched down at London Airport from Abadan on Friday, 8 April 1960, it ended not only the last flight ever to be made for BOAC by the Argonaut, but also the end of an era, during which it acted as the backbone of the Corporation's operations during the critical decade of transition from pistons to jets. On retirement, they had flown an impressive total of 512,864 hours, travelling an estimated 107 million miles and carried 870,000 passengers.

The profitable and successful performance the Argonaut had given BOAC was primarily due to the combined efforts of a very good team of maintenance engineers which saw technical problems tackled with the minimum of delay that ensured they were serviceable and flying as much as possible. For example, in the mid-1950s, the fleet achieved 9.96 hours utilisation each day and were confined to the hangar for the shortest possible time for essential maintenance.

However, their withdrawal from BOAC service was far from the end of the Argonaut's flying career. With a range of some 3,000 miles, they brought all the major European tourist destinations within reach and very quickly, the aircraft found a new lease of life with secondary operators where they were to have even longer careers. At least five went to the Danish operator, Flying Enterprise, nine examples, including Hotel Golf, were purchased by Gatwick based Overseas Aviation and four were sold to the Rhodesian Air Force.

In BOAC service, the passenger layout was either 40-seat 'Majestic Class' or 50-seat 'Baronet Class' – later increased to 54. This low seating arrangement reflected the long haul North Atlantic and Empire routes undertaken by the Corporation and the need to carry a much heavier fuel load. But the ingenuity and resourcefulness of the independent airlines – where every seat of course reflected revenue – managed to cram in up to 78 seats which without doubt pitted safety against space.

In charter operation, the Argonaut – which as airliners go was now well into middle-age – acquired the reputation of a somewhat troublesome aircraft and at times seemed to possess a mind of its own. It was regarded by its crews as a nice aeroplane, but heavy on the controls. One pilot commented that flying the aircraft was a bit like dancing with your great aunt! For the engineers who had the responsibility of looking after these big, and sometimes cantankerous airliners and keep them flying described the type as a proverbial 'can of worm'. In fact, if the truth be known, the Argonaut had the dubious distinction as the only known transport aircraft whose overall performance deteriorated with age.

The take off on a fully laden Argonaut was a somewhat fraught experience for the passengers and crew, and indeed observers on the ground. It certainly liked plenty of runway and when it finally managed to lumber into the air, its rate of climb was decidedly sluggish to say the least. As the minutes passed, the crew and passengers alike would turn to their respective windows, look down and say to themselves: "Yes, the houses are definitely getting smaller!"

Added to all this was the Argonauts depressing propensity for dripping copious amounts of engine oil and hydraulic fluid on the apron and it was not unusual for ground engineers to have drip trays at the ready as the aircraft taxied in to place under the offending engines. But hardened aviation buffs, especially lovers of the propliner, would insist: "She's not dripping oil, she's marking her territory!"

Engine problems and malfunctions were to disrupt its service life thereafter and it wasn't unusual to find them regularly limping back to the airport of departure on three engines after an in-flight shutdown and became the butt of derisory jokes. One aviation commentator went so far to describe the Argonaut as good three-engined aeroplane and one long-serving Argonaut pilot reckoned that – according to his log book – he had spent more time flying on three engines than he had on four!

A typical example of the many incidents to blight its later years is the one cited below by one youngster flying off on holiday with his parents.

One of my earliest memories of a family holiday by air was to Majorca in 1965 in an Air Links Argonaut from Gatwick. I was already by this time a young spotty spotter complete with anorak! Ah, the joy of air transport by four historic Merlin engines.

By Le Mans southbound, I noticed on looking out of the cabin window liquid streaming over the port wing. Five minutes later, one of the engines was shut down and the captain announced that we were returning to Gatwick. When we touched down, there were at least three fire engines cruising up and down the taxiways with their crews anxiously looking in our direction.

We disembarked and forty-five minutes later, we were told that the technical problem had now been sorted out. We took off again and this time got as far as Brighton before we returned to Gatwick for the same charade. Two frustrating hours later, we were asked to re-embark. Cue: Many stout protective fathers who grouped together and refused to let their families fly on that clapped out old crate again. Eight hours later, a Douglas DC-7 – clearly not in great demand – was flown over from Ireland and off we went on holiday without further ado.

The largest operator of ex BOAC Argonauts was Overseas Aviation who began operations in March 1957. Besides the nine Argonauts bought from BOAC, an additional number of the North Star version were purchased from TCA. Overseas expanded rapidly by some 600 per cent – unparalleled in UK independent airline history and became one of Europe's largest charter operators; because of its sheer size, it naturally dominated the inclusive tour business. However, it became too big too soon and in the summer of 1961, the company ran into serious financial difficulties. When the Shell Company refused to refuel their aircraft on the ground at Malaga Airport due to unpaid bills, it was discovered that some of their staff had not been paid for weeks and in addition, the airline hadn't paid any landing fees. Consequently, at the end of August 1961, the airline collapsed with debts of £500,000 grounding its entire fleet.

It was around this time that Derby Airways – who would be re-branded as British Midland Airways in 1964 in readiness for relocating to East Midlands Airport – were in desperate need of pressurised four-engined equipment which would hopefully bring down the seat-mile costs and, more crucially, enable them to quote keener prices to the large inclusive tour agents in what was now becoming an increasingly competitive business. But like the majority of the independents of the era, lack of finance was always going to be a limiting factor. Unaccountably, they rejected outright the tried and tested Douglas DC-4, no matter how cheap they might be and after further consideration they decided on the purchase of two well maintained Douglas DC-6A passenger-cargo aircraft offered for sale by American Airlines. But with the sudden demise of Overseas Aviation, they quickly changed their minds and opted for the lower priced Argonauts offered in a liquidation sale by Lombards – the controlling bank. Purchasing five aircraft, they were ferried to Burnaston aerodrome where two were cannibalised for spares and the remaining three, Hotel Golf, Hotel Sierra and Hotel Yankee, entered service on inclusive tour charter flights from Manchester, Birmingham, Bristol and Cardiff.

Why British Midland settled on the Argonaut, when it was manifestly inferior to the DC-6, was a complete mystery to everyone in the aviation business. It was well known that the seat-mile costs of the Argonaut were 50 per cent higher than that of the DC-6, and the cost of overhauling the Merlin engines – provided no trouble was found – was considerably more than the equivalent Pratt and Witney engines of its Douglas counterpart. But British Midland seemed to have no interest in detail – especially economic detail. Captivated by the thought of purchasing a fleet of five aircraft for a rock-bottom price, no doubt clouded their judgement. What seemed at first as an attractive deal turned out in the end to be disastrous in both financial and operational terms. Even so, cheap as the deal seemed, the purchase was still a huge financial undertaking for the company.

The choice of the Argonaut was disastrous one and a decision in hindsight they came to deeply regret, mainly because of their unreliability and high operating and maintenance costs. Another negative factor was that in the whole of its service life with BOAC, no correct operating procedures for the Merlin engine had been arrived at and as a result, the Argonauts suffered a long series of in-flight engine failures and exploded exhaust systems. These technical problems with the Merlins were so common they weren't even recorded as an incident in the technical log. Because of insurmountable delays and diversions one large tour operator – Hourmont Travel of Cardiff – transferred all its business to the rival airline Cambrian, and remember this was the era when if you arrived at your destination within 24 hours of schedule, you were considered on time. Because of the high operating costs and engine malfunctions, BMA seriously examined the possibility of replacing the Merlin engine with the Rolls-Royce Dart turboprop – an idea which in the end came to nothing. Despite all the negative aspects, there was no going back, and like it or not, the Argonaut would have to remain British Midland's mainliner for the foreseeable future.

Even in British Midland ownership, with its excellent engineering staff and facilities, technical problems continued to plague the type and did nothing to build up the operational prestige of the company. The following account by one British Midland passenger is typical of the numerous technical problems and associated delays that were regularly encountered during the busy holiday season:

I flew on the ill-fated Hotel Golf approximately six months before the Stockport crash. We managed to get airborne from Ringway Airport on the third attempt for Ostend. After only about ten minutes in the air, one of the starboard Merlins decided to have a fire. We were diverted for an emergency landing at East Midlands Airport where, after a successful landing, the aircraft was unceremoniously towed away to a hangar and all the passengers were deposited in the staff canteen and fed cold ham and chips.

Argonaut 'Hotel Golf' seen here at Manchester Airport a few weeks prior to the accident.

A four-hour wait ensued, until Hotel Golf's sister ship Hotel Yankee arrived, which should have operated the East Midlands-Jersey flight. This was allocated for our continued journey, and the Jersey bound passengers informed of an indefinite delay to their flight. The second leg of our journey was not however without incident, as on landing at Ostend both tyres on the port undercarriage burst!

It soon became obvious to British Midland engineers that the Argonaut was a tad tail heavy, and in a bid to improve longitudinal trim Hotel Golf was stripped inside. The rear lounge was ripped out to be replaced by relocated toilets which seemed to solve the problem. At the same time, the passenger cabin was modified with two additional windows being cut into the forward fuselage allowing an extra row of seats to be added, increasing the original Overseas Aviation seating plan of 72 to 75. In 1964, this was further increased to 78 with a seat pitch of 31 inches; those who bemoan the lack of legroom nowadays, remember it was just as bad in the old days. All these seating and other modifications, of course, had airworthiness approval from the Air Registration Board and reflected the shorter sectors flown by the aircraft and the need for lighter fuel load.

It was immediately obvious that the Argonaut could not operate commercially from Burnaston which had no proper runway – just a close mown strip – and was totally unsuitable for heavy airliners like the Argonaut that had higher tyre pressures and landed faster. The Argonaut required a proper runway for commercial operations so the aircraft were more or less based at Birmingham Airport where the company leased hangar space; the aircraft only returning to Burnaston for heavy winter maintenance and crew training.

During its time with British Midland, Hotel Golf had suffered two recorded incidents. The first occurred in June 1965 when a wingtip struck a hangar whilst the aircraft was being towed on the airfield. A second more serious mishap occurred on 6 March 1967 at East Midlands Airport. The aircraft had just completed a local test flight, and upon touchdown, the nose wheel collapsed into its bay resulting in substantial damage to the underside of the nose, two inboard propellers and engines. Damage was also sustained underside to the fuselage sides caused by fragmentation from the propeller blades. As a result, the aircraft was pulled from service for extensive repairs carried out on site by Field Aircraft Services. On completion, the aircraft was functionally flight tested by Captain Marlow on 12 April and was returned to service in time to operate that summer's heavy charter schedule.

Plagued by the soaring costs of operating and maintaining the aircraft, which was now haemorrhaging company profits at an alarming rate, a decision was made by the British Midland board on 1 January 1967 about their future use. It was decided to withdraw two of the Argonauts at the end of the 1967 holiday charter season and retain only one aircraft – which happened to be Hotel Golf – as a back-up aircraft. Besides their unreliability and operational costs, there were other reasons for their withdrawal. One was that Rolls-Royce had notified the airline that because of uneconomic costs and a shortage of usable spares, they would not be prepared to continue to overhaul the Merlin engines beyond 1967. Another factor was that in the late 1960s, suitable aviation fuel – Avgas – was beginning to become a scarce commodity at airports across Europe. The board also decided that from 1968 onwards the airline would operate an all turbo prop fleet.

Chapter Eight
Dire Warnings of Things to Come

"Aviation in itself is not inherently dangerous… But it is terribly unforgiving of any carelessness or neglect."

Captain A G Lamplugh

The tragic story of Hotel Golf's violent end at Stockport can be traced directly back to the early years of the Argonaut operational service with BOAC. Between 1953 and 1954, the airline suffered a number of incidents involving inadvertent fuel transfer in flight, fortunately none of these incidents resulted in disaster.

Briefly explained, inadvertent fuel transfer is fuel unintentionally transferring itself from one tank to another through an improperly closed cock, with the very real possibility of starving one or more engines of fuel. BOAC corresponded with Canadair, the manufacturers, regarding their concerns, and in turn, Canadair consulted with Douglas and asked for their views. Douglas said that there had been some problems with the fuel system in the early years on the DC-4, but they had no further complaints since operators learned how to maintain and rig the control system.

Canadair narrowed down the BOAC incidents to incorrect rigging of the cables and pulleys within the system and after a special drive on safety, the problem seemed to have been resolved to the satisfaction of the airline. According to Canadair, the BOAC incidents were the only ones on record and failed to understand the true implications of the problem. Believing it wasn't a serious hazard, they didn't issue a service bulletin, made no changes to the Argonaut operational manual and sent no warnings to other operators of the type; as far as they were concerned, the problem only seems to have applied to BOAC who knew about it. As the regulations stood at the time, BOAC had no obligation either to report these incidents to the Air Registration Board or any other relevant authority. However, for BOAC their troubles with the fuel system were far from over.

On 5 July 1957, one of their Argonauts, Hotel November, showed anomalous inadvertent fuel transfer on a flight to Singapore. After landing for refuelling, the captain very properly refused to continue the journey, and accepted a considerable delay until he had been given a satisfactory explanation as well as having the fuel system checked by engineers. Although various possibilities were explored, no final conclusion was reached. The Singapore incident is the last one officially recorded in BOAC service, although during my research, I found some hearsay evidence from their flight crews that they experienced some 'odd' things happening in the fuel system during flight. Regrettably, the real underlying problem was never fully addressed and remained lurking under the surface to strike again; and strike again it did on the morning of Sunday 4 June 1967 over Stockport.

The Argonaut's fuel system, identical to that of its parent, the Douglas DC-4, is a complex and technical piece of plumbing, but the essentials are not difficult to understand. The system comprises of four main tanks located in the wings. The number

1 tank supplied the number 1 engine, whilst number 2 supplied number 2 engine in the port wing. This arrangement was repeated in the starboard wing, with number 3 tank supplying number 3 engine and number 4 supplying number 4 engine. To further complicate matters, there were also cross feed lines which connected all the tanks and enabled any engine or combination of engines to be fed fuel from any individual tank.

In the cockpit, the four levers controlling fuel tank selection were mounted on the raised centre pedestal on the captain's side just ahead of the port throttle levers, whilst the two levers controlling the cross-feed cocks were in the corresponding position on the co-pilot's side. The location of both sets of actuating levers on the flight deck was so awkward that a pilot restrained by his seat harness could easily put one or more levers in the wrong position. Just a slight error in the positioning of a cross feed lever – by as little as a quarter of an inch – could create a situation in which a cross feed cock would be improperly closed, allowing for a substantial amount of fuel migration from one tank to another without the flight crew being aware.

The selector levers were designed to click into position when they were set correctly, but because of natural wear during its 18-years of operational life, they were neither audible nor felt. The primary reason for the detents was to ensure that the fuel cock does not leave its selected position due to vibration or other unintentional reasons. Many British Midland pilots, interviewed after the accident said that the midway detent was easily detected, but the forward and aft positions could not be felt at all, and during flight, they would simply push and pull the lever as far as it would go; some even admitted that they didn't even know there were detents in these positions. A test pilot from the Accident Investigation Branch found that when pushing the cross-feed lever from the midway to the forward off position, he was tending to leave the lever 10 degrees short of the shut off position. It was a built-in trap that seemingly nobody within British Midland was aware of.

It was common knowledge amongst British Midland engineers and flight crews that when Argonauts had been standing for long periods on the airfield, fuel was found to have transferred itself from one tank to another. The following incident involving Hotel Golf just a month before the Stockport accident is a typical example and is described here by Captain Peter Austin:

On a return flight from Beauvais in Hotel Golf on 4 May 1967, we landed at Birmingham Airport in the late afternoon. Before going off duty, I asked the engineer to have the aircraft refuelled with 1,000 gallons in the four main tanks in readiness for an early start the next day. On arrival at the airport the following day, I completed the paperwork for my flight to Rotterdam and boarded the aircraft. I was informed by my First Officer, Roger Wise, that he had discovered 200 gallons of fuel had transferred overnight from the number two main tank to the number two auxiliary tank. I asked him if he was sure that the fuel cock lever was closed after refuelling the previous day, and he assured me it was. I then asked the engineer if he was certain the fuel had been put into the right tanks, and he confirmed that he had. I had heard of fuel transference happening to Argonaut aircraft on the ground, but I have never knowingly experienced it myself and certainly not in flight; our engineers have always been adamant that this cannot happen.

British Midland engineering staff believed that this inadvertent fuel transference was a known idiosyncrasy of the aircraft and was mistakenly ascribed it to mishandling of the fuel selector levers by maintenance personnel when working in the cockpit. Pilots and engineers fervently believed that inadvertent fuel transfer in flight was an impossibility, but if a close examination of the Argonauts fuel logs had been undertaken, it would have led to the discovery that fuel transfer in the air was in fact a common occurrence, ready to catch out the unwary, fatigued or both, as the following incidents clearly demonstrate.

The Abadan Incident

On 28 January 1966, Hotel Golf's sister ship Hotel Yankee, returned to East Midlands Airport via Brindisi and Amsterdam with Captain Harry Marlow in command. On landing, item number 10 of the defects entered in the technical log after the flight, and signed for by the commander, reads: 'On two occasions, using 1 and 4 auxiliary tanks each with 200 gallons, both tanks ran dry after 50 minutes. The missing fuel transferred itself to 1 and 4 main tanks. At the time, 1 and 4 auxiliary booster pumps were running and 1 and 4 auxiliary tanks selected.'

The following day ground engineers dealt with the defects. The relevant entry in the 'action taken' column, signed for by the supervising engineer reads: '1 and 4 auxiliary tanks refuelled to 150 gallons. Fuel pipe removed, fuel cocks checked and adjusted. Ground run undertaken using auxiliary tanks and found no fuel transference'.

On the face of it, the Abadan incident was very much like inadvertent fuel transfer in flight, but the engineers after testing the system found everything satisfactory and came to no positive diagnosis of the cause of the defect. But the problem didn't go away

The Beauvais Incident

On Saturday 13 May 1967, just three weeks before the Stockport accident, Hotel Golf was found at Beauvais Airport to be suffering a fuel leak in the number 4 main tank. The following day, after temporary repairs to stem the leak, the aircraft was flown back empty to East Midlands Airport under the command of Captain Hunt. On this flight, the number 4 engine was deliberately shut down and feathered (feathering an engine is when the three individual propellers of the propeller unit are turned edge on to the slipstream to reduce drag). For 15 minutes in every 20, in order to keep fuel distribution even whilst flying on three engines, Captain Hunt fed engines 1, 2 and 3 from their respective tanks, and for the remaining 5 minutes, he fed all three engines from number 4. Captain Hunt observed that when the number 4 tank was selected to off, and number 3 selected to on, the fuel pressure rose not only on the number 3 pressure gauge but also on number 4. This should have been a clear indication that the tank selector lever for the number 4 tank was not properly closed.

On landing at base, the commander duly entered this anomaly in the technical log. The following day a British Midland engineer – as with the Abadan incident – checked the fuel system and found nothing amiss. After a ground run, he entered in Hotel Golf's technical log in the 'action taken' column – 'Fuel cock checked and found satisfactory'. Here again, as with the Beauvais incident, no identification of the actual cause of the trouble had been positively diagnosed.

We come now to what has been called the Palma incident, which occurred just seven days before the Stockport crash. What transpired on that flight was of such a striking nature, that if the facts had been effectively reported and investigated, it would have led to the discovery that inadvertent fuel transfer, causing fuel starvation to one or more engines was a very real danger. Even at that late stage, warnings could have been given to British Midland pilots operating the Argonaut, to keep a careful watch on the outer main fuel tank states. If such a warning had been given, then Captain Marlow would have been in a better position to avoid or at the very least, cope with the emergency thrust upon him only one week later.

The Palma Incident

On the morning of Sunday 28 May, Hotel Golf was in position at Ringway Airport ready to operate British Midland's regular holiday charter flight to Palma. The aircraft was under the command of Captain Barry Fleming with First Officer Roger Wise acting as his co-pilot. Also flying as part of the crew was Brian Gifford, an experienced, although not certificated Flight Engineer. He was carried on the aircraft primarily to perform engineering duties, such as supervising the refuelling and any routine maintenance that was required during the period the aircraft was on the ground at Manchester and Palma.

When Captain Fleming entered the cockpit that morning, he found a note left by the previous crew posted on the instrument panel, which conveyed the information that the number 4 fuel contents gauge was substantially under reading by some 75 gallons. But no entry of this defect had been recorded in the technical log which was in breach of duty under the provisions of the Air Navigation Order of 1966.

Hotel Golf had been refuelled with the standard load for the Palma run, namely, all four main tanks full and 100 gallons each in number 1 and 4 auxiliary tanks. The aircraft took off at 10:07 with a full passenger load and after attaining cruising altitude, set a course on the first stage to Palma. At 11:00 using the fuel tank selector levers, Captain Fleming switched from main tanks to auxiliaries; at 12:05, he switched back to main tanks in order to balance the fuel load. The engines were now being fed fuel from their own tanks, number 1 engine from number 1 tank, number 2 engine from number 2 tank, and so on. But unknown to both pilots, one of the cross-feed levers was left a few degrees out of position and consequently, fuel from the number 4 tank was being inadvertently transferred through a slightly open fuel cock down wing to the adjacent number 3 tank.

At 14:50, when the aircraft was flying over the Perpignan region, Roger Wise became concerned about the low reading on the number 4 main fuel tank contents gauge, then showing only 350 lbs. appreciably lower than would normally be expected at this stage in the flight. Even for allowing for a substantial under-reading – with a consumption of about 450 lbs per hour – this was cutting the fuel for number 4 engine rather close. There was nearly an hour to go before reaching Palma with the possibility of having to hold there before landing. The First Officer asked Captain Fleming if he would like to cross feed fuel from the number 3 tank to number 4 for a time, since this was showing a much higher reading. Fleming replied that it was not necessary, as he had been informed the number 4 contents gauge was substantially under reading, and besides, with full tanks on take off from Manchester, logically there must be enough fuel in tank number 4 to reach Palma safely with a reserve.

In the holding pattern over Palma, Roger Wise, still concerned about the now extremely low reading showing on the contents gauge, turned to Brian Gifford in jump seat behind and asked him to keep his eye on the fuel pressure gauge for the number 4 engine and inform him at once if it started to fall further, so he could immediately cross feed fuel from number 3 tank to maintain the fuel supply to number 4 engine.

When Hotel Golf was approaching the runway threshold, something the engineer did was understood by the First Officer to be a warning that the fuel pressure in the number 4 gauge was falling. He immediately moved the starboard cross feed selector lever to the midway inter-engine position to maintain a fuel supply to the number 4 engine. He could not, from his position restrained by his seat harness, reach across to shut off the number 4 main tank selector lever without interfering with Captain Fleming's handling of the throttles on the final stages of the approach. The effect of the cross feeding was immediate and increased the pressure in the number 4 tank. Hotel

Golf touched down almost immediately afterwards. As soon as the undercarriage kissed the runway, Roger Wise breathed a sigh of relief – it had been a near thing.

Captain Fleming attached no great importance to what his First Officer had told him about the cross feeding, because he was utterly convinced that having departed Manchester with full main tanks there must be plenty left on landing at Palma. After engine shutdown, Roger Wise, who still harboured concerns about the fuel state in the number 4 tank asked the Engineer to check the fuel uplift. This he did, noting down the quantities put into each tank to fill it to the brim on the refuelling receipt, as well as the total uplift, which is all he would normally have to record. The figures he got from the refuelling were in litres, and the First Officer used his navigational computer to convert this into imperial gallons. He was staggered at the result. To his utter astonishment, it showed that number 4 tank had less than 14 gallons remaining on landing – a perilously low amount. After checking that the total fuel uplift, which approximated the estimated burn off for the outbound flight, Roger Wise erroneously came to the conclusion that there must have been a mistake about the figures he was given because it just didn't make any sense. He rejected the result of his calculation as impossible. It never occurred to him at the time to work out the individual fuel uplift for the remaining three tanks. If he had, he would have discovered that the missing fuel from number 4 tank had transferred itself during the flight down wing to the inboard number 3 tank.

On the return flight to Manchester, Roger Wise kept a watchful eye on the fuel system. He noticed no abnormalities, except for the substantial under reading he now believed to be present on the number 4 fuel contents gauge and the fact that the number 3 fuel gauge became unserviceable during the flight. The remainder of the journey passed without further incident. Hotel Golf landed safely at Manchester, and after off-loading its passengers returned to base at East Midlands Airport; landing there just before midnight. After engine shutdown, Brian Gifford, on Captain Fleming's instructions, entered as defects in the technical log that the number 3 fuel gauge was unserviceable and that the number 4 gauge under reads by 400 lbs.

The following day British Midland engineers dealt with these defects and took appropriate corrective action. But not a word of what transpired on the final approach to Palma, or the extraordinary result of the fuel uplift calculation reached British Midland's Chief Pilot, Captain Fenton or his deputy Captain Wallace for further investigation. Under the provisions of the Air Navigation Order, Article 7, it was the absolute duty of Captain Fleming or his First Officer to record this startling incident in the technical log. It was a highly regrettable omission that would soon lead to catastrophic consequences. The parallels between the Palma incident and the subsequent accident at Stockport one week later is obvious. Palma was an incident *too* many and should have sounded the warning bells that all was not well with the fuel system; in effect it was a full-dress rehearsal for Stockport.

Chapter Nine
Beware the High Ground

"Yankee Kilo…you have my field in sight?"
Perpignan Air Traffic Control

Early on the evening of Saturday 3 June, Captain Ron Pullinger, a 46-year-old airline pilot, employed on a seasonal contract with the independent airline Air Ferry, sauntered into the crew operations room at Manston Airport, near Ramsgate, to complete a flight plan and to be briefed about the weather over his intended route. In about an hour's time, he was due to fly 83 holidaymakers on a charter to Perpignan, which at the time was a major hub for holidaymakers going to the South of France.

Captain Pullinger lived locally and was a well-known and popular figure in the Thanet area. After service as a pilot with the RAF from 1940 to 1948, he flew with British United Airways on Britannias and with Morton Air Services on DC-3 Dakotas before taking up his current contract with Air Ferry in January 1967.

The mundane charter schedules might not hold the same glamour and excitement as flying with the RAF, but they were certainly not without their moments of incident and danger. Many commercial pilots of the period describe civil flying as long periods of boredom punctuated by moments of sheer terror. Although he was a pilot of very considerable experience, with 10,400 hours to his credit, only 241 of those were spent in command of large four-engined transport aircraft. He had landed at Perpignan on 12 occasions during 1958–59 and once in 1965. He had not been to the airport again before 28 May 1967, when, as aircraft commander, he had made a daytime landing. Reports from both British United and Air Ferry were favourable, and the report of the person responsible for authorising his qualification as commander on the DC-4 was in particular praise regarding his airmanship.

In the operations room, Captain Pullinger met up with Bill Isaacs, his First Officer assigned to the flight. Bill, aged 61, was a great character and a veteran aviator, having made his first solo flight way back in 1934. He was stationed in Burma pre-war where he joined the Burma Volunteer Air Force and he became a much in demand instructor. When Burma was overrun by the Japanese, his unit was sent to India where Bill served as a Lieutenant flying on communications duties. After a further period of instructing, he joined 31 Squadron and was attached to the staff of Field Marshall Wavell as his personal pilot on a Lockheed Lodestar, and in 1944, he was deservedly awarded the Air Force Cross for his outstanding war-time service.

After demob, he easily made the transition to civil flying, obtaining his Commercial Pilots Licence in 1955, and thereafter, flew for a number of British and foreign airlines. Every year from 1963 onwards – because of upsurge in seasonal holiday charter flights – Bill would turn up at Manston Airport from his home in Palma Nova to fulfil a summer contract flying as co-pilot for Air Ferry. Shortly before the accident, he received the happy news that his partner in Palma had given birth to a daughter, an event that gave him immense joy and satisfaction. It was one of the many tragedies resulting from the subsequent crash that he did not live to see and hold his new daughter.

The two stewardesses rostered on the flight were Catherine Dunn, aged 22 from County Durham, and Patricia MacCann, a 23-year-old Yorkshire girl. Catherine was only on the Perpignan flight by sheer chance due to a late change of the roster because she 'trip traded' with another stewardess. In light of what subsequently happened, her colleague who had requested the switch, harboured a lot of guilt, suffering many conflicting emotions in the ensuing months and years. Fate and chance have always played a part in aviation disasters, tragically for Catherine this was yet another example.

Air Ferry was another one of the many independent airlines that had sprung up in the early 1960s to take advantage of the expanding and lucrative inclusive tour business. The company, a subsidiary of Leroy Tours, began operations on 30 March 1963 with a series of charter flights to more than twenty holiday destinations across Europe. When Air Ferry's first summer season came to an end, it had carried over 120,000 passengers during seven months of operations. It was a promising and prosperous start for the fledgling airline.

The Saturday evening flight to Perpignan was a regular seasonal charter to transport tourists on a 31 guinea (£32) holiday on the Costa Brava. The aircraft allocated for the flight was a 23-year-old DC-4 – radio call sign Yankee Kilo – with the capacity to carry some 84 passengers in noisy, lumbering comfort at a sedate 180 knots. It was this very same aircraft that operated Air Ferry's very first operational flight in 1963 from Manston to Palma.

Yankee Kilo began life as a military Douglas C-54 and was delivered to the USAAF on 15 January 1944. Post war, it was variously described as a Skymaster or a DC-4 with the civil serial N56006; the aircraft served with Pennsylvania Central Airlines and Capital Airlines. During 1955, the aircraft was sold to the small American supplemental carrier, General Airways, and a year later, took part in the Hungarian Airlift. In 1960, Liverpool based Starways bought and registered the aircraft in the UK as G-APYK.

Yankee Kilo spent the 1960 season on inclusive tour work flying from Liverpool, Manchester and Glasgow to holiday destinations all over Europe. In 1961, Starways leased the aircraft with a flight crew to the Belgian flag carrier, Sabena, for United Nations use in the war being waged in the Belgian Congo, where the aircraft was responsible for ferrying relief supplies and UN troops around the country. This work took its toll on the aging airliner, suffering substantial damage in a wheels-up landing at Elizabethville on 23 July 1961. The aircraft received temporary repairs on site before being ferried to Prestwick via Palma for more comprehensive repairs by Scottish Aviation.

At the start of the 1962 season, the Starways operational DC-4 fleet stood at only two aircraft – Echo Zulu and Yankee Kilo – and it became necessary to lease another DC-4, because Yankee Kilo had suffered yet further damage after landing short at Liverpool Airport following a crew training flight in May. After extensive repairs, it returned to service the following October and Starways were quick to sell on the unlucky airliner to Air Ferry.

There is some dispute as to why Starways put the aircraft up for sale, and the real reason was never ascertained. But rumour circulating in the aviation fraternity at the time has it that the aircraft had been purchased without import duty, on condition that it was only used on international flights. With the importance of Starways domestic route network, this would no doubt have been a considerable restriction on the airliner's use and profitability. Another rumour was that the airline simply wanted to replace what they believed was an unreliable, accident-prone aircraft, with a more reliable one previously flown and maintained by a well-established airline.

According to the available records, Yankee Kilo suffered more than her fair share of technical problems and incidents, for example, on 25 May 1967, on a holiday flight to Basle, it was struck by lightning causing some damage to the starboard aileron. During its five years of service with Air Ferry, it had flown a total of 6,001 hours and carried 122,633 passengers without serious mishap.

With the flight plan and documentation completed, Captain Pullinger and his First Officer left the operations room and strode out across the tarmac to the waiting aircraft. Entering the cockpit, they settled in their respective seats and began the normal pre-flight preparations and checks. Meanwhile, the stewardesses, Catherine Dunn and Patricia MacMann, welcomed onboard the 83 excited and chattering holidaymakers.

At 6:10, the door was sealed and the four engines were fired up, a few minutes later, Yankee Kilo received taxi clearance and 17 minutes later, the DC-4 took off into the evening sunshine in good time and with no technical delay. The aircraft headed out over Dover and held there until 6,000 feet was reached before proceeding onwards to Lydd. Yankee Kilo crossed the coast near Beachy Head at 7,000 feet and was then handed over to Paris Air Traffic Control. The French coast was reached at 7:24 and Chartres at 7:51. From there, the flight progressed normally and without incident to Chateaudun at 8:00. At this point, an Invicta Airlines DC-4 – Papa Mike – also flying from Manston to Perpignan, was some ten miles ahead of Yankee Kilo and at a slightly higher altitude. On reaching Nevers at 8:28, Captain Pullinger reported that he was climbing to 9,000 feet in readiness to clear approaching high ground. The aircraft was then passed from Paris to Marseille Control before reporting at Clermont Ferrand at 9:03 and then at Mende at 9:25. At this point in the flight, visibility was reasonably good, threatened by nothing more than the approaching darkness. With both pilots methodically checking the instrument readings and navigation, the flight seemed in all respects routine and uneventful.

Yankee Kilo had made this journey many times before, but very soon, this familiar routine charter flight would change to one of terrible proportions. It was shortly after passing Mende that, unaccountably, the aircraft began to deviate markedly from the prescribed flight plan, a deviation that would take it south west of Perpignan and dangerously towards the high ground of the Pyrenees.

With the highest peaks above 11,000 feet, this massive 270-mile-long mountain range stretches from the shores of the Mediterranean Sea on the east to the Bay of Biscay on the west and makes a natural formidable boundary between France and Spain. It is a geographical area that can produce extremes of weather making flying conditions at times most unpleasant for both aircraft and crew. It could be particularly dangerous in darkness with spectacular electrical storms ready to catch out the unwary, inexperienced, and even those aviators who profess to know the area well. It was already well known as a notorious graveyard for aircraft.

It was also after passing Mende that some areas of doubt seemed to exist in the radio transmissions: Yankee Kilo called Marseille Control stating that it would be abeam Montelimar at 9:44. Marseille immediately queried this and asked for confirmation that this should be Montpellier, Montelimar being practically on the same parallel as Mende. In response, Yankee Kilo corrected itself and answered: 'Sorry… Montpellier'. Shortly afterwards, Captain Pullinger gave his estimated time of arrival at Perpignan as 10:10. Marseille Control again queried this message and in a questioning tone transmitted: "10:10?"

Yankee Kilo answered: "Affirmative."

At 9:43, the aircraft reported to Marseille Control that it was abeam Montelimar at 9,000 feet and gave 9:53 as the estimated time of arrival at Papa 3 (an entry point into Perpignan TMA). This ETA was appropriate but made the estimated time of arrival at Perpignan even more difficult to accept. The controller, who had corrected the transmission Montelimar to Montpellier, asked the aircraft to maintain 9,000 feet and call again at Papa 3. This point was reached at 9:50 and Marseille Control last contact was to clear the aircraft to descend to 7,000 feet and asked Yankee Kilo to change frequency and call Perpignan Approach Control for their landing instructions.

Two minutes later, at 9:52, Yankee Kilo called the Perpignan controller and still gave 10:10 as their estimated time of arrival, although both the Marseille and Perpignan controllers considered this to be an error. The aircraft was requested to call again on reaching 7,000 feet. At 9:55, the aircraft duly reported passing 7,000 feet in the descent and Perpignan Approach told it to continue descending and call again on reaching 5,000 feet. From then on, some confusion arose between Air Traffic Control and the aircraft. The Perpignan approach controller's broken English, spoken in strong French accent lacked clarity, and coupled with the fact he was not using standard aviation phraseology no doubt led to misunderstandings between the controller and the aircraft.

At 10:00, Yankee Kilo reported that it was approaching 5,000 feet. Perpignan acknowledged receipt and transmitted in heavily accented English: "Yankee Kilo, five zero...have you my field in sight?" The aircraft asked for repetition of the transmission and the controller repeated: "Have you my field in sight?"

The aircraft replied: "Roger, we'll advise...field in sight." Having apparently understood from this ambiguous message that Yankee Kilo had the runway approach lighting in view, the controller instructed them to report downwind for runway 33 for a visual approach and landing.

At 10:04, Perpignan asked Yankee Kilo for its present flight level and more particularly: "Have you my field in sight?"

The aircraft replied: "Yankee Kilo, negative at this moment. We will be with you in about five minutes."

The controller obviously did not understand and asked again in broken English: "Yankee Kilo, you have not my field in sight?" The reply, heavy with static and barely audible on the air traffic recording sounded something like: '...that...is affirmative'. The controller misunderstood the call and told the aircraft again to report downwind for a landing on runway 33, then, a few seconds later Yankee Kilo asked for QDMs (magnetic headings). The controller was surprised by this and asked the aircraft to repeat. There was no reply to this transmission or any of his subsequent calls. It seems the crew of Yankee Kilo were far off course when they began their descent and unknowingly, in the darkness, were heading away from the airport directly towards the dangerous and unforgiving high ground of the Pyrenees. It would appear from all the later radio transmissions that the crew had never positively identified the airport.

Villagers in the little town of Vernet-les-Baines heard the airliner pass overhead 'extremely low' and continue up the valley with its landing lights on. It was after the landing lights were switched on that the anxious crew picked out the steep, rocky mountains illuminated directly ahead. Both pilots knew they were in serious trouble and from then on totally lost control of the situation. In a desperate bid to escape the mountains, they endeavoured to turn back on a reciprocal heading by making a sharp left-hand turn with an extreme angle of bank. In the cabin, the terrified passengers, with no warning from the crew as to what was happening, grasped at the seat armrests and each other anxiously wondering what their fate would be. It was during this stomach-turning manoeuvre that the port wing, outboard of the number one engine, struck a rocky spur of the Canigou Massif with disintegrating force. On contact, the entire port wing broke away from the fuselage and fragmented over a sparsely wooded plateau. The rest of the aircraft with its human cargo, streaming cherry-red flames from the severed wing root, followed a ballistic trajectory across a ravine and violently slammed into a near vertical rock wall, 450 metres north of the first point of impact. Eyewitnesses saw the mountainside flash red in the blackness of the night as the aircraft exploded in a pyrotechnic display. Within a split second, all 88 passengers and crew on board were reduced to mutilated humanity. The location of the crash – estimated to have taken place at 10:06 British Summer Time at an altitude of 3,800 feet – was some thirty-five miles from its planned destination.

Rene Pideil, Mayor of the tiny mountain village of Py, less than half-a-mile from the crash scene, was relaxing at home watching television when he heard the heavy drone of the airliner overhead. Fearful of yet another crash in the area, he said: "I rushed outside to see the aircraft with its landing lights on circling above trying to escape the mountains. I then saw it plough into the mountainside. There was a terrific flash and explosion followed by a huge mushroom cloud like an atomic blast."

The fact the DC-4 had substantially deviated from the usual coastal route for holiday charter flights, a navigational error seemed the most obvious explanation for the accident. But the question that had to be asked: was this due to pilot error, or lack of ground aids? Perpignan Airport was surrounded by high dangerous peaks and the area was well known by pilots for heavy turbulence, added to all this was the Airport's substandard runway lighting, approach radar and the poor English spoken by the air traffic control personnel. Having said that, Invicta's DC-4 Papa Mike, flying just ahead of Yankee Kilo, did not report any particular difficulty with any of the navigational aids or indeed the weather and landed safely at 10:00 p.m.

The first of the rescue teams made the tortuous ascent to the crash site as dawn was breaking with the forlorn hope of finding some alive in the still burning wreckage. It soon became clear because of the extreme violence of the crash and all-consuming fire that there could positively be no survivors. The only sign of the 88 passengers and crew were a few torsos, limbs and other unidentifiable human remains.

The passengers who came from all over the UK, had included an infant, two entire families from Yorkshire, some children and seven young men aged between eighteen and twenty from south London who had decided to make their first flight together. A five-month-old baby – left in the care of relatives – was orphaned when her young parents died. Others killed were first-time flyers from the North West, including two 20-year-old plumbers from Manchester – Billy Rafferty and Terence McGowan who were the best of mates and lived on the same street.

One young woman booked on the flight with her mother had a vivid premonition of the forthcoming disaster and decided in that instant to leave the coach taking them from Victoria to Manston Airport. Her mother, going to see her other daughter – a holiday rep with Lyons Tours was waiting at Perpignan to meet the flight – continued her journey alone and became an unfortunate victim of the tragedy.

Everyone at Manston was naturally stunned and shocked by the events. The Invicta Airlines DC-4s – Papa Mike – which had preceded the Air Ferry flight was parked next to Yankee Kilo on the apron and the two groups of passengers boarded their aircraft at the same time. One of the Invicta ground stewardesses had exchanged some good-natured banter with the group of young men from London who were larking about in good humour at the end of the Air Ferry queue. After hearing news of the dreadful accident, she could not get their happy and innocent young faces out of her mind. The seven lads had planned the holiday over pints in their local pub, the Fox and Hounds in Sydenham. Landlord, Arthur Cooper, after hearing about their tragic deaths, said: "They were a marvellous, jovial and well-mannered bunch of lads – not an ounce of nastiness in any of them. All they wanted was a bit of fun."

The accident was of course front-page news in all the Sunday papers and back at Manston, the senior officer on duty in Traffic, not wanting to alarm those about to fly out, tried to ensure there were no Sunday papers on sale in the terminal. This he achieved, although of course many arriving passengers on the coaches had already purchased their papers on the journey.

Some of the passengers' families came to Manston in the days following the accident; traumatic visits for them all and for the Air Ferry staff who met them. Other visitors were from the Accident Investigation Branch, Farnborough, a presence that would last for some time.

High ground accidents in the '50s and '60s were recognised as the deadliest threat to commercial aviation, in which highly qualified and experienced pilots fly perfectly functioning aircraft into mountainous terrain with devastating consequences. These types of accidents are clinically termed by air crash investigators as CFIT, Controlled Flight into Terrain.

The Perpignan disaster in itself was shocking enough, but who then could have predicted, or even imagined, the terrible events that were to follow just twelve hours later at Stockport.

Chapter Ten
Holiday Reps, Aircrew and Airports

"Charter a plane, put a couple of ads in the newspapers and the public would come rolling in."

Travel Pioneer – Vladimir Raitz

In the 1950s, air travel abroad was still regarded as the preserve of the wealthy well-connected elite, far beyond the means and aspirations of the average person; for most Britons, the thought of flying off to holiday abroad was an outrageous concept. In 1951, only around one in 14 Britons holidayed abroad, and even in 1961, the figure was only one in nine. The vast majority of British people had never flown and of those who had, most had done so during military service.

By the mid-sixties, the cheap 'inclusive tour' holidays by air – continental holidays as they were then called – were suddenly opened up to millions of ordinary people and soon became a must-have purchase for the adventurous tourist. Throughout the decade, more and more sun-starved Brits, sick of the dismal English weather and bad-tempered boarding-house landladies, gave up the traditional seaside resorts of Blackpool, Bridlington and Brighton in exchange for the sunshine and new excitements of the Spanish Costa's. In these exotic resorts, they found themselves booked into hotels much more palatial and opulent than their own homes; even jerrybuilt hotels seemed luxurious in an era when many people still lived in houses with outside toilets and no running hot water. Above all else, the inclusive tour holiday was relatively cheap – holidaymakers could eat and drink for practically nothing and there were free excursions provided by the tour company to take in the sights, and of course, freely spend hours baking in the fierce Spanish sunshine. They flew off pale-faced from regional airports all across the UK to return home two weeks later sporting healthy Mediterranean suntans, clutching straw hats, bottles of duty-free alcohol and cigarettes, along with exotic stories of overseas adventures to regale their family and friends.

The concept of marrying up an airliner load of seats with a block of hotel rooms to make up a package holiday was by no means a new idea; it was first practiced by a number of travel companies in the immediate post-war years. However, it was Vladimir Raitz, a Russian émigré, who is the person reputed to be the original inventor of the package holiday, and in 1949, he registered Horizon Holidays as a limited company. "What could be simpler?" he said. "Charter a plane, put a couple of ads in the newspapers and the public would come rolling in." And roll in they did. Raitz, whose first brochure was just four pages long, initially wanted to organise package holidays to Corsica but was prevented from doing so by the Civil Aviation Act of 1947, which gave the British flag carrier – British European Airways (BEA) – the monopoly on all European flights, despite the fact that BEA didn't actually fly to Corsica. It took Raitz from October 1949 until March 1950 to persuade the Ministry to grant him a licence to operate holiday flights to the island; but the licence came with the ludicrous restriction that he only carried students and teachers!

In May 1950, he chartered a clapped-out war surplus 32-seat Dakota, complete with crew, bullet holes and flak damage. At the same time, he cut a verbal deal with a Spaniard running a tented encampment on a beach in Corsica. For around £32, he offered his adventurous clients an all-inclusive holiday under canvas. With a refuelling stop in Lyon, the whole journey took a bone-jarring six hours.

That first flight to Corsica effectively gave birth to the greatest phenomenon in travel history. From that point on, the British inclusive package tour industry gathered momentum and within a few years, Raitz was flying holidaymakers to beach resorts in Majorca, Sardinia and Malaga. His vision sparked a revolution in how the British would spend their holidays in the decades to come, but it took another ten years for it to fully take off.

Another pioneer in the industry was J H Wilson who owned the Liverpool-based Cathedral Touring Agency and the local airline Starways. In 1952, he started operations out of Liverpool with pilgrimage tours to Lourdes using Dakota aircraft. The following year, Wilson diversified into general package tour operations with holiday flights to Bilbao. By 1958, due to high demand, the Lourdes pilgrimages were operated six days a week on the larger DC-4 and by 1961, Starways were flying both Dakotas and DC-4s from Liverpool to Basle, Biarritz, Malaga, Oporto and Palma.

People quickly realised that for the same amount of money they were spending on a holiday in Britain, they could fly off on a holiday to Spain where the sunshine was almost guaranteed, added to all this their spending money went much further; suddenly, holidays had become more colourful and exciting.

To tempt aspiring holidaymakers, travel agents churned out bright colourful holiday brochures with flattering colour images of luxury hotels – many of which had not yet been built – remember there was no Trades Description Act in those days and travel companies could be very devious in their claims. Unfortunately, this new breed of holidaymakers were unwittingly the guinea pigs for the travel industry and many would suffer the consequences in many of the air crashes that plagued the early years. All the statistics show that civil aviation was a hazardous business in those days and the number of accidents and fatalities were legion. For example, in the twelve years between 1955 and 1967, there were thirty-five fatal accidents to British operators alone, killing 1,123 – a shocking record.

Skytours, Global, Lunn-Poly, Sunflight, Riviera, Clarksons, Luxitours and Gaytours were just some of the companies that sprung up overnight to take advantage and cash in on this new profitable market, filling aeroplanes and hotels with people. It was a cutthroat industry and only the fittest would survive. Many quickly floundered and went to the wall due to the heavy discounting that many travel companies and charter airlines relied upon to get the contracts.

One North West travel company operating in this sector was Liverpool based Arrowsmith Holidays. Founded in the late 1940s by travel pioneer Harry Bowden Smith, it was his company that first brought cheap foreign travel to the working-class masses of the industrial northwest. Ruefully, Harry would often boast that his greatest triumph was 'introducing British fish and chips to the Spanish costas!' The company quickly prospered and at the beginning of 1967, he struck a deal with British Midland Airways to operate a series of 29 return charter flights throughout the season to Palma, with a total contract value of £38,000 – a substantial amount in those days.

One of the most popular destinations for aspiring tourists seeking sunshine and relaxation was Majorca, the largest of the Balearic Islands, which well into the twentieth century was nothing more than a sleepy impoverished backwater. It was regarded, especially by the British holidaymaker something of an exotic destination. By the mid-sixties, the Swedes, Germans along with the British, made Spain the top holiday destination, becoming the most visited country in the world. The first British package holidaymakers touched down in Majorca as early as 1952 and the island soon proved to be an irresistible attraction. With its almost guaranteed sunshine; stunning coastline; historic monasteries; colour washed windmills and houses along with the finest food and wine, made it a holiday idyll that captivated the holidaymaker. The island proved so popular that during the peak season tourists would dwarf its own population. Even as late as 1967, the island was still enchanting and unspoilt – but that would drastically change in the ensuing years, becoming synonymous with sangria, straw hats, stuffed donkeys and loutish behaviour.

The upsurge in the package tour sector also provided profitable opportunities for the up and coming independent charter airlines. With a plethora of cheap war-weary Dakotas, well past their prime and achingly slow, they were eagerly snapped up along with a pool of ex-military pilots readily available; these independent operators were more than anxious to grab their share of this lucrative new venture.

These charter airlines were the trailblazers in this rapidly growing industry and taking advantage of the surge in demand they managed to do some profitable work filling the skies with tourists. Many of these companies operated old and creaking aircraft that were barely legal, just maintaining the required permissible level of safety demanded. As these new charter airlines flourished, the British flag carrier, British European Airways, winced as its market share for their scheduled services fell dramatically.

The independent airline sector was a high-attrition industry in the 1960s, most companies operated on a knife-edge and it was a very real struggle for survival. It was a tough business with narrow profit margins, and in order to show a profit for the discounted fares charged by the travel companies, the aircraft and their crews were worked mercilessly hard throughout the summer season. The schedules were deliberately kept tight, refuelling stops and turnarounds at airports were short, and frequently there were no aircraft held in reserve if one suddenly became unserviceable – which was a regular occurrence. They were aggressive operators – they had to be to stay in contention with their rivals and stay in business. They had no choice during the busy summer season to fix what was legally essential and get their aircraft back in the air. It was an incessant demand to 'keep 'em flying' – after all, their aircraft made no profit when stuck on the ground waiting for spares and repairs.

In the mid-sixties, the package holiday was still a pretty basic and haphazard affair, with dilapidated hotels, run by indifferent hoteliers with facilities that were archaic and at times non-existent. Former holiday rep, Susan Maddocks, who was based on the island at the time, gives a fascinating insight into what it was like in those pioneering days.

I remember the first year I worked as a rep for Arrowsmith Holidays. At the time, the company chartered the Dan Air Ambassador – the same type of aircraft that was involved in the Manchester United Munich air disaster in 1958. This airliner was then known as the Elizabethan and soon after it was renamed the Ambassador – presumably for PR reasons and British European Airways, the airline involved wasted no time selling off the remainder of the fleet to Dan Air and other charter operators. Being a twin-engined airliner, it had a restricted range and required at least one refuelling stop at Perpignan. Arrowsmith also chartered the British Midland Argonaut and the Caledonian Airways DC-7.

The Caledonian was the elite Saturday night charter from Manchester. However, something always seemed to go wrong with this flight – tyre burst on landing, someone opening the door on take off and a long list of technical problems and glitches were just some of the things I remember. And every Saturday, late into the night, I could be found patiently waiting at the airport for a replacement aircraft to arrive. Unfortunately, because the DC-7 held 104 passengers, there was always a dozen or so passengers left over because the replacement aircraft were always smaller. We coached these poor holidaymakers to airports all over the country – Gatwick, Liverpool, Prestwick to name a few – in the unlikely event that they could get a flight. Of course, we never told them anything, we just herded them through passport control and onto a coach, waved them goodbye before they could ask any questions and we quickly cleared off with a new batch of clients for more of the same.

I clearly remember an incident involving the now long defunct travel company Mercury Direct, who unwittingly booked some of their clients into a brothel! When the rep paid them a visit a few days after their arrival to see how they were getting on, she was absolutely mortified to discover the place was an absolute hovel and the holidaymakers were terrified to go out after dark – and to cap it all the so-called hotel manager had a trolley for a foot!

I also recall one hotel in Arenal, which for some inexplicable reason always had accommodation available when we were in a fix with over bookings – which were often in those days – and proved to be a lifesaver for us reps at the time. That is until someone realised that the same clients had been sitting on the hotel steps and living out of their suitcases for a week. We discovered that the hotel owner had a fleet of ramshackle vehicles waiting outside the backdoor – including donkey and cart and a motorcycle and sidecar. He just herded all the new arrivals straight through his overbooked hotel to the backyard and dispatched them all over the island, and then couldn't remember where he had sent them. Two girls were eventually located in an unfinished villa with workmen still tiling the bathroom on an isolated rocky headland. They had been sternly warned not to go out between the hours of 10 and 12 in the morning because the Guardia Civil had rifle practice, and as there wasn't a road in sight, they had to climb down a steep hillside in the dark to get to the only guesthouse where they could eat. Still, that was far better than some of the German travel agencies who just dropped their clients off at hotel building sites and told them they would pick them up in a couple of weeks.

It was a horrendous yet exciting time being a holiday rep in that era where every day was always full of incident. I remember some of the Clarkson's girls constantly being sent home with nervous breakdowns, and you had little or no help or support from England. When one of my clients suddenly dropped dead on a coach excursion, I got a message from my manager's wife telling me to sort it out myself and not to bother him as he had a headache. This involved identifying the body, getting someone to come over from Barcelona to embalm him, finding a lead-lined coffin and organise a flight back to the UK on a scheduled carrier. I also had to see a judge who asked a couple of cursory questions and then decided he had had a heart attack. Then on top of all that, I had to arrange for the poor grieving widow to fly home. Not something a lot of 20-year-olds nowadays could do.

I well recall the terrific number of aircraft fatalities in the 1960s, it was absolutely horrendous, especially involving the independent charter airlines where aircraft and crews were often overstretched and overworked, and the regulations governing air safety were much more relaxed than today. I remember one year taking a flight from Valencia to Palma on a battered old, World War Two Dakota that had seen better days. The flight was booked to capacity but the captain allowed an extra 12 passengers on board and we stood up hanging onto the overhead luggage rack for dear life all the way there, including take off and landing!

Some unbelievable things happened in those early years and no one was ever censured or sued. I suppose looking back, I was lucky to survive it all.

Captain Harry Marlow lived in a comfortable detached house in the leafy suburb of Beeston, Nottingham, with his wife, Bobbie, and their two sons, Robert 9 and Stephen 15. In 1967, he was 41 and had been a commercial pilot with British Midland Airways and their predecessor Derby Airways for eleven years.

Like many pilots of his generation, he first learnt to fly in the RAF during the Second World War. In 1943, he was posted to Canada where in peaceful clear blue skies, he learned the rudiments of flying on the docile and forgiving single-engined Harvard trainer. His flight training was rigorous and fatiguing, flying up to five flights a day over the vastness of rural Canada. Besides practical flying instruction, he had tuition in navigation, basic aeronautics and engineering; it was the start of his love affair with aviation. With a natural aptitude for flying, he was graded an above average student by his instructors and had no difficulty gaining his wings as a Sergeant Pilot in 1946. On his return to the UK, he was posted to 19 Squadron at RAF Church Fenton near York, which at the time was a front-line fighter station in the defence of northern England and one of the first to operate jet aircraft. Church Fenton proved to be an attractive posting for it was there he underwent a conversion course to fly the new powerful and agile Meteor jet fighter. Highly rated by his instructors, he eventually became a member of the elite Meteor aerobatic team – a forerunner of the Red Arrows. His RAF record describes him as an 'exceptional and conscientious pilot'.

On leaving the RAF in 1954, he qualified for his Commercial Pilots' Licence the following year. With so many good experienced pilots available in the immediate post war years, looking for work with the scheduled and independent carriers was difficult, with only exceptional pilots being recruited. However, because of his aptitude and experience, he made an ideal recruit and soon landed a job with Skyways flying as First Officer on Avro Yorks, Hermes and Dakota aircraft. In 1956, he secured a position closer to home with British Midlands predecessor – Derby Airways – at Burnaston aerodrome in the Midlands. Within a year, he was promoted to junior captain on Dakota and Marathon aircraft and in 1958 became Captain in Command; soon after, he qualified to fly the turbo-prop Viscount and Argonaut. Harry Marlow liked the Argonaut, after bucketing about the sky in Dakotas; he enjoyed the comfort and speed offered by the pressurised Argonaut and Viscount with their ability to fly above the worst of the weather.

By the early summer of 1967, he had amassed an impressive total of 10,197 flying hours, of these, 2,009 were on the Argonaut. In the January of that year, his Instrument Rating and Instrument Approach Proficiency were checked and renewed and he also underwent route competence checks. His last medical before the accident was on 18 April which showed no adverse factors that would affect his ability to carry out his duties as an airline pilot. There can be no doubt that he was an exemplary and conscientious pilot with immense experience and fully competent to command Argonaut Hotel Golf from Manchester to Palma and return on the night of June 3/4.

However, it must be recorded that Harry Marlow was involved in two landing accidents just three weeks apart in 1964; one minor the other far more serious. The first occurred in September when his First Officer was at the controls of a Dakota carrying 13 passengers. A heavy landing was made in good weather at Guernsey Airport, the aircraft bounced heavily on touchdown and both propellers struck the ground when his co-pilot pushed the control column forward and overcorrected. The propellers and both engines were so badly damaged that the aircraft had to be pulled from service for extensive on-site repairs. Although shaken by their experience, none of the passengers were injured. Reputedly, after the aircraft came to a halt in a morass of aircraft bits, Harry Marlow turned to his First Officer and said with a grin: "You know, we must really have a chat about these dodgy landings of yours!"

Fifteen days later, he was in command of Dakota – Juliet Victor. The aircraft departed Hamburg at 18:00 hours on a return charter flight to Burnaston aerodrome, carrying a party of 36 members of the Derby Licensed Victuallers' Association and guests back from a conference. The main part of the flight was routine and uneventful. He made contact with Derby air traffic control at Burnaston giving their ETA at the airfield as 9:00 p.m.

With an October chill in the still air and clear skies and the River Trent close by, the weather forecast indicated that the formation of radiation fog over the aerodrome was a distinct possibility soon after sunset. Because Burnaston had no permanent runway lighting, nothing more sophisticated than gooseneck flares were used to illuminate the grass runways in poor visibility and at night. These flares, which looked like giant watering cans with a burning wick in the spout and fuelled by paraffin, were laid out the length of the runway prior to the arrival of the aircraft.

The normal procedure for an aircraft approaching Burnaston at night was for the flight crew to first locate the River Trent and follow this as far as Burton-on-Trent, then follow the railway line as far as the Hilton Gravel company's brightly lit neon sign, then pick up the A38 and follow the road as far as the aerodrome. On occasion, even car headlights were used at the end of runway to assist a landing. Without doubt, this was a potentially hazardous technique, and one that would remain British Midland standard drill at Burnaston right up to 1965, when the airline relocated its operations to East Midlands Airport.

The weather conditions prevailing at Burnaston were passed to the aircraft as: Surface wind calm, visibility two kilometres, no cloud. Captain Marlow began his descent towards runway 10, during which visibility rapidly began to deteriorate and the controller noticed bands of fog rolling across the aerodrome. Losing sight of the threshold lighting Harry Marlow elected to overshoot at 500 feet. He informed the tower that he would make another approach, this time to runway 28, and requested 'Very' lights (flares) to be fired from the runway threshold to aid his approach. Ground staff was dispatched with instructions to fire the lights when the controller signalled with a green Aldis lamp from the control tower. However, the Dakota had made its second approach and was in the process of overshooting before they were in position. Captain Marlow positioned the aircraft for a third approach, but again this was aborted at 600 feet. He later claimed that he did not remember making this approach, but according to the co-pilot who did, the overshoot was carried out because the aircraft was not properly aligned with the runway.

As the aircraft climbed away, the controller radioed the aircraft with information that the visibility was further deteriorating and extensive fog patches were on the aerodrome. On being given this information, Captain Marlow should have seriously considered diverting to Birmingham his alternative, but undaunted he elected to try a fourth long visual approach to runway 28. Commencing the approach from 4 miles out at 1,000 feet, he maintained visual reference by ground lights and traffic on the A38. When the aircraft was a mile and a half from the threshold at 700 feet, he requested Very lights to be fired because the runway lights were still not visible. Passing over Findern village at 500 feet, three quarters of a mile from the threshold, he saw the Very lights arc across the night sky and the first half of the runway lighting. A slight turn to the right was made to align the aircraft with the runway centre line and Juliet Victor, with the undercarriage down and flaps extended, swept over the perimeter fence at 85 knots.

Drifting to the left, the aircraft touched down heavily on the port undercarriage, bounced, briefly became airborne and entered a bank of fog. Captain Marlow immediately lost visual reference with the runway and the Dakota struck the ground hard 70 yards further on collapsing the port undercarriage leg. The aircraft travelled across the airfield in a wide left-hand turn and collided with the perimeter fence.

At the threshold, the ground personnel who fired the Very lights saw the aircraft pass overhead with the engines throttled back and then disappeared into the fog and presumed a landing was being made; seconds later, they heard a sickening thud. The aerodrome fire tender alerted by the noise drove down the runway, where visibility was between 30 and 100 yards. The aircraft could not be seen on the runway and was eventually located on the southwest boundary of the airfield. The aircraft was extensively damaged, but fortunately, there was no fire and all the passengers and crew evacuated the aircraft without serious injury. It was clearly a case of bent metal and hurt pride. Nevertheless, it was a disquieting experience for all concerned.

At the subsequent inquiry, Harry Marlow said in his defence that he could see all the runway lighting clearly from two miles out – 'then everything suddenly disappeared' – a common occurrence in radiation fog. Experience over the years has shown that surface fog on an otherwise clear night can lead the most careful pilot into disastrous errors of judgement when anticipated visual references fail to appear. Flying in these conditions required the eye considerably longer to appraise a potentially dangerous situation.

Captain Harry Marlow (author's archive).

The findings of the investigation board criticised Captain Marlow, in that, after three abandoned approaches, and the information given to him by air traffic control about the existence of fog patches on the aerodrome 'it would have been prudent for him to divert'. Was this 'bash on regardless' attitude a hangover from his barnstorming RAF days? RAF trained pilots tended to be intrepid flyers, rarely perturbed by bad weather conditions and were taught to fly 'by the seat of their pants' which had been all right in the service that taught them their trade, but it was certainly out of place in a commercial airliner. The report also went on to censure British Midland Airways for the approach lighting at Burnaston, which did not meet with the required standard laid down in civil aviation regulations. Since the airline was responsible for the operation and upkeep of the airfield, they had a measure of direct control over the facilities it provided for its aircraft.

As a result of his misfortune, Captain Marlow was demoted to the rank of First Officer. The Board of Trade required that he should not again be employed by the company as a pilot in command until he had undergone a flight test witnessed by an examiner from the Civil Aviation Flying Unit. He subsequently passed that test and was reinstated as captain in June 1965 and thereafter, flew regularly without further incident or criticism.

It is a matter of pride for a pilot to depart and land on time, added to this was the fact that a degree of pressure was put upon the commander to deliver his passengers on time at the planned destination rather than divert, which would involve additional expense for the company. Unscheduled diversions tended to cause friction within the airline and stress on the aircraft commander, and quite possibly on that foggy night, Harry Marlow felt obliged to at least make an attempt to get the aircraft down. In those days, it was always a case of commercial pressure versus operational pressure, and it was this pressure that could, and sometimes did, cloud a pilot's judgement which in turn can very easily lead to disaster. The cost-conscious independent airlines, like British Midland, were acutely aware that safety does not increase profits and would not spend money unnecessarily on safety unless forced to do so by law. There is no doubt that these companies employed shrewd corner-cutting operational methods, but always made sure they stayed just within legal requirements – but no more than that.

This type of accident in poor visibility, when a pilot has tried unsuccessfully to get in but continues to press on regardless instead of diverting has been the cause of numerous fatal crashes over the years. For example, one foggy night in April 1965, the pilot of a British United Airways Dakota told Jersey approach control that he was just going to come down and have a look, and then divert to France, where all the other aircraft had gone. The pilot made one approach, overshot, and informed the controller that he was 'a bit near the old steeple!' – apparently, he had narrowly missed a church – undaunted he pressed on for another attempt. This time, he crashed killing all but one on board.

And, the same again in 1965. After two overshoots, an Iberian Constellation struck an earth-moving machine at Tenerife Airport on the third attempt to land. Six crew and twenty-four passengers lost their lives. These accidents graphically illustrate the terrible consequences which follow repeated attempts to land an aircraft in adverse weather conditions.

The events culminating in the Stockport air disaster began on Saturday 3 June. On that morning, Harry Marlow, taking advantage of his last day of leave, rose at 9:30, indulged in his passion by playing a round of golf at his nearby club. He then returned home, lunched, read the newspapers, watched some sport on the television in the afternoon before retiring to bed with a novel; this was his usual practice before a night flight. He arose from his brief sleep at six, showered, changed into uniform and after a light meal, set off to drive the 70 miles to Manchester Airport. On the journey, he made a minor detour, calling in at the British Midland operations room at East Midlands Airport to collect some documents as previously arranged, but on arrival found they had already been sent on. He continued his journey via Ashbourne, Leek and Macclesfield arriving at the airport at nine o'clock. With just an hour to go before the scheduled departure time, he reported directly to the operations room where he met up with Chris Pollard, his First Officer for the flight.

The flight to Palma was a regular charter service operated during the summer season. Harry Marlow had flown this particular route for the past nine years, first with Dakotas and then on Viscounts and Argonauts, so he was well versed with the route and procedures that the flight entailed. He described the long arduous flight with refuelling stops on the way in the old unpressurised Dakota as 'a flog', and even the direct flight in the much larger pressurised Argonaut was still a long and gruelling five-hour trip.

The First Officer rostered for the Palma flight was Chris Pollard; at just 21 years old, he was considered remarkably young to be an airline pilot. With his boyish face and Cornish accent, he loved aviation with a passion; in fact, he is best described as an aviation fanatic and becoming a pilot was his boyhood dream. What prompted his interest in aviation is difficult to say, there being little flying activity in Cornwall at the time to stimulate the imagination, apart from the annual air show at the Culdrose Royal Naval Air Station near Helston, which his family often attended. An occasional visit to London with his parents would find Chris wanting to spend the whole day aircraft spotting on the observation deck above the Queens Building at Heathrow. He was skilful with his hands and started to model plastic aircraft kits before moving on to build powered balsa wood models, whose engines he would spend many an hour patiently coaxing into life before flying them up on Dartmoor.

First Officer Chris Pollard (author's archive).

In his early teenage years, he devoured avidly as many books as he could on aviation, and was particularly stimulated by Philip Cleif's *Airway to the Isles,* which concerns the air route to the Scilly Isles. Cleif was based at Roborough Airport, Plymouth, in the early 1960s and was one of the instructors that taught Chris to fly. By his mid-teens, he lived and breathed flying; in fact, it became an obsession. He taught himself the principles of aerodynamics and took flying lessons at the age of 13 on Tiger Moths and Austers, gaining a private flying licence as soon as he was legally able to fly solo, in fact he could fly before he could drive a car. He felt energised by flying and knew that he had found his niche in life.

He had many other interests, including sport and amateur dramatics, but from a career point of view, he was not interested in anything desk-bound or too academically based. Nothing but a life with the airlines really appealed, so at the age of 18, he applied to the London School of Flying at Elstree where he studied assiduously the theory and honed his flying skills for his Commercial Pilots Licence. He progressed well there, and although his father first financed his studies, British Midland Airways, who recognised his talent and potential, sponsored him over the last part of the course.

There was not the slightest trace of nervousness in his flying. He was quick to learn and sailed through his practical and theoretical tests without difficulty. There is a report that says he passed out at the top of his group and was highly regarded by his instructors as an above average student with considerable promise, but being the modest chap he was never made anything of this.

He joined British Midland in October 1966, settled in well with his colleagues, making many friends and was universally respected and liked by everyone. Despite his relative youth, he was technically very capable and quickly qualified to fly as First Officer on Dakota, Viscount and Argonaut aircraft. He now found himself in that enviable position of his hobby being his job. On top of all this, he had recently become engaged to Helen Jones, a British United Airways ground stewardess at Gatwick Airport, so all was perfect in his personal life too. Tragically, it would soon come to an abrupt and tragic end.

The third member of the flight crew was 32-year-old engineer Gerald 'Taff' Lloyd who hailed from Kegworth, near East Midlands Airport. After serving in the Fleet Air Arm, he joined Derby Airways in 1962. He was an experienced, although not certificated flight engineer and flew as part of the crew in order to perform ground engineering duties when the aircraft was away from its home base. Nicknamed 'The Flying Spanners', these engineers had no official duties to perform in the air, but in order to help out the crew during the flight, they would fill in the instrument readings in the fuel and technical logs, and, if asked to do so by the Captain or First Officer, would operate various switches and levers in the cockpit, such as the radiator shutter controls and fuel booster pump switches during the approach check prior to landing. He would normally occupy the jump seat behind the pilots but quite often, they would stand up in the cockpit. Alan Beardmore, who crewed on the Argonaut recalled: "I spent many hours in the cockpit and used to stand up on the step behind the pilots for take off and landing. There was a jump seat available, that could be fitted on the structure between the seats but the problem was you couldn't get the attachment pins out once the cabin was pressurised and it got in the way during the flight when trying to reach the switches and circuit breakers on the overhead panel."

If airline pilots are the charismatic stars of the aviation world, then the airline stewardess is the consummate professional, epitome of glitz and glamour that oozed sophistication. Back in the '50s and '60s, air travel still conveyed a sense of wonder and awe; it was new and exciting to most people. Being a stewardess in this period possessed a certain kind of prestige and was one of the most sought-after positions for a young woman; the competition to get one of these jobs was fierce. Even with the lowly independent operators, such as British Midland, it was tremendously exciting and a lot of fun in an era that was still regarded as the 'golden age' of flying, long before the disparaging term cabin crew or trolley dolly came into general use. But it was far from an exotic lifestyle flying between far-flung locations. The aircraft were old and many were unpressurised so flew at a much lower altitude, seldom above 10,000 feet where the worst of the weather was encountered. This made most passengers nervous, especially those on their first flight and many were air sick – including the stewardess – who would have her work cut out calming the distraught passengers.

In the early days, Derby Airways cabin crew could be counted on the fingers of one hand, and if it became necessary to take on a new stewardess, the selected candidate was simply given an ill-fitting uniform and told what to do before her first flight. But by 1960, it was becoming apparent that some kind of formalised training was going to be essential if the airline wanted to promote a professional image to its passengers. Under the chief stewardess, a new intensive course of instruction lasting approximately three weeks was introduced – this seemed so glamorous and exciting at the time that the BBC came down to film it.

Ann Harvey, to fulfil her passion for travel joined Derby Airways as one of the company's first stewardesses in 1959 serving on Dakota aircraft. The qualifications and guidelines for the job included: weight proportional to height, should be no shorter than five feet four inches, neat in appearance and have a first aid qualification; and if you spoke a second language all the better. It was flying from Burnaston Airport's badly rutted grass airstrip that her life of adventure really took off. She describes the era with fondness.

Creature comforts were minimal in those days. The cramped and noisy cabin may have smelled of oil and vomit, but we were expected to maintain a fragrant demeanour, even down to wearing stiletto heels for the entire duration of the flight. Being a stewardess during that period was more about status than money. The pay was poor, so to supplement my meagre income, I devised a few wheezes along the way, for example: we were expected to look our very best at all times and were given an allowance to have our hair done once a week. Well, I didn't see anything wrong in the way I did it myself, so I pocketed the money and it came in very handy!

One of my pre-flight jobs was to check that the pins and covers protecting the undercarriage and sensor probes had been removed. Then, after counting that all the passengers were aboard, I would walk up the cabin pop my head in the cockpit and report to the captain: 'Five locks, two pins and thirty-two souls strapped in', so he knew it was safe to depart. Finally, just before take off, I would dish out barley sugar sweets to help the passengers alleviate the pressure in their ears as the aircraft gained altitude.

During many a flight, I could often be found – to the bemusement of passengers visiting the cockpit – sitting up front at the controls flying the aircraft whilst the pilot put his feet up and took a break. He told me: "If you can drive a car, you can fly a plane." But he did select the autopilot until I had proved myself capable of flying manually. I remember he was very particular about his propellers; once on the ground after engine shutdown, they had to be turned by hand so that both were at exactly the same angle as one another. I also recall one other captain who at the end of a flight when we were approaching our base at Burnaston, would circle the giant cooling towers near his home to signal to his wife that it was time to get lunch ready! I don't think many pilots would get away with that today.

Flying in those days was very much a social event and a real occasion. People would dress the part as if they had been invited to a Royal garden party or were going off to spend a day at the races. Men always wore suits and women wore heels, hats and gloves. For the independent airlines, like Derby, image and presentation was paramount, so meals were served on china plates on starched white linen and passengers were given the best silverware and glasses. Flying may have been noisy and uncomfortable but it was a wonderful time to travel. However, I did experience some hairy moments. For example, in Luxemburg a cabin window blew out on take off and I quickly reacted by moving the screaming passengers away from the lashing slipstream to safer seats. When I went to tell the captain about the incident, he snapped: "Well, I hope you bloody well did something about it." *Charming*, I thought, but let him off because he later recommended me for a commendation.

The stewardess rostered for the Palma flight was 25-year-old Julia Partleton. In her requisite elegant light grey form fitting uniform, complete with airline badge and wings, immaculate hair and make up, she fitted all the criteria required for an airline stewardess; personable, gregarious, charming and well groomed. Added to all this she was psychologically stable, physically fit, calm and decisive, never known to panic in an emergency and was certainly not ruffled by the odd surly and demanding passenger she came across from time to time.

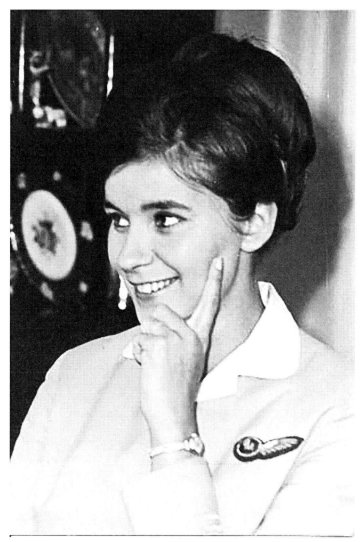

Stewardess Julia Partleton (author's archive).

Julia was born in Ruskin College, Oxford in 1942, her mother having being evacuated there from Stockwell, London during the blitz. Sadly, her mother died of TB in 1946 and she was then brought up by her grandmother until she too died, leaving Julia to fend for herself from a very early age. Although she seldom spoke of this part of her life, it undoubtedly had a profound effect on her, making her very proud, independent and determined, underneath which was a kind and caring person, champion of the underdog and passionately fond of animals.

Her first job after leaving school was as a secretary at London's St George's Hospital, but she soon found the work wasn't demanding enough to satisfy her driving ambitions. She became unsettled, impatient and anxious to move on with her life. Realising things were never going to improve; she seriously began to consider her choice of career. Such was her personality that if she wanted to do something in life she went out with determination and achieved it. She was a young woman of sensitivity, intelligence and ambition, and to her everything seemed possible. So in 1964, looking for new adventures and the chance to travel, she took charge of her life, applied for, and was accepted as a stewardess with Derby Airways. She wholeheartedly embraced her newfound independence and from that point on her life changed beyond all recognition.

By this time Derby Airways had set up a stewardess training school headed by a senior stewardess where the new recruits undertook six weeks of intensive training, mainly in the Burnaston Airport departure lounge, as it was the only heated area in the complex, but training was constantly interrupted each time an aircraft was due to depart. The syllabus covered basic aerodynamics, safety procedures, evacuating the aircraft, first aid, serving from the bar, and of course, and more importantly, what to do in an emergency.

She had no difficulty passing all her examinations and practical tests and sailed through her yearly proficiency check in February 1967 which covered the most important aspect of the job – safety procedures and how to prepare for any type of emergency that maybe encountered in flight and on the ground. If all this was not enough, she also had the natural ability to calm fractious passengers, travel-weary children and to subtly calm the nervous first-time flyer, at the end of all this she could still descend the aircraft steps looking like an advertisement for the airline.

The records show that she worked hard and had various commendations as a stewardess, by all accounts from friends and colleagues this was the happiest time of her life. She eventually became a training stewardess; a role in which she was very strict and very much to the book. But in her social life she was a totally different person and she could be quite wild at times. There is one amusing story from this era where she accepted a dare of dubious merit – to ride a pushbike through the lounge bar of a local hostelry which was the regular haunt for off duty airline crews. This she did without hesitation and as a consequence of the escapade was duly barred from the establishment. Clearly, she worked hard and played hard, but as soon as she donned her uniform, she was a true professional with passenger safety and comfort her primary concern.

Assisting Julia on the flight was 21-year-old steward Tony Taylor from Leicester. Little is known about him other than that prior to joining the airline he worked as a barman in a London hotel. It was there one day, in the early part of 1967 that quite by chance he got into conversation with Julia's training stewardess. Bemoaning to her how dull and boring bar work was, she suggested that if he wanted travel and excitement, he should apply to British Midland, who at the time was in the process of recruiting. He jumped at the opportunity. Within days of submitting his application, he received a letter requesting him to report for an interview at the company offices at East Midlands Airport and soon after, to his delight, he had been accepted as a cabin steward. Just a few months later, after successfully completing his training, he was regularly flying to holiday destinations all over Europe. In the light of what subsequently happened just months later, the stewardess, who had made the suggestion forever after regretted that chance conversation at the hotel bar.

Steward Tony Taylor (author's archive).

On Saturday, 3 June, Hotel Golf's crew, apart from Captain Marlow, met up at East Midlands Airport at 8:00 a.m. to take advantage of the company transport to Manchester Airport where on arrival they took up rooms in the Excelsior hotel, just a stone's throw from the airport. After a light breakfast, they retired to their rooms where they slept prior to the evening flight. They rose at 7:00 pm and after a meal, they walked the short distance to the Airport to check in.

Hotel Golf, the ill-fated aircraft at the centre of our story rolled off the Canadair production line at the company's Dorval factory in Montreal in 1949 and was ferried over to the UK for crew training and check out. In BOAC service, it was given the registration letters G-ALHG – radio call sign How George – after the phonic alphabet of the time which was later changed to Hotel Golf after the last two letters of the registration. Up to Saturday 3 June 1967, it had flown a total 32,850 hours in its 18 years of hard operational life.

The previous day – Friday 2 June – Hotel Golf, under the command of Captain Austin, suffered technical problems at Manchester Airport. At 9:00 p.m., the aircraft, with 77 passengers on board, was about to depart for Genoa. Whilst carrying out the usual pre departure engine tests, he discovered a fault in the constant speed unit on the number 3 propeller. The captain had no option but to shut down the engines and disembark the passengers. On examination by engineers, the faulty unit was found to have seized solid so justified its removal and replacement. After a two-hour delay, Hotel Golf took off and flew to its planned destination without further incident, returning to Manchester early on Saturday morning where it was parked in the south side bay to await the evening flight to Palma. At 7:00 p.m., the aircraft was coupled up to an airfield tractor unit and towed the short distance to gate 4 on the International Pier in readiness for Hotel Golf's penultimate flight. An hour later, cabin crew, Julia Partleton and Tony Taylor climbed the stairs and entered the cabin to begin the routine preparations prior to the boarding of the outbound passengers.

Ringway Airport, as it was then known, is situated on the southwest boundary of the city on the edge of the vast Wythenshawe housing estate. The Airport was officially opened for business on 25 June 1938 by the Air Minister of the day, Sir Kingsley Wood, who incidentally opened British Midland's original base at Burnaston in 1939. However, with outbreak of hostilities the following year, it ended the airport's brief involvement with civil flying for the duration. Although it was never a front-line RAF station, it played a major role during the war as a centre for aircraft production and the home of the Parachute Training School with some 60,000 paratroopers being trained there.

When civil flying recommenced in 1946, the wartime buildings and hangars were quickly converted to handle an ever-increasing number of passengers and freight services. The first scheduled airline operations commenced in June 1946 when an Air France Dakota arrived from Le Bourget Airport, Paris. The Airport was promoted to international status on 28 October 1953 when the Belgium airline, Sabena, introduced the first scheduled service to New York using a DC-6B with a refuelling stop at Gander – the flight time to Gander was a gruelling 10 hours 22 minutes against strong headwinds.

In the early days, getting to the airport was no easy task, with few cars and little in the way of public transport; passengers would hop on a special airline bus from the city centre. Despite the increasing number of passengers using the airport, it was still antiquated with passengers having to sit it out on wicker basket chairs in draughty corridors awaiting their flights. However, in 1962, all this changed when the original wartime airfield gave way to an imposing new terminal which heralded a new era of burgeoning traffic growth. The new complex consisted of a new 130-foot-high, ten-storey control tower integral with the main building structure and twin passenger piers, the upper decks of which were provided for spectators giving uninterrupted views of every part of the apron and runway.

After passing through the main automatically opening entrance doors into the traffic hall, departing passengers were confronted with 30 airline check-in desks with television monitors relaying up-to-the-minute departure and arrival information. The main feature in the concourse, and the centre of interest for arriving and departing passengers alike, were four huge 'mega drip' Venetian glass chandeliers. Located around the concourse were banks, shops, information service desks and even a post office. In keeping with its greatly enhanced status, the powers that be decided that the name Ringway was far too parochial and adopted the grander title of Manchester International Airport which today ranks as one of the busiest in Europe.

Chapter Eleven
Palma Bound

"Hotel Golf is rolling."

Captain – Harry Marlow

Captain Harry Marlow and his First Officer, Chris Pollard knew each other well, having crewed together on 21 previous flights, the most recent being on 11 January. With a mixture of experience and youthful raw talent, they made up a flight crew par excellence and fully competent to operate the flight to Palma and return. In the operations room, they began the mundane activities that precede any routine charter flight; there were load sheets, navigational maps, weather forecasts and other paperwork to attend to before the flight plan to Palma could be filed.

The weather in the latter part of May and early June was very unseasonable, especially at the height the Argonaut operated, and there was no surprise that the forecast showed a cold front approaching Western Europe predicting low cloud and rain with the possibility of isolated thunderstorms over northern Spain which the airliner would overfly *en route*. The forecast for the return journey was not much better with the prospect of rain and drizzle over much of England, but there was certainly no hint of menace in the forecast.

After completing and filing their flight plan, both pilots sauntered across the apron in the late evening sunshine to the waiting aircraft. The Canadair C-4 Argonaut, Hotel Golf, allocated for the flight couldn't have looked smarter. With a recent repaint and sporting the new British Midland two-tone blue livery, it certainly belied its eighteen years of hard service plying the world's airways. The cabin interior had also been refurbished, it was bright and cheerful offering great passenger appeal with company blue fabric seats, creamy-white head restraint covers and warm restful lighting – even the cabin windows were curtained.

Argonaut cabin interior (author's archive).

Chris Pollard ascended the stairs, entered the flight deck and eased himself into the right-hand seat. Reaching up, he switched on the overhead lights and got stuck into the least glamorous duty of airline flying – paperwork. It was the cockpit interior that betrayed Hotel Golf's true age; it was in a shoddy condition, it looked and smelled distinctly old-fashioned. The black paintwork of the instrument panel housing a myriad of dials and switches was badly chipped and the distinctive odour of hydraulic fluid, rubber and leather pervaded everywhere. As Chris Pollard dealt with the pre-flight details, Harry Marlow made his routine walk round departure check, inspecting the aircraft from nose to tail, wing tip to wing tip – an examination which would normally take no more than five minutes. He checked the wings and propellers for any evidence of damage – he saw none. But on inspecting the main landing gear, he was unhappy about the condition of one of the tyres. Taking no chances, he ordered the ground crew to have it changed. The flight, due to depart at 9:30 pm, was now running some 40 minutes late, Captain Marlow hoped for a speedy turnaround at Palma to make up the lost time.

Leaving the engineer Gerald Lloyd to supervise the wheel change, Harry Marlow climbed the stairs, joined Chris Pollard in the cockpit and settled himself in the big green leather upholstered crew seat, now scuffed and worn with hundreds of thousands of miles flown. His first task was to leaf through the technical log and check there were no reported defects carried over from the previous flight, satisfied there were none, he signed the load and trim sheets; they were now ready to depart.

In the departure lounge, the crackle of the tannoy announced that the Palma flight was ready for boarding. In response, husbands and wives, obviously 'dolled up' in their smart suits and best dresses – in this era, flying was considered something of a social event – stood up, gathered their hand luggage and made their way to passport control and after completing the formalities were ushered to the departure gate. By the time the passengers had been boarded and the door sealed, the sun had long since slipped below the horizon and darkness began to descend casting long shadows over the airfield. With the passengers seated and settled, Julia Partleton, in accordance with her duties, positioned herself at the front of the cabin and with smiling efficiency, she gave the passengers the routine well-rehearsed safety drill, pointing out the location of the

130

emergency exits and requested that they read and study the *'Flight Details and Souvenir'* booklet located in the seat pocket in front. In addition, she told them that in the unlikely event of ditching in the sea, their life jackets could be found under their seats. After checking the number of passengers tallied with the load sheet, she reported the details to the captain then took her seat next to the steward in the rear and strapped herself in ready for departure.

Seated at his console behind the green-tinted glass of the control tower, the air traffic controller gave Hotel Golf their departure clearance and issued their taxi instructions. Harry Marlow acknowledged receipt and went through the routine checks and drills; both pilots looked through their respective side windows to make sure there was no obstructions to the propellers before engine start up. The magneto switches were flicked on and the number 3 engine starter button pushed, in response the 13-foot diameter three-bladed Hamilton Standard propeller reluctantly turned a few silent revolutions, coughed twice before bursting into life, sending a shudder through the airframe. The same procedure was followed for the other three Merlins and a few minutes later with all the propellers thrumming in unison, Hotel Golf began taxiing out to the runway threshold.

A not uncommon site for passengers flying on the Argonaut – a shutdown engine and feathered propellers (Graham Norman).

The sun had now slipped below the western horizon and darkness began to descend over the vast expanse of the airfield as the airliner picked her way between the sparkling green taxiway lights towards the runway threshold. On reaching the holding point, Hotel Golf was ordered to wait to allow for a Cambrian Airways Viscount which was fast approaching the threshold on finals. As soon as the Viscount had touched down and cleared the runway, the voice of the controller crackled in the pilots' headsets: "Hotel Golf cleared for take off." Harry Marlow acknowledged receipt and steered the aircraft on to the runway and lined up the snout of the Argonaut on the centre line.

All four throttle levers were pushed forward simultaneously and the four snorting piston engines revved up to a crescendo. With all cockpit checks completed, they were

131

ready to depart. As the airliner slipped its brakes, the controller heard the voice of Harry Marlow crackle over the radio: "Hotel Golf is rolling."

Take off on the Argonaut could be a long and fraught business. Packed with passengers and a full fuel load, it certainly liked plenty of runway before it was willing to commit itself to the air. As the airspeed needle flickered at 110 knots, Harry Marlow made a long backward movement of the control column and Hotel Golf unstuck from the runway at 10:06 p.m. British Summer Time and climbed away in the falling darkness, the bright runway lights gently slipping away beneath the tail. Forty minutes later, Hotel Golf reached its cruising altitude of 9,000 feet and joined the Amber One Airway on the first stage of yet another routine charter flight to Palma.

Chapter Twelve
The Last Flight of Hotel Golf

"We were looking forward to going home. Who was to know what was to follow."
Survivor – Harold Wood

As the fragmented remains of the Air Ferry DC-4 continued to burn and smoulder on the rocky slopes of the Pyrenees, Hotel Golf steadily eased her way southward over the darkened French countryside. For the passengers looking out into the night, there was little to see, aside from the flickering stubby blue flames from the Merlin manifolds illuminating the engine cowlings and the occasional clustered lights of the sleeping towns and villages that appeared through the breaks in the cloud.

With French Air Traffic Control conversing with the crew at regular intervals giving routine weather and position reports, everything seemed to be progressing precisely according to the flight plan. However, entries being made in the fuel log by Gerald Lloyd were showing abnormalities in the aircraft's fuel flow and distribution. For example, during the second hour of the flight, more fuel was being drawn from the port side tanks than the starboard and this position was reversed during the third hour. However, as on previous flights it went completely unnoticed by the crew.

In the cabin, the passengers, fatigued by the incessant throbbing of the engines, fitfully dozed as the long hours passed. Forward in the darkened cockpit, the lights were turned down, only the green luminescence glow from the orderly rows of instrument dials casting a ghostly light over the pilots' faces. Ahead through the cockpit windows, they could just about discern the approaching jagged outline of the higher peaks of the Pyrenees, an area that often-spawned nightmarish electrical storms and torrential rain of exceptional intensity; thankfully, tonight it was clear and calm.

Five hours after departing Manchester, rain began to lash the cockpit windows as the Argonaut began its gradual descent towards Palma. The disembodied voice of the Spanish controller broke the stream of static on the radio to give the crew their landing instructions and shepherd Hotel Golf down to intercept the glide scope. With the undercarriage down and flaps extended, the aircraft groped its way through the drizzle towards the diffused runway lighting. It was a tricky approach and called for some skilful flying. Throttling back the engines, Harry Marlow gently nudged the rudder bar to compensate for the crosswind as the airliner floated over the perimeter fence sinking the last few feet to gently kiss the rain-soaked runway. With a squeal of protest from the brakes, the Argonaut slowed, turned off onto the taxiway and ambled towards the cluster of buildings that made up the passenger terminal. It was 03:20 a.m. British Summer Time.

As soon as the outbound passengers had disembarked, Harry Marlow and Chris Pollard left the aircraft and hurried through the rain to the terminal building for refreshments before filing their flight plan for the return journey. In their absence, the engineer, Gerald Lloyd, now on 'spanner duty', sheltered from the rain under the wing and supervised the refuelling. In total, he uplifted 9,203 lbs, the equivalent to that burnt off on the outbound flight, which would be more than ample for their return with a substantial reserve, if for any reason they had to divert to their alternative Birmingham. As with the Palma incident, one week earlier, the engineer made no calculation to ascertain the amount of fuel remaining in each of the four main tanks on landing. It is highly likely that if Harry Marlow had ordered the tanks to be physically dipped before refuelling commenced, it would have led to the alarming discovery that the starboard outer tank was almost empty on engine shutdown – the missing fuel having inadvertently diverted down wing to the inboard tank through a misaligned fuel tank selector lever.

Because of the delayed departure from Manchester, Harry Marlow wanted a smart turnaround in order to make up lost time, as the aircraft was required for another flight from Ringway later that day. After a brief refreshment break, he walked over to the Traffic Office to check the passenger list and return load whilst Chris Pollard went over to the Met Office to pick up the latest weather forecast before lodging a flight plan with the Air Traffic Control. When all the necessary paperwork was completed, they headed back to the aircraft in the early morning rain, climbed the stairs and took their places on the flight deck. It had been agreed that Chris Pollard would fly the return leg to Manchester. This was pretty much standard practice for air crews at the time so that the first officer gets the chance to fly, building up his flying hours, getting a feel for the routes and learning the procedures, in the hope of one day being promoted to captain.

The early summer dawn had broken over Palma as the transfer coaches arrived at the airport and off loaded the bleary-eyed holidaymakers clutching their bags of holiday souvenirs and duty free for friends and relatives back home.

David Ralphs remembers:

Both Alan and I had a wonderful holiday on the island, making new friends, excursions, entertainment, exotic food and even barbeques – which were unheard of back home in those days. We arrived at a rainy Palma Airport just as dawn was breaking and entered the departure lounge, which, despite the early hour, was extremely crowded with holidaymakers waiting their flights home. After about three quarters of an hour, our flight was called and everyone piled onboard the rickety old airport buses for the short journey out to the aircraft – it was raining steadily at the time in complete contrast to the perfect sunny weather we had enjoyed during the holiday.

On leaving the coach I ran over to the aircraft; ran up the stairs to find I was the first passenger on board. I made my way down the length of the aisle towards the front and chose a pair of seats; third row from the front on the right-hand side. Alan, having seen to our luggage then joined me taking the aisle seat beside me.

Occupying the seats in front of David were Vivienne Thornber and her friend Susan Howarth. Vivienne like Susan had been brought up in the cramped streets of Nelson, a typical Lancashire mill town that was interchangeable with so many others in the north of England. In those days, it was a place of dreary uniformity where people were born, worked and died, without ever leaving the confines of their hometown. Their only respite from the drudgery and toil of everyday working life being the annual Wakes week holiday – a tradition going back to the 19th century – when the booming mills and engineering firms shut down for a fortnight. For the majority, the seaside town of breezy Blackpool was the favourite destination. Others, with more extravagant ambitions, upmarket Southport beckoned, whilst a handful of others would hop on a coach to one of the many new holiday camps that had gained great popularity in the immediate post war years.

However, for Vivienne and Susan, like many young people growing up in what was termed the swinging sixties, they wanted nothing more than to reject the boring and traditional and embrace something better and more exciting. With aspirations far beyond the confines of the Lancashire town of their upbringing, they wanted to broaden their horizons, and for them, Blackpool wasn't the only holiday option available. With their youthful enthusiasm and yearning for new adventures, they decided to book one of the popular, and much advertised, all-inclusive package holidays to Spain where the sunshine was almost guaranteed.

At home on cold, dank, miserable winter evenings, they passed their time flicking through dozens of glossy travel brochures. They were quickly captivated by the flattering and often misleading photographs of fantastic out-of-this-world hotels, along with exaggerated descriptive copy designed to entice the prospective tourist. After much deliberation, they decided on a ten-day all-inclusive holiday in Majorca, which seemed not only exotic, but existed in another dimension, light years away from their home environment.

They paid their deposits and applied for their passports, which was practically unheard of for ordinary people in that part of Lancashire; it was something that had always been the reserve of the wealthy upper-class elite. They knew of few people who had been on a foreign holiday, stayed in a plush hotel, or flown in an aeroplane, but they soon would – and all this for £40. Full of excitement, they began to lose their inhibitions from the very moment they fastened their seat belts. They never considered for one minute, when they booked the holiday, whether the aircraft they were about to fly on was safe and airworthy, or even the nightmare possibility of an air crash. As far as they were concerned, they were young, indestructible and would live forever. Vivienne told me about their holiday of a lifetime:

It was the first time I had ever flown. I remember it was an awfully long night flight; some five hours as against just over two hours today by jet. It was a lovely experience and I really enjoyed it. We landed in Palma early on the Thursday morning and from there we were taken by coach to the Hotel Balmes in Can Pastilla. I remember Susan opening the bedroom window and singing out at the top of her voice *Granada*, I don't know why, but I suppose we were both very excited and just being silly.

We met up with some really nice lads from Liverpool and got very friendly with them during our stay. They had been there a week prior to us arriving so they were able to show us the sights and we went with them several times to the beach at Arenal and had a whale of a time.

For both girls, their holiday had been a glorious culture shock, opening up a whole new world from anything they had experienced before. They savoured everything about the sun-drenched island; sumptuous food; exotic excursions, making new friends and picture-perfect weather. It had been a great adventure, an experience that did not disappoint as Vivienne enthused in a handful of postcards she sent home.

Dear Mum and Dad,

Had a great journey here and we arrived at 4:30 a.m. Weather absolutely fantastic so we are taking the sunbathing easy the first few days. The hotel is fabulous and the courier is really nice. I'll write in greater detail later, but just thought I'd let you know we're both OK.

This place is just out of this world.

Love, Viv.

All good things come to an end and both girls were downhearted on the final day before zipping up their suitcases and leaving for home. But as exuberant as ever, they were determined to squeeze the very last bit of enjoyment out of what had been a fabulous and memorable holiday; as far as they were concerned, it was still party time. "The last night of the holiday," Vivienne said, "found us dancing in an open-air night club just across from our hotel. I remember looking up and watching the aircraft flying overhead and thinking, *it wouldn't be too long before we would be up there on our way home – worst luck.* I clearly remember the last song they played before we left the club was *Pretty Women* by Roy Orbison. That was the point when we knew the holiday was well and truly over. We then walked back to our hotel to pick up our luggage and await the coach transfer to the airport. Of course, we didn't know then what we were in for."

When the passengers boarded the aircraft, where they chose to sit largely dictated whether they survived or died. Harold Wood remembers how he came to choose those lucky seats that would save his and his brother's life:

We had a wonderful holiday in Majorca; good weather, fantastic sights, friendly locals and excellent food, and now we were looking forward to going home. Who was to know what was to follow? I remember we arrived at the airport in good time and on entering the departure lounge it was buzzing with holidaymakers waiting for their flights home. Billy and I played pocket chess with some people we had made friends with on holiday until the announcement for our flight was called over the tannoy. We were then bussed out to the waiting aircraft. In those days, there was no assigned seating so it was one mad scramble to get the best seats. Billy and I worked our way forward and grabbed two seats on the right near the front; Dad went forward and found a vacant seat at the very front of the cabin. I remember that in the row directly behind us were schoolgirls Fiona Child and her friend Christine Benton.

Just before engine start up, Harry Marlow's voice crackled over the cabin tannoy and made an announcement to his passengers: "This is your captain. I would like to apologise for the delay in taking off due to a technical fault and hopefully, we will be soon on our way." A technical fault, as most regular air travellers will know, is a convenient phrase to cover just about every possible problem, technical or not, which can prevent them from departing on time. Whatever the glitch was, it seems to have been quickly resolved because a few minutes later, the Merlin engines coughed and spluttered into life. Harry Marlow called the tower for their taxi instructions and very soon, Hotel Golf was trundling away from the embarkation point in the early morning rain.

With the four Merlin engines throbbing in unison and water vapour streaming off the propeller tips, Chris Pollard lined up the Argonaut in preparation for take off. Holding the aircraft against the brakes, he opened up the throttles for a final power check, satisfied that all was in order, he slipped the brakes and Hotel Golf barrelled down the wet runway; the wheels dispersing great waves of standing water. The runway lights flashed by in a blur and on reaching 110 knots, Chris Pollard pulled back on the control column to haul Hotel Golf aloft towards the dull cadaverous sky. It was 5:06 British Summer Time.

Generally, flying is inherently boring, so in order to pass the long hours of the homeward journey, the passengers chatted with each other, a few played cards, some dozed, others flicked through magazines. A handful gazed down through the cabin windows at the spectacular, yet inhospitable jagged peaks of the high Pyrenees that slowly passed beneath as the aircraft slipped unnoticed into French airspace. Somewhere down below amongst the forbidding crags, rescue parties were making their torturous climb towards the smouldering wreckage of the Air Ferry DC-4 to recover the remains of the dead.

The first part of the homeward journey was flown at 9,000 feet where the outside temperature was near to freezing. But within the cocoon of the pressurised fuselage, it was excessively warm, as Vivienne Thornber recalls: "One thing I remember about our flight home was the cabin being very hot and stuffy, a lot more so than the outward journey. Because of the heat and the fact we had been up most of the night, Susan and I kept dozing off, as did some of the other passengers. In fact, the steward had to wake us both up to serve breakfast."

David Ralphs also recalls the oppressive heat in the cabin:

For the first few hours, the flight seemed normal, with the exception of the air conditioning which was not at all satisfactory. As the flight progressed, the atmosphere grew steadily hotter and uncomfortable – in fact, it was stifling. I first removed my jacket and then my waistcoat. On looking around the cabin, I noticed that other passengers were also removing articles of clothing and many were commenting on how hot and claustrophobic the conditions were.

Glancing along the wing from my window seat, I noticed a rivet that appeared to be loose and was moving up and down in its aperture, this naturally held my attention and I remember continually been drawn to it throughout the flight.

After clearing the high ground of the Pyrenees, Hotel Golf began a gradual descent to 6,000 feet in the region of Agen in southern France and would maintain this altitude for the remainder of the flight until the descent and let down into Manchester Airport.

As the aircraft toiled northwards, the flight seemed routine and uneventful, but entries jotted down in the fuel log by Gerald Lloyd were showing some disturbing features for fuel consumption and distribution. For instance, in the 39 minutes from taking off and climbing away from Palma, fuel should have reached the engines in equal amounts from all the main tanks. But in fact, twice as much fuel was being consumed from the port tanks as from the starboard ones. Then for the next hour – 5:45 to 6:45 – Hotel Golf consumed an equal amount of fuel from the tanks on both sides. At 7:45, when the next set of figures was entered in the log, the aircraft had consumed 900 lbs from the number 4 starboard outer tank as compared with only 100 from the number 1 port outer. Indeed, more fuel appeared to have been drawn from the number 4 tank than from all the other tanks combined. It remains an unfathomable mystery why any of the crew, especially the engineer, who was making the entries in the log, failed to notice these glaring abnormalities. No further fuel readings were taken after 7:45; but the readings of the engine instruments were recorded at 8:45.

At 8:00 a.m., Julia Partleton and Tony Taylor began serving breakfast to the passengers, most of whom were fitfully dozing trying to catch up on missed sleep and many had to be gently nudged awake. As the passengers were tucking into their bread rolls and coffee, Hotel Golf approached Abbeville, the last reporting point in France. From this point on, responsibility for the flight passed from French air traffic control to that of the United Kingdom. Harry Marlow input the new frequency, flipped on his mic and called up London Airways who would route the aircraft over the English Channel and south east England and onwards to Manchester.

Hotel Golf: *London, Golf Alpha Lima Hotel Golf, good morning.*
London: *Hotel Golf, go ahead.*
Hotel Golf: *Hotel Golf, Abbeville three six, flight level six zero. Lydd five five Rochester, Daventry, Lichfield, Manchester.*
London: *Hotel Golf, so cleared, maintain six zero.*

Hotel Golf departed the French coast and thundered over the moody grey corrugated waves of the English Channel on a course that would intersect the coast at Lydd on the final leg of the journey home. Soon after, the airliner crossed over the white cliffs of the Kent coast into the featureless grey overcast, and on over the rain-soaked orchards and hop fields of the Kent countryside. As rain lashed the windscreen Harry Marlow made a routine call to London Airways with his flight details.

Hotel Golf: *London, Hotel Golf, check Lydd at five six, flight level six zero, estimating Rochester at five zero.*
London: *Roger Hotel Golf.*
Eight minutes later, at 09:04, the aircraft approached the outskirts of Rochester.

Hotel Golf: *London, Hotel Golf, check Rochester at five zero, flight level six zero, estimating the Park at one five.*
London: *Thank you Hotel Golf, call airways now on one two four decimal six. Good day.*

Hotel Golf: *One two four decimal six. Good day.*

The aircraft was now passed on to the next controller along the route, who would guide them as far as Daventry. Harry Marlow changed frequency and established contact.

Hotel Golf: *London, Golf Alpha Lima Hotel Golf.*
London: *Hotel Golf.*
Hotel Golf: *Good morning, check Rochester at zero five, flight level six zero and estimating the Park at one five.*
London: *Roger Hotel Golf.*

From this point on, the journey was very much routine and uneventful. At 9:32 the aircraft was handed over to Preston Airways who would direct the flight as far as Manchester before handing over to the approach controller in the Manchester tower. With Chris Pollard flying the aircraft, Harry Marlow changed the radio frequency and called the Preston controller to give his Daventry report and forward estimate for Litchfield.

Hotel Golf: *Preston, Hotel Golf, good morning. Daventry three two, flight level six zero, Litchfield at four five, Manchester. Over.*
Preston: *Roger Hotel Golf. Runway in use two four.*

Coming in range of his East Midlands base, Harry Marlow made a routine call to Peter Eyre, the duty controller on the company frequency with his flight information, number of passengers, ETA at Manchester and the aircraft's serviceability for its next flight. With the camaraderie that existed within the company, both Harry and Peter shared some good-natured banter over the radio before the aircraft travelled out of range on its last leg to Manchester.

When Hotel Golf passed abeam Litchfield, Harry Marlow began to make a number of errors in his radio transmissions, first with Preston Airways, and later with Manchester approach control. There can be no doubt that both pilots were suffering some degree of tiredness, Harry Marlow more so, having had little sleep in the previous twenty-four hours.

The problem of fatigue is particularly important to a pilot. Not only does he or she work long and irregular hours, but as distinct from almost any other profession, theirs calls for peak performance when the workload is at its highest and fatigue at its worst.

During long hours of flying, the subtleties of fatigue gradually reduce the mental alertness of any airline pilot, reducing his efficiency and judgement without him realising it. Tiredness is an invisible killer and has the same effects on mental reasoning and physical coordination as alcohol does and may well prove to be the explanation of those accidents which have been previously put down to 'pilot error'. It can make well-qualified conscientious pilots commit almost unbelievably stupid errors, poor judgement, over confidence and slips in competent handling of the aircraft.

Hotel Golf: *Echo Golf, passed errr… Litchfield five five, estimating Congleton at errr… Sorry, four five, Congleton at five four, over.*

The Preston controller, presumably drawing Harry Marlow's attention that he had given the wrong call sign for his aircraft at the initiation of his call, transmits with emphasis: 'HOTEL GOLF…'

Preston: *Hotel Golf radar. The runway in use is two four, maintain flight level six zero to the Mike Charlie Romeo Beacon via Congleton.*
Hotel Golf: *Roger.*

At 09:51, Preston Radar were dealing with a BEA Vanguard – radio call sign Echo Delta – which also required routing into Manchester and needed to descend through the Argonaut's flight level. For obvious safety reasons, Preston called up Hotel Golf to check their position.

Preston: *Hotel Golf, what are your flight conditions?*
Hotel Golf: *Errr… I have Echo Delta in sight.*
Preston: *Roger, are you happy if he's to go through your level, he'll be number one at Manchester?*
Hotel Golf: *Affirmative, he's passed us.*
Preston: *Hotel Golf, continue your approach on one niner decimal four. Good day.*

The wipers, working overtime, slapped hypnotically across the rain spattered windscreen as the Argonaut tracked northwards through the drizzle-laden clouds towards the Congleton navigational beacon. Having now vacated the Preston frequency, Harry Marlow contacted the Manchester approach controller who would vector Hotel Golf onto the Instrument Landing System (ILS) down through the overcast for a landing on runway 24.

The ILS, as its name suggests, is a landing aid whereby the ground station transmits two radio beams. In using the ILS, the pilot follows two needles on the instrument dial – one vertical to keep the aircraft in line with the runway centre line, and one to keep to the correct glide path down to the runway threshold. The ideal situation was to keep both needles forming a cross in the centre of the dial. The ILS, despite its name, is merely an approach aid and is not normally used under 300 feet.

At 9:56, Harry Marlow pressed the transmit button and called the Manchester control tower.

Marlow: *Hotel Golf is just coming by Congleton, any instructions? Over.*
Tower: *Roger Hotel Golf, you're re-cleared to flight level five zero (5,000 feet) heading zero three zero.*
Marlow: *Right three three zero and we're steering three two five and released to five zero.*

Harry Marlow makes another error in repeating back the heading. The alert controller quickly corrected him.

Tower: *Actually, zero three zero Hotel Golf.*
Marlow: *Right zero three zero and down to five zero.*
Tower: *Correct.*
Tower: *Hotel Golf, radar, continue descent to three five zero (3,500 feet) QNH and report passing five zero. (5,000 feet).*
Marlow: *Roger, three five on one zero two zero, will check through five.*

Again, Harry Marlow made another mistake in repeating back the QNH setting. The vigilant controller brought it immediately to his attention.

Tower: *ONE... ZERO... TWO... FIVE... Hotel Golf.*

Harry Marlow, realising his error, immediately corrects himself and transmits: *One zero two five... Sorry!*

These slips in communications certainly showed some hesitancy on his part and tiredness may well have affected his concentration during this critical stage of the approach and may well have reduced his efficiency at the time when he was called upon to think and act quickly when faced with the emergency.

Flying at 200 knots, Hotel Golf passed through the 4,000-foot mark in the descent. It was now time for the crew to begin the routine approach check, in preparation for landing. This involved, amongst other things, opening the radiator shutter flaps, setting the altimeter millibar adjustment, extending the wing flaps to 15 degrees and switching on the main fuel tanks booster pumps. The approach check, which was a standard routine drill, was about to turn into a nightmare.

The controller, watching intently the progress of the aircraft on his radar screen saw that the aircraft had settled some half a mile to the left of the localiser and was not flying a course that would lead to an interception on the ILS. He called the aircraft to query whether the ILS signal was indicating on their instruments.

Tower: *Hotel Golf, seeing you well left of centre line, are you receiving the ILS?*
Marlow: *Errr, yes, will turn right a little.*

In response, Chris Pollard gently banked the aircraft a few degrees to starboard to intercept the ILS beam, then, as part of the approach check, he reached forward, and with his left hand pushed against the fuel cross feed selector levers located on his side of the flight deck, to physically verify that they were in the main tanks on, cross feeds off position. However, in applying slight pressure to 'touch confirm' that the cross feed was indeed off he unknowingly moved the levers – about the thickness of a pencil – to the fully closed position. At that moment, the number 4 engine, with its main tank already exhausted, was still operating normally by drawing fuel back through the slightly open cock from the inboard number 3 tank. With the cross-feed levers now properly closed, a series of events assailed the crew with bewildering rapidity. Within a few seconds, the number 4 engine sucked final drops of precious liquid from the fuel line, and at 10:01 and 55 seconds the engine, now starved of fuel, ceased to deliver power; the propellers windmilling uselessly in the airflow.

Shutting down an engine and feathering its propeller had to be the most rigid and most practised of all cockpit drills and it was clearly understood by both pilots what

140

had to be done if further trouble was to be avoided. If it was a straightforward engine failure, then it could be worked around during the overshoot procedure, and at this point, there was no reason for alarm. With little information coming from the cockpit instruments, Harry Marlow wrongly assumed it was the number 3 inboard engine that had failed, shut it down, and elected to abandon the approach.

The loss of the number 4 engine through fuel starvation and with the number 3 engine shut down caused a tremendous amount of drag that induced the aircraft to markedly swing to the right. To counter the swing and keep the aircraft on a straight course, Harry Marlow tramped hard down on the rudder pedal to apply full opposite rudder.

As the aircraft turned to the right away from the approach path to the airport, puzzled passengers exchanged apprehensive looks and the cabin filled with surprised nervous murmurings. Those seated on the port side who noticed the runway approach lighting sailing by on the murky horizon, anxiously turned to their fellow passengers and asked, "Why are we turning away from the airport?" Although not immediately panicked by the turn of events, a handful of the passengers became increasingly edgy.

At this point, David Ralphs remembers glancing across the aisle at fellow passenger Mr Tomlinson, who he had become friendly with during the holiday. "I noticed he was holding what appeared to me a small portable air band radio. He seemed to be intently listening in on the conversation between the crew and the control tower and he looked rather confused about what he was hearing. At that point, I turned away to look out of my window. Through breaks in the clouds, I saw the main road between Stockport and Manchester, which I was very familiar with having travelled along it at least once a month on business."

With this abrupt and inexplicable loss of power, Harry Marlow thoughts began whirling round in tight circles trying to make some sort of logical sense about what was happening to his aircraft. He was acutely aware that he was confronting a problem that he hadn't encountered before in his long career of airline flying.

Chapter Thirteen
Six Miles from Home

"Hotel Golf is overshooting; we've got a little bit of trouble with RPM."
Captain – Harry Marlow

All professional airline pilots implement what they think is the correct course of action for averting an accident, and it is all too easy – with the benefit of hindsight – to say they should have done this or they should have done that. We will never know for sure what occurred on the flight deck when the number 4 starboard outer engine abruptly ceased to deliver power; there were no cockpit voice recorders installed in civil aircraft in those days to tell us. What we do know, from all the available evidence, is that when Harry Marlow realised they had suffered an engine failure, he – as protocol decreed in any emergency – instinctively responded and took over control of the aircraft from Chris Pollard. At this point, he had no reason to believe that what had just occurred constituted a major emergency but, as a precaution, he made the deliberate decision to abandon the approach, go round, and try to sort the problem out.

What happened next is a matter of conjecture, but the following sequence of events fits in with the known facts. It is quite probable that Captain Marlow did not fully understand the problem from the limited information coming from his instruments and acted prematurely. Mistakenly believing that it was the number 3 starboard inner engine that had failed, and not the number 4 outer, he shut off its fuel, and ordered Chris Pollard to feather the propellers. He then found that after 'cleaning up' the number 3 engine, it had not eased the handling problems normally associated with a single engine failure, and he was also rapidly losing height, which he should not have been with three engines under power. Although puzzled by the behaviour of the aircraft, there was no indication to either pilot that they were in a life-threatening situation.

Given the height and position of Hotel Golf in relation to Manchester Airport at the time of the emergency, it would have been possible for Harry Marlow to reach the runway and land safely, even with one engine feathered and the other windmilling. It is clear from the radio transmissions that he was certainly perplexed by what was happening and he took the deliberate decision to overshoot. He saw this as the safest action to take in the circumstances that were known to him. However, this decision would soon have far-reaching and fatal consequences.

Both pilots had experienced single engine failures in flight before – indeed, it was a regular part of their training – but this particular problem during the approach phase was certainly puzzling. To lose two engines on the same side of an aircraft within 20 seconds of each other is a most unusual event, and the fact that it occurred when the aircraft was at low altitude and at low air speed constituted a grave emergency.

There is no doubt that the number the 4-engine failed first because of fuel starvation, its own tank empty due to inadvertent fuel transfer during the homebound flight. If Harry Marlow did in fact misidentify the engine, it would have taken him some considerable time to realise his mistake – if indeed he ever did. Once the correct identification had been made, there was in theory ample time available to sort out the mix-up, but with two engines 'out' on the starboard side he was fully occupied in controlling the aircraft and trying to maintain height and heading. The remaining workload, navigation, communications and engineering greatly exceeded the capability of the First Officer, Chris Pollard.

At some point during the overshoot, the mistake was realised, the number 4 engine was feathered and the number 3 propellers unfeathered – as was discovered after the crash – but for some unknown reason, power was not restored to the number 3 engine in time to prevent the accident.

What follows is the final seven minutes of the flight, from the time the emergency occurred until impact at Hopes Carr, which were accurately recorded by the flight data recorder and the airport Air Traffic Control tape, which was recorded as a matter of routine.

The approach controller called the aircraft to ascertain it was closing with ILS.

Tower: *Hotel Golf is six miles from touchdown. Established?*

Hotel Golf did not respond to this transmission and the controller was not unduly concerned, as occasional breaks in communications were not abnormal. After waiting a few seconds, the controller called again.

Tower: *Hotel Golf radar, do you read?*
Marlow: *Hotel Golf is overshooting; we've got a little bit of trouble with RPM.*
Tower: *Roger Hotel Golf.*

This was the first reference to any kind of problem, and by this time, nearly a minute had elapsed since the second engine had failed. The controller was not overly anxious that the aircraft had initiated an overshoot procedure, although not an everyday occurrence, it did occur from time to time if a pilot was not entirely satisfied with his approach for whatever reason. Overshoots do not constitute an emergency, unless the pilot indicates that such a state exists, and Harry Marlow's transmission that he was abandoning the approach gave the controller no concerns that an emergency had arisen and he dismissed the incident as essentially unthreatening.

The controller gave the aircraft instructions in order to position for another approach.

Tower: *Hotel Golf make a left turn onto a heading one six zero climbing to two five zero feet.*
Tower: *Hotel Golf, why are you overshooting?*
Marlow: *We've got a little bit of trouble with RPM...will advise you.*
Tower: *Roger Hotel Golf.*
Marlow: *What was the left turn onto?*

To his surprise, the controller on looking at his screen saw that Hotel Golf had already initiated a twenty-five degree turn to the right, and not to the left as instructed. In order to try and expedite positioning the aircraft for another approach, he ordered the aircraft to continue turning right, and gave them a new heading to steer. The airspeed had now decayed to 114 knots, and the altitude had fallen off alarmingly to 1,300 feet, with the altimeters continuing to steadily unwind.

From the radio transmissions, there was nothing abnormal in the tone of the pilots' voices, which suggested they were alarmed by what was happening to their aircraft, but the content suggested that they were at any rate puzzled by its behaviour, and quite possibly at this stage had not diagnosed the true cause of the problem. Although instructed to climb to 2,500 feet, the aircraft was in fact steadily losing the struggle against gravity.

Suddenly and unexpectedly, Hotel Golf broke free of the overcast, and from now on could be seen by ground-based witnesses, who, on hearing the heavy drone of the Merlin engines shot apprehensive glances skyward. Beyond the rain streaked cockpit windshield, the crew were faced with an industrial panorama spread out in all directions as far as the eye could see. Harry Marlow shot a glance at the altimeter and gasped at the frightful information it portrayed. With two engines on the starboard side inoperative, the aircraft was seriously disabled, but Harry Marlow had no reason to believe, at this point, that he couldn't sort out the problem and make it safely to the airport for an emergency landing. Given sufficient altitude and time, they would have eventually no doubt worked out what exactly was going on, but unfortunately, they did not have that luxury.

At 10:04, John Hamilton Greenacre, a 20-year-old bank clerk, was standing outside his terraced house in Hawley Street in the Levenshume district. Leaning against a wall idly smoking a cigarette and contemplating the day ahead, when he was startled by the discordant noise of the Argonaut approaching.

I immediately identified the aircraft as a DC-4 type flying roughly in a northerly direction approximately following the line of the A6. It was very low just skirting the bottom of the low cloud in the area. The engine noise sounded rough and one of the engines seemed to be backfiring. I could plainly see the letters BM on the tail fin and saw that the undercarriage and flaps appeared to be in the up position. All four propellers were turning and it was flying with its wings level. Apart from its low altitude and loud engine noise, I noticed nothing abnormal about the airliner's behaviour. It finally disappeared from my view over the rooftops on an even keel without altering direction.

Julia Partleton, after stowing and securing the catering equipment in the galley, slowly walked the length of the cabin from the rear, checking as she went that all the passengers had complied with the 'FASTEN YOUR SEAT BELTS – NO SMOKING' sign that had been illuminated. Reaching the forward bulkhead, she tapped on the cockpit door before entering. Leaning in, she gave the crew a 'thumbs up' that all was in order in the passenger cabin and they were ready for landing. She saw the engineer, Gerald Lloyd, standing up flicking switches on the overhead panel and Captain Marlow was sitting in the left-hand seat with his hands on the control column and appeared to be flying the aircraft. Everything she observed during that brief visit gave every appearance of business as usual and saw nothing untoward that suggested an emergency was taking place.

Closing the door behind her, she returned to her seat at the rear and strapped herself in next to Tony Taylor in preparation for landing. As soon as she was settled, the steward turned and whispered in her ear: "I don't think we are going to get in."

Julia, assuming he was referring to the weather, replied: "Don't be so silly – everything is fine." But on stealing a glance out of the window at the passing rooftops, she thought to herself that they were a bit lower than usual at this stage of the approach. A few minutes later, after peering intently out of the window at the trailing edge of the starboard wing, Tony Taylor turned to her again, and with a note of concern in his voice said: "He's now taken the flaps back up." Julia, who had flown with Tony Taylor on previous occasions regarded him as a rather nervous individual, she ignored his comment, said nothing and calmly sat back to await touchdown.

By this time, Hotel Golf's airspeed had further decayed to a jaw dropping 111 knots and was still continuing to lose altitude; height and speed are a pilot's best friend – frighteningly, Hotel Golf had neither.

In the airport control tower, it was a busy time – radar tracking and vectoring aircraft onto the approach as well as clearing others for take off. It was now nearly a minute since Harry Marlow had informed the approach controller that he was overshooting. The controller had no concerns at this point that the aircraft and its 84 souls on board might actually come to grief. Having just dealt with a KLM Electra, he turned his full attention back to the Argonaut.

Tower: *Hotel Golf, please advise when you are ready to recommence your approach.*

With no immediate response, the controller sensed that there was something not quite right, so he called again to ascertain their flight conditions.

Tower: *Hotel Golf your position is seven miles, bearing zero four zero of the field. What is your level now?*

Harry Marlow's reply was immediate and shocking.

Marlow: *HOTEL GOLF… ONE THOUSAND!*
Tower: *UNDERSTAND… ONE THOUSAND?*
Pollard: *AFFIRMATIVE.*

The controller was absolutely staggered by the dramatic content of this message. After checking on the radar that the height given was correct, he immediately put the full emergency procedure into operation and the airport fire service was given the known details of the aircraft's position on final approach to runway 24. He then cleared the surrounding air space; instructing inbound aircraft to turn away and take up a holding pattern to keep the airways clear for the developing emergency. Then, in a calm and deliberate voice, the controller called the aircraft:

Tower: *Roger, turn right heading one eight zero. Hotel Golf, can you maintain height?*

Harry Marlow reported back with tepid reassurance: *Errr… Just about.*

Another ground-based witness to observe the troubled airliner was off duty Manchester Police Constable, Alan Faulkner. Having served four years in the Air Training Corps followed by National Service in the RAF, he was an expert witness to the unfolding drama he observed from outside his terraced home in the Gorton district.

Just after ten o'clock on that morning, my attention was drawn to the sound of a piston-engined aircraft flying close by. I looked up and saw the airliner suddenly emerge between two rows of houses travelling approximately in a north-easterly direction at an extremely low altitude, much lower than I have seen any aircraft in this area. I have never heard aircraft engines so erratic; they sounded like a car engine when one cylinder was misfiring. This made for a distinct chugging noise. It gave me the impression that some of the engines were working correctly but that one or more were not. As it passed by, I could clearly see the large black letters BM stencilled on the tail fin. Because of the uneven note of the engines, I started to look for the propellers, but because of the angle of the aircraft to my line of vision, I could only see the starboard side. The propeller of the outer engine seemed to be turning at normal speed but the inner prop appeared to be very much slower as I could clearly make out the individual blades as they rotated. The tail of the aircraft was slightly down with the nose up which gave the impression that it was having difficulty maintaining height. As the aircraft flew away from me, it began a gradual turn to the right heading towards the Audenshaw reservoir before disappearing from view behind the rooflines.

The calm and laconic voice transmissions from Harry Marlow gave little hint of the high drama-taking place on the flight deck as he struggled to cope with, and indeed make sense of the problem he was encountering.

Tower: *Hotel Golf, continue your right-hand turn, heading two zero zero, maintain as much height as possible.*

The airspeed had now decayed to an alarming 98 knots causing the aircraft to buffet and shudder in the airflow and was in immediate danger of stalling and falling out of the sky. Even with full take off power now applied to the remaining port engines, it wasn't enough to halt the airliner's inexorable descent. Captain Marlow's sole devotion was airspeed and to avoid the stall at any cost. Without warning, a fearsome vibration shook the aircraft as it teetered on the edge of stalling. Harry Marlow knew this was not the time for delicate airmanship; it was a time for quick decisive 'seat of the pants' flying with a liberal dose of adrenalin thrown in. In a desperate effort to keep Hotel Golf airborne, he instinctively thrust the control column abruptly forward, forcing the nose down allowing the aircraft to claw back vital airspeed. However, in carrying out this manoeuvre, he sacrificed 341 feet of precious altitude in just 15 seconds. Clearance above the ground was a shocking 285 feet. Harry Marlow watched the airspeed needle creep up with agonising slowness but was still struggling to keep the aircraft under control and maintain altitude. He pressed the transmit button on his control column and made a disquieting transmission to the controller:

Marlow: *Hotel Golf, we're unable to maintain height at the moment.*

Tower: *Roger, you're eight miles from touchdown, closing from the right.*

Desmond Rea, a 35-year-old gas board official, knew a thing or two about aviation having served three years in the RAF. On that morning, he was reading the Sunday papers in his lounge when he heard the Argonaut thunder directly over his house in Denton rattling the doors and windows. Throwing the paper aside, he rushed outside into his garden and was riveted by the incredible sight of the Argonaut staggering along close to stalling speed.

I was astounded to see a large four-engined commercial airliner flying over at an extremely low altitude. I could clearly read the words British Midland along the top decking of the fuselage and the large black letters BM on the tail fin. As I watched the aircraft flying away the tail dropped and the nose rose, it gave me the distinct impression that the pilot was desperately trying to gain height. The undercarriage was up and all four propellers were turning. I noticed nothing abnormal about it apart from its extremely low height, which I estimated to be about 300 feet or less and the extremely loud noise of the engines. I continued to follow the progress of the aircraft until it was lost to my view behind houses in the Haughton Green district.

Tower: *Hotel Golf, I've lost contact with you, due to your height, adjust you're heading on the ILS and report established.*

Pollard: *Hotel Golf, we have the lights to our right and we're 800 feet this time, errr…just maintaining height.*
Tower: *Roger Hotel Golf.*

Chris Pollard's transmission: 'we have the lights to our right' was not the runway lighting as he assumed; it is extremely doubtful the pilots could have seen the airport approach lighting from their position, having regard to the visibility prevailing at the time which was only 1,500 metres in rain and drizzle. What he probably saw was the street lighting of central Stockport diffused by mist and drizzle which mistakenly made him believe they were a good deal nearer to the Airport than they actually were.

Terrain clearance was now 290 feet.

Marlow: *Hotel Golf; will you get the emergency on?*
Tower: *Affirmative, the emergency has already been laid on.*
Marlow: *Ta.*
Marlow: *Errr…what's the position from the field?*
Tower: *Seven and a half to run to touchdown.*
Marlow: *Thank you.*

Despite the extreme stress of the situation, Harry Marlow still had the courtesy to say a respectful 'thank you' to the controller. Considering the grave emergency, both pilots were struggling with their voices remained calm and clear, however, listening back to the tape recording, as I have done many times, you can clearly detect a distinct note of resignation in their voice transmissions from this point on.

Hotel Golf had now described a complete circle to starboard, intercepted the ILS localiser and was now settled back on a direct approach to the Airport.

The next witness to the unfolding drama was 41-year-old Iain McIntosh who lived in Woodley on the eastern outskirts of the town. In his statement later given to the accident investigators, he reported:

I was standing on the first floor of my house when I heard the heavy drone of approaching piston engines. My first thought was that they were Rolls-Royce engines in a York transport aircraft which I had flown in frequently during my RAF service. I immediately went over to the north facing bedroom window and on looking out in the direction of Hyde, I saw what appeared to be a DC-4 airliner flying very slowly and in obvious trouble. It was very low, about 150 feet above a mill chimney situated in the Tame Valley which is roughly northeast of my house. It was in a nose up, tail down attitude and the wings were slowly rocking up and down – perhaps ten degrees each way. From my observation, it gave me the distinct impression that it was really struggling to remain airborne.

Tower: *Hotel Golf, I have no radar contact with you, you are cleared to land, surface wind two seven zero, twelve knots.*
Marlow: *Hotel Golf.*

At this point, the Precision Approach Radar – which due to an improvement in the weather earlier, had been taken out of service for a minor technical adjustment – was now operational again and enabled the controller to see a contact at the very bottom of the elevation display.

Tower: *Hotel Golf, I now have contact; six miles from touchdown.*

On being given the distance from the runway threshold, Harry Marlow responded with a despairing 'HOW FAR?' Immediately, the controller repeated the distance, pronouncing each word slowly and distinctly with added emphasis: '*SIX... MILES*'.

As the emergency progressed, all of Harry Marlow's efforts were immersed in keeping the aircraft under control. He was now literally standing up in his seat continuously exerting a pressure of some 200 lbs with his left foot on the rudder bar to keep the rudder hard over to the left to counteract the asymmetric thrust from the two port engines which were now operating on full take off power; every rivet, nut and bolt of the airframe creaked and strained in protest.

The adrenalin was now running high in the cockpit. Harry Marlow, his eyes continually scanning the altimeter and airspeed indicator, was now despairing, he had neither height nor speed to clear the urban sprawl of the town centre that lay directly ahead, let alone make to the airport. He had known for some time that the game was up and was now desperately seeking for somewhere to put the aircraft down, he knew that a crash landing anywhere in the town, home to thousands of people, would be nothing but sheer catastrophe causing heavy loss of life on the ground.

By now, there were scores of people standing in the red-bricked streets below, drawn from their homes by the thunderous roar of the approaching aircraft. With their eyes turned skyward, they stood and stared, mesmerised by the unfolding drama. In parks and recreation grounds, Sunday morning football matches that had just kicked off abruptly stopped, as players, referees and spectators all stared up in horrified fascination as the airliner, clearly in difficulties, thundered overhead at less than 300 feet.

Barrington Wood, a 40-year-old probation officer, witnessed the final agonising stages of the flight. As was his habitual practice on a Sunday morning, whatever the weather, he was to be found walking his dog in Woodbank Park on the eastern edge of the town centre. On hearing the heavy drone of aircraft engines, he took a terrified look over his shoulder and was awestruck to see a large piston-engined airliner emerge out of the drizzle. The tumult grew louder as he watched its progress in fascinated horror. As it slowly passed by, just a few feet above the dripping trees, he could plainly see the outlines of the passengers framed in the cabin windows. As suddenly as it had appeared, it was lost from his view as it dipped down below the tree line on the park boundary. Moments later, he heard the snarling roar of the engines cease abruptly; he stood rooted to the spot waiting for the sound of impact that was surely to follow.

Shattering the Sunday morning peace, Hotel Golf was now flying perilously low over the endless rows of houses along the length of Turncroft Lane, its turbulent wake rattling roof tiles and windows as it headed for the very centre of Stockport. Immediately ahead, pointing like a dagger, and closing by the second, loomed the intimidating sight of a 300-foot high factory chimney. Harry Marlow reacted to the approaching danger with amazing coolness, deftly tilting Hotel Golf's 117-foot wingspan to the left to avoid the collision.

Up to this point, there was little sign of restlessness amongst the passengers; they seemed oblivious to the dire emergency taking place on the other side of the cockpit door. However, in the final the minutes a quiet anxiety began to set in; it was an almost imperceptible sense that something bad was going to happen. They had felt themselves descending, then turning and climbing and then suddenly, they were being buffeted as the aircraft edged on the stall. More worrisome was their close proximity to the ground, but even then, no one realised just how serious the situation was.

At this point, sleepy-eyed Vivienne Thornber chanced to glance out of her rain flecked cabin window and was alarmed to see the huge green gasholder, stark and menacing, pass by at the same level as the aircraft. With her eyes firmly glued to the window, she saw the rooftops of houses and factories becoming disconcertingly bigger, getting closer, so close that 'I could almost count the roof tiles'. She knew then that something was drastically wrong.

Pollard: *Hotel Golf, we're now 500 feet.*
Tower: *Roger, your height should be 1,850 feet.*
Pollard: *Hotel Golf roger.*

There was a distinct note of resignation in Chris Pollard's voice in this final transmission from the crippled aircraft. The 500 feet altitude he reported was the altimeter reading set at sea level, their true height above the terrain was well under 300 feet. At this point, the ground begins to rise sharply towards the town centre, and even if they could maintain their present altitude, the aircraft would soon converge with the rising ground with devastating consequences. With terraced streets and factories slithering rapidly below, Harry Marlow realised their position was hopeless. He knew then it was time to put the aircraft on the ground.

Meanwhile, from her seat in the tail, Julia Partleton noticed a male passenger two rows in front looking very pale and clearly unwell. With just minutes remaining before touchdown – or so she thought – she could have quite easily ignored him, stayed seated and done nothing. But being the professional she was, she released her seat belt and walked forward to the cramped galley situated amidships on the port side to get him a glass of water. It was perhaps a slight inconvenience, but it was a decision that undoubtedly saved her life.

Turning on the tap, she heard the port side engines labouring heavily and felt the aircraft pitching which she put down to turbulence. Suddenly, without forewarning, she felt the aircraft lurch sharply to the right. Steadying herself against the galley partition, she glanced out of the window and was astonished to see the glistening rooftops just a few feet below.

Vivienne Thornber, her eyes now firmly glued to the window, grew increasingly nervous and uncomfortable as the aircraft staggered over the town. Her anxiety further increased when she saw a succession of chimney pots flash past her window in a blur. The realisation finally registered on her senses that they were going down. Describing those final nightmare moments, she said: "We were so low that we seemed to be opposite the bedroom windows, then without warning, the aircraft banked violently to the right and the engines spluttered. I knew then we were going to crash and was gripped by the terrifying realisation that I could die. I turned to Susan, grabbed her hand and screamed: 'Oh my God.' These were the last things I remember. Then everything went black."

Harold Wood, seated two rows behind Vivienne, had been looking forward to touching down at the airport, although it had seemed an age since the 'Fasten Your Seat Belt' sign had been illuminated.

I can vividly remember as we were approaching Manchester, the almost overpowering smell of perfume wafting down the cabin, which I thought was strange, as I hadn't noticed it during the flight. I reached up for the air conditioning nozzle, then without any warning, the aircraft swung abruptly to the right with the wing pointing almost to the ground. Looking out of the cabin window, I caught a fleeting glimpse of a chap coming out of a newsagent and getting into a white van parked in the street below, it was so close I could read the registration plate. The man looked up and for a split second, our eyes met. I then felt the stomach-lurching sensation of the aircraft plunging to earth. At this point, I felt very nauseous; I turned away from the window and reached for a sick bag. That is all I remember until I found myself coming round in the wreckage of the cabin.

On the flight deck, the cataclysmic final seconds of the flight were now being played out. The whole airframe began to shudder and tremble as it teetered on the edge of the stall from which, at this height, there could be no possible recovery. The dials on the instrument panel became a confused blur as it vibrated on its rubber mountings. Directly ahead, almost completely filling the rain-splattered cockpit windows loomed a deadly obstruction – a cluster of four 16 storey 150-foot-high residential tower blocks that were home to scores of families. To the right quarter, emerging out of the drizzle was the 125-foot high tower of St Mary's Parish Church in the market place – there could be no possible way through. Harry Marlow had exhausted every trick he knew to keep the aircraft flying, and like any pilot, faced with a dire emergency he had only split seconds to react.

After a seven-minute battle to save his aircraft, Harry Marlow gave up the unequal struggle to stay in the air. Out of the corner of his eye, ahead and to his right, he saw a tiny splash of greenery amidst a brick panorama. It was a bold gamble, but in reality, he had no other option. He reacted quickly. With calmness and coolness, he slammed back the throttles cutting the power to the two port engines. As the propellers spluttered to a stop, he yanked the control yoke hard over to right as far as it would go in a stomach-sickening downward turn towards the patch waste ground. With terrible finality, Hotel Golf impacted the ground.

In the glass-turreted airport tower, the approach controller, numbed and unbelieving, stared blankly at his radar console watching the luminous green sweeping hand showing no return blip. The airliner had completely disappeared off the screen at a range of six miles from the airport. Presuming the worst, he vainly continued to call the aircraft at regular intervals desperately hoping for a response:

Tower: *Hotel Golf, no radar contact…*
Tower: *Hotel Golf, radar, do you read?*
Tower: *Golf Alpha Lima Hotel Golf, do you read?*

The airways were silent. The only reply in the controllers' headset was the mocking hiss of static. There would be no reply. Hotel Golf had struck the ground at 10:09 and five seconds British Summer Time.

As the silent minutes passed by, the controller could no longer avoid the crushing truth, that flight BD 542, with 84 souls on board, had come down in the vicinity of Stockport town centre, some six miles short of the runway threshold. The mood inside the control tower was sombre and subdued. There now began a flurry of activity as the air traffic staff stowed their headsets and frantically began writing notes and closing out their logs. The audiotape of the communications between the aircraft and tower was immediately impounded for the investigation that was surely to follow. It was all routine procedure that they had trained for; an attempt to preserve all the data as a crime scene might be.

Chapter Fourteen
It Was on the Cards

"It is a capital mistake to theorise before one has data."
Sherlock Holmes – *A Scandal in Bohemia*

There is no doubt that air disasters make gruesome and tragic headlines, and yet, it is a strange and macabre paradox that they also save lives, for every advance in air safety has come about by what has been learnt from previous accidents. It is through the painstaking, logical and ingenious detective work of the air accident investigators that they almost always discover the cause, and by so doing, prevent another accident and loss of life in similar circumstances. It is their dedication to the job that makes the present-day high level of aviation safety a reality. Because of the nature of its work, it could be truthfully said that the Air Accident Investigation Branch is the only government department trying to put itself out of work.

After a rather quiet week of regular office hours, the AIB staff left for home on Friday evening hoping for a relaxed uninterrupted weekend. A chance to spend time with their families, potter in the garden, dabble in their hobbies and attend to a multitude of neglected household tasks. But late on Saturday night, their telephones began to ring with urgency. The investigators on call knew with sinking hearts what the call would inevitably mean.

On receiving the news of the Air Ferry DC-4 crash in France, the AIB 'Go' team sprung into action like a well-oiled machine and duly arrived in Perpignan the following day. It was strictly a French investigation because under the International Civil Aviation Organisation rules, it generally falls to the country where the accident occurred to lead the investigation. However, because the accident occurred to a registered UK operator, and the fact that all the passengers and crew were UK citizens, the AIB was expected in the circumstances to assist.

Then to compound matters came the totally unexpected news of the Stockport accident which put great pressure on the resources and staff of the AIB. With limited technical staff available, another accident investigation team was quickly assembled and dispatched to Stockport within a few hours.

The investigation team was headed by the Senior Inspector of Accidents, Geoffrey Wilkinson; a distinguished aeronautical engineer, a pilot for 21 years and a graduate of the Empire Test Pilot School. He was a systematic and methodical man and his investigative methods were highly precise with tremendous attention to detail. There could be no one better to lead the investigation. He was assisted by Chief Investigating Officers, Eric Newton; Richard Clarke; Reginald Feltham and William Tench.

Eric Newton, ex-engineer and ex-pilot, had more than 25 years' experience in aircraft accident investigation. A Fellow of the Royal Aeronautical Society, he was calm, well dressed and always ready to question everything under the sun. His job was to liaise with the senior inspector in charge and in particular, investigate the propellers, feathering units, constant speed units along with the electrical controls.

Richard Clarke was put in charge of the wreckage analysis. He had the responsibility for the examination of the airframe, flying controls, all cockpit readings and the landing gear and flaps. All the other groups involved with the investigation would keep him in the picture, co-operate generally and supply him with their individual reports.

Team member, Reginald Feltham, was an experienced pilot as well as a qualified engineer. His discipline was the Flight Data Recorder and he would be responsible for the recovery of the unit from the wreckage, supervise the playing back of the recording and turn the recording into tabulated data. From the information obtained, he would compile a report with his conclusions.

Responsible for the overall supervision of the investigation was William Tench, Deputy Chief Inspector of Accidents for the past twelve years. Tench had an extraordinary career in aviation. He first learnt to fly in 1940, and served as a pilot with the Fleet Air Arm during World War Two. From 1947 until 1955, he flew with KLM before joining the AIB. He once described the job as '…a fascinating challenge, occasionally exciting but always involving patient, even monotonous examination of every aspect of the accident – the tedium of which may erode those qualities of tenacity, imagination and perseverance which are fundamental to the effective investigator'.

All of the above investigators were free to engage – with no expense spared – any expert from outside the Branch who, in their opinion, could best assist them with their particular problems. Those listed above were the principle players, but there were many other individuals assisting the team working away diligently in the background.

The investigators methodology in the initial stages of any investigation was remarkable simple. On being notified of an accident, they would arrive at the scene, as soon as was possible, which normally would be a matter of hours. Their first assignment would be to walk around the crash site taking photographs, mapping the wreckage distribution, take detailed notes, locate the flight recorders, seek out any eyewitnesses, interview survivors – if any – and most importantly, secure the scene and preserve any evidence for the forthcoming investigation and subsequent inquiry.

Ideally, that is how it should pan out, but when the seasoned AIB team were escorted by the local police to the crash site, they were appalled and dismayed to see that the rescue workers in their frantic rescue and enthusiasm to clean up the crash location had completely destroyed the scene. The wreckage is the most tangible evidence an investigator can get his hands on. Even the tiniest scrap of metal or smashed component is of vital importance to solving the riddle of why the aircraft crashed. It was nothing less than a major blunder and highly likely that vital evidence had already been destroyed.

Nevertheless, they were diligent and undeterred in their task to find evidence and spent a number of hours on site sifting through the grotesquely twisted remains, making notations, taking measurements, with a burning desire to uncover the cause of the crash.

Preliminary examination of the wreckage showed that the undercarriage was retracted in the locked-up position and the flap selector lever was set at ten degrees down. From the position of the radiator shutter actuators and the fact that each engine was selected to its own fuel tank, the investigators believed that the crew were carrying out their approach checks when the emergency occurred. It was also noted that the rudder trim tab was fully adjusted to the left. In the remains of the cockpit, the rudder trim control wheel, located on the cockpit combing, was also at the equivalent setting indicating a selection of 12 divisions nose left, which is the maximum deflection of the tab. These positions clearly showed that the pilot was applying maximum left rudder, as one would expect him to do in an endeavour to overcome the swing to the right caused by the two failed engines on the starboard side. The remainder of the wreckage was so severely burnt and melted by the intense heat that no useful evidence could be found to help the investigators. This preliminary on-site examination yielded little, if any, information that was of value to progress the investigation. With little to go on, the task facing the AIB men seemed a daunting one.

The location of the crash, in the centre of a densely built-up area, was the worst possible place to try to put an aircraft down with any expectation of survival. The investigators knew immediately that it pointed to the crew being faced with overwhelming circumstances which left them little, if any choice but to put the aircraft down in that particular place.

In these early stages of the investigation, the theories and speculation expounded by the media must be put aside and they knew by experience not to jump to conclusions, to take nothing for granted and always use the investigators rule of thumb – always doubt the obvious. They were under no illusions that the investigation was going to be a difficult one and one of considerable technical complexity that would fully occupy their minds in the weeks and months to come. Although they didn't know it at the time, the case would become epic in the annals of the Air Accident Investigation Branch.

The investigation was not a linear path, but a giant jig-saw puzzle, that over the coming weeks and months would gradually come together to form a picture. They would have to sift and evaluate all the available evidence without emotion and eliminate all the engineering red herrings and hopefully discover the cause.

One of their first tasks was to interview the best-placed eyewitnesses who saw the aircraft in difficulties at various points under the flight path, right up to the time of impact. However, their evidence, and that of the survivors lying in the infirmary gave the investigators no real clues as to why Hotel Golf had suddenly within minutes lost speed and height over Stockport.

One vital witness, Captain Harry Marlow, who was pulled out of the wreckage alive, suffered numerous injuries, including lacerations of the face, a fractured jaw and a serious head injury causing retrograde amnesia causing him to remember little, if anything, of the flight beyond Congleton Beacon. He was interviewed by an investigator in hospital the following day. The interview began with some routine questions about the return flight from Palma. He was then asked about his decision to abandon the approach and overshoot. What he told them, allowing for the fact that he was still severely shocked and under sedation was highly significant. He said that he couldn't hold the aircraft straight 'even with rudder' and had been trying to find somewhere to 'put the aircraft down'. But most telling of all was his question to the interviewing officer. "Which engine was it?" This, and the evidence from his recorded conversation with the air traffic controller that he was having a 'little bit of trouble with RPM' and the fact that Hotel Golf was rapidly losing speed and altitude, suggested trouble with the engines or propellers. This led to an initial suspicion that either number 3 or number 4 propeller had gone into reverse pitch or alternatively had run away in an uncontrollable over speed condition; consequently, the engines and propellers received special attention.

Following this line of inquiry particular scrutiny was also paid to the Rolls-Royce Merlin engines and associated components. The battered remains of the four power plants were removed from the wreckage and transported by road to the Scottish Aviation base at Prestwick where Rolls-Royce engineers performed a full strip down inspection of the engines' 3,000 individual parts to determine if there had been any pre-crash malfunction or mechanical defect. Each component was cleaned, examined and, in some cases, x-rayed. The results of this meticulous examination revealed that there was no evidence of over speeding, the oil supply was functioning normally and that engines 1 and 2 on the port wing were operating normally at the time of impact, engine number 4, the starboard outer was stopped, and made a new discovery about number 3 – it was probably windmilling – that is the propeller was being turned by the airflow and not by the engine. From all the available evidence, they could not find any mechanical reason for the failure of these two engines to deliver power.

Having drawn a blank with the power plants, attention now switched to the propellers and associated equipment to see if there was any evidence of pre-crash defect or failure which might have affected control or governing of RPM. After being disentangled from the wreckage, they were taken to the Hawker Siddeley Dynamics workshops at Stevenage, where engineers tried to ascertain the blade pitch angles on impact. Because of the severe damage sustained in the crash, it was not possible to determine this from the blades alone; they had to resort to impact markings on the faces of certain mating components which permitted the blade angles at impact to be determined with accuracy. By this method, they were able to conclude that the number 4 propeller was feathered and numbers 1, 2 and 3 were in the normal operating pitch. Again, as with the engines, there was no evidence of pre-crash failure or malfunction.

At this stage, all that was known with any certainty was that Hotel Golf was flying with two out of its four engines out of action for no obvious reason. Against this indisputable evidence was the fact than none of the eyewitnesses who saw the aircraft during the last few minutes of flight, speak of any of the propellers being stationary. There were nine such witnesses, and of those, four had served in the RAF and one in the Fleet Air Arm. Human observation and eyewitness statements – the investigators knew from experience – can be notoriously unreliable and misleading, and in this instance, their conflicting evidence about the propellers was regarded as unreliable, which is not surprising since they were all presented, some more suddenly than others, with the astonishing and alarming sight of a large four engined airliner, flying at very low altitude over a densely built-up area.

However, in the tail of the aircraft there was a reliable witness – the Flight Data Recorder. Habitually referred to as the black box, it was in fact a bright fluorescent orange armoured sphere. In the UK, passenger-carrying aircraft above a certain weight have been fitted with flight data recorders since July 1966 and proved to be a massive advance in air accident investigation. The Midas flight recorder fitted to Hotel Golf – crude by modern day standards – was made of several layers of hardened steel and designed to withstand the impact forces and fire of almost any crash. It recorded each second of the flight – airspeed, altitude and compass heading. If it was operating correctly up to time of impact, the investigators would be able to discover what had transpired during those last seven minutes of the flight. The information it contained could be vital to solving the riddle of the crash.

The recorder was recovered undamaged from its location in the aft part of the fuselage under the tail on the day of the accident and immediately flown to Royston Instruments headquarters in Byfleet, Surrey, for immediate decryption. On examination, the thin magnetic recording tape was found intact and had been running right up to the time of impact. That tape could now be played back and would tell the investigators about the performance of the aircraft, the timing of every alteration in speed, altitude and heading, and at what point Harry Marlow lost power on those two starboard engines. From the readout, Reginald Feltham of the Accident Investigation

Working Group was able to accurately reconstruct the last part of the flight. The results conformed closely to the eyewitness's accounts and helped fill in the gap, which resulted in Harry Marlow's inability to remember anything about the flight beyond Congleton.

The readout showed that the number 4 starboard outer engine failed first, followed twenty-seconds later by number 3 – just before Captain Marlow radioed the tower that he was overshooting. The airspeed then decayed to 110 knots and the behaviour of the aircraft from then on was consistent with the crew being faced with a major emergency involving severe control difficulties that were never overcome. But as factual information to progress the investigation this added nothing, and gave no answer to the main question – why were two of Hotel Golf's engines inoperative? The answer had to lie somewhere in the aircraft itself. Despite so far drawing a blank, the investigators remained diligent and undeterred in their task to find answers to what was turning out to be a baffling case.

On 7 September, now some three months after the accident, the investigators were still no nearer to solving the puzzle of why the Argonaut had crashed. It was decided to carry out flight tests on Hotel Golf's sister aircraft, Hotel Yankee, which British Midland had put at their disposal. The object of these test flights was to establish the minimum control speeds with the aircraft in the same configuration as that of Hotel Golf in the last seven minutes of flight – that is with the two starboard engines shutdown.

In good weather, Hotel Yankee took off from British Midland's base at East Midlands Airport. Flying the aircraft from the left-hand seat was the very experienced David Davies, the Chief Test Pilot for the Air Registration Board; occupying the right-hand seat was Captain Sidney Fenton, British Midland's chief pilot acting as co-pilot. Also carried onboard acting as observers were members of the Accident Investigation Branch.

David Davies was a wise choice to undertake the test flight; at the time, he was probably the most experienced pilot around who could evaluate the flying characteristics of the aircraft. He joined the ARB as Chief Test Pilot in 1949 and flew and evaluated all the new British post war airliners, including the Vickers Viscount, Bristol Britannia and the world's first jet airliner, the de Havilland Comet. He went on to check out all the British and American jetliners which followed: VC 10, Trident, One-Eleven, Boeing 707, Douglas DC-8, DC-9, DC-10 and not forgetting the supersonic Concorde.

His general assessment of the controls was that the Argonaut was a rather heavy aircraft to fly, but that so long as all four engines were operating, there was no serious criticism to make. However, with one or more engines inoperative, its control characteristics were such, that though acceptable for transport aircraft when the Argonaut was first offered for certification in 1949, it would not be accepted if offered up for certification in 1967 because of the higher standards then in force.

No passengers were carried on board Hotel Yankee, but enough sandbags were in place to simulate exactly the same load that was carried by Hotel Golf on that final flight. On this test flight, it was hoped to discover at exactly what speed the aircraft would stall carrying this weight, how it would behave at very low speeds with two engines shut down and whether it would have been possible for Harry Marlow to reach the airport after the emergency arose.

Climbing to 4,000 feet – and because of the very real dangers that might be encountered during the test – they flew over the most deserted countryside they could find. On reaching altitude, the first thing that was checked was the stall – the moment when the aircraft flies so slowly that the wings stop providing enough lift to keep the aircraft airborne. All four engines were throttled back, and as the airspeed dropped below 100 knots, Hotel Yankee began to buffet as the airflow broke away from the wings. With the aircraft in imminent danger of stalling and spinning uncontrollably out of the sky, Davies opened up the throttles; put the nose down and with increased airspeed, the aircraft recovered and flew on. With the aircraft flying level, they shut down and feathered the number 4 starboard outer engine. This is how Hotel Golf would have been with only one engine stopped and how the propeller was found after the crash. In this configuration, the aircraft found no difficulty in maintaining airspeed, height and heading. Next came the most potentially dangerous part of the test flight. With ten degrees of flap extended and the number 4 engine shut down and its propeller feathered, they shut down the number 3 engine and allowed the propeller to windmill in the airflow. In this configuration, Hotel Yankee's airspeed rapidly decayed and the aircraft was unable to maintain height without the application of take off power to numbers 1 and 2 engines. To maintain adequate directional control and reduce the rudder foot loads to a manageable level, the speed would need to be increased to 120 knots. These two actions, had they been adopted by Captain Marlow, should in theory, have enabled Hotel Golf to have reached Manchester Airport and make an emergency two-engined landing. However, Captain Marlow could only have achieved this result by sacrificing height which, as we know, he had precious little to spare in the final stages of the flight. Furthermore, he could not have been expected to take these actions unless he appreciated that two engines had failed. One must also bear in mind that he would be intensely preoccupied exerting considerable physical strength on the rudder bar to keep the aircraft under directional control. In the flight test, it was calculated that the rudder loads exceeded 200 pounds foot force and could not be held for longer than a few minutes, and on this flight, Davies had to ask Captain Fenton to assist in holding the rudder pedal down to keep the aircraft on a straight course.

The results of the test flight revealed that during the emergency that overtook Hotel Golf, Harry Marlow would have been totally occupied trying to control the aircraft and the remaining workload would have greatly exceeded the capability of Chris Pollard. There is little doubt that had the emergency occurred at 10,000 feet as opposed to 1,500 feet the crew would have eventually worked out exactly what was happening to the aircraft and quite possibly saved the situation.

It became evident from the flight data that with two engines 'out' on one side – even with the aircraft carrying a relatively low payload – it was not possible to keep the aircraft on a straight and level course at low speeds, even with full left rudder and rudder trim selected. Even if the minimum safety speed was maintained, with one propeller feathered and one windmilling, this would still result in a steady loss of height. For the investigators, they had proved what they believed to be true, but discovered nothing new and were no further forward. They still could not find the answer to why those two starboard engines failed when there was nothing mechanically wrong with them. They knew that instances of double engine failure on one side of an aircraft – and within seconds of each other – were sufficiently rare that it was beyond doubt that they must be interrelated, but were at a loss to know why. The mystery only deepened. After nearly two decades of service, was there some hidden, still unknown characteristic within the aircraft that had caused the accident? The investigation team were working under tremendous pressure to find the cause before another Argonaut suffered the same horrific fate.

In their search for answers, the investigators left no stone unturned and even looked at the possibility of fuel contamination from the fuel tanker which refuelled the

Argonaut as the following account by an Air Ferry pilot flying out of Palma Airport that morning suggests:

I was flying a DC-6 – November Oscar – out of Palma that morning and refuelled from the same tanker as the British Midland Argonaut – in fact, I emptied the tanker and had to finish with another one. Before take off we had a magneto problem and had to return to the ramp to get it fixed. It turned out to be a leaking oil seal in the distributor. Once it was cleaned out, all was well and we departed Palma for home.

Many months later, I was hauled into the Chief Pilots office to meet two 'men from the ministry' and was given a very thorough grilling by these guys. They quizzed me uphill and down dale telling me that I must have had engine trouble all the way home. I told them I did not and stuck to my guns. They then confided in me that they were going down the road of fuel contamination as being the cause of the Stockport accident. My testimony, of course, destroyed their theory once and for all and sent them scurrying back to the drawing board.

Within days of the disaster, some 40 tons of wreckage and components had been gathered together, loaded onto RAF Queen Mary trailers and transported by road to the Royal Aircraft Establishment at Farnborough for painstaking examination.

Situated on the south side of Farnborough airfield, in an area known as Berkshire Copse, and close to where aviation pioneer S F Cody prepared and flew his string-and-canvas flying machine, is a huddle of buildings used for the reconstruction and examination of the remains of crashed aircraft. It is a place of intense activity and urgency. There in a vast hangar – well concealed from inquisitive public view – the remains of Hotel Golf were, as far as it was possible, painstakingly reconstructed like a giant macabre 3D jigsaw puzzle. Slowly over the coming weeks, under the direction of investigating officer Richard Clarke, it would be painstakingly sifted and evaluated.

In October, with the opening of the Public Inquiry only a few weeks away, the pressure was mounting on the investigators to step up their efforts and find answers. At this point in the investigation suspicion fell more and more on the Argonaut's fuel system as the main cause of the accident – in fact for a few of the investigators it had for some time become suspect number one. To support this theory, the investigators decided to examine the fuel logs for the British Midland Argonaut fleet and from this analysis came an entirely new line of thinking. It had been suggested by some that inadvertent fuel transfer, causing fuel starvation to one or more engines, might have been a factor in the cause of the crash, although most aviation experts, including British Midland pilots and engineers, considered this was highly unlikely to occur in flight and was wholly without foundation. The evidence was flimsy at best, nevertheless, the investigators, working on the old Sherlock Holmes maxim that: *when you have eliminated the impossible, whatever remains, however improbable, must be the truth.*

In 1967, there were nearly 900 aircraft in passenger carrying service worldwide with fuel systems very similar, if not identical with the Argonaut. They included the Douglas DC-4, DC-6, DC-7, DC-8 and the Carvair – therefore, it was imperative to investigate this line of inquiry before another aircraft with the same fuel system suffered the same appalling fate as Hotel Golf.

At East Midlands Airport, another British Midland Argonaut – Hotel Sierra – was being used to carry out ground tests on the sparking plugs taken from the number 3 engine of Hotel Golf – the engine that windmilled. There was some doubt about the condition of these plugs recovered from the wreckage, but on test, they were found to be perfectly serviceable. With the aircraft still available, Captain Fenton, the Chief Pilot of British Midland and Captain Wallace, the Flight Safety Officer, along with members of the investigation team decided to test a long shot in endeavour to prove or disprove the fuel starvation theory.

They put fuel into the main and auxiliary tanks, started up all four engines. And whilst the aircraft was on the ground, they positioned the two cross feed levers controlling the flow of fuel from different tanks to different engines to see if it might be possible for the fuel to be drained out of one tank into another without the pilot knowing. Engineers and pilots said it couldn't possibly happen but the investigators had their doubts – certainly, it was worth trying.

In cockpit the cross-feed lever, which allows any engine to draw fuel from any tank, was left open by just a fraction of an inch – a gap so small that neither pilot could see it from where he sat. The four engines ran together steadily using up fuel. If there was any truth in the theory then sooner or later, one tank would run dry and one or more of the engines would stop. For the investigators watching on the apron, it was just a matter of patiently waiting to see what would happen, and if an engine did stop, which one would it be? It was quite chilling for the observers on the ground to see the number 4 starboard outer engine suddenly shut down and the propellers windmill slowly to a stop. However, with engines 1, 2 and 3 running off their own tanks with the cross-feed lever slightly open and with number 4 tank empty, it proved impossible to induce number 3 engine to fail, either by fuel starvation or ingesting air from the empty number 4 tank. This was good solid evidence that the investigators were right in their fuel starvation theory. They didn't know it at the time, but after months of investigation and speculation over the causes, it was possible that they had now come within sight of the end of the investigation. The key it seemed to solving the riddle of the Stockport air disaster was in the cross-feed levers and that gap of a quarter of an inch – and it pointed to one cause alone – fuel starvation.

From this test and others like it, the investigators were able to say with some certainty that if the cross-feed levers are left not quite shut then a substantial amount of fuel can flow from an outboard tank to its inboard neighbour due to the dihedral angle of the wings. This could also explain why fire damage was greater on the port wing – there being less fuel in the starboard wing.

In the light of this evidence, the fuel and instrument logs for the British Midland Argonaut fleet was closely analysed and shockingly revealed numerous incidents of inadvertent fuel transfer in flight, none of these had been diagnosed as such at the time. So grave were the implications the investigators immediately alerted all airlines operating aircraft with similar fuel systems to keep a close eye on the fuel contents gauges and if in any doubt dip stick the tanks before flying.

And basically, that was all that was known with any certainty when the Public Inquiry into the causes and circumstances of the accident to Hotel Golf opened in London.

Chapter Fifteen
Public Inquiry

"After the aircraft has crashed, everyone knows how she might have been saved."
Proverb

There were two forms of air accident investigation undertaken in Britain in 1967. The most common was an Inspector's Investigation at the discretion of the Chief Inspector of Accidents, the other was a full-scale Public Inquiry ordered by the government minister responsible for aviation. Typically, aviation accidents that call for a public inquiry are those involving multiple deaths. In this instance, the Stockport disaster was deemed so serious and stimulated a great deal of public interest that a Public Inquiry was the only option, in that the public has a right to know what happened and particularly in the Stockport case, why it was allowed to happen.

A public inquiry accepts evidence and conducts its hearings in a public forum. The role of the inquiry is an attempt to discover the causes and circumstances and hopefully restore public confidence by carrying out a fair investigation into the events. It should be forward looking and identify any lessons to be learnt and make any recommendations necessary to safeguard the public. A Public Inquiry into a serious aviation accident is normally conducted under an independent Commissioner, usually an eminent member of the legal profession and supported in his task by members of the flying and engineering professions who would act as assessors.

In the main, despite good intentions, public inquiries are a complete waste of time and public money, where quite often the needs of the technical investigation tends to be overlaid by legal considerations in that there is greater interest in proving who was not to blame than establishing actual or probable reasons for the accident and rarely achieves anything but to line lawyers pockets at the tax payers expense.

The slow grinding wheels of the Stockport inquiry – at vast expense – was a seemingly endless procession of witnesses and aviation experts filing through the inquiry room that naturally produced much rhetoric, where a great deal is said over many weeks and months, without enhancing air safety one jot. Most of the proceedings were merely to allow the public to see that this particular accident was being taken seriously by those responsible for air safety in the UK. In the end, the Stockport inquiry did little, if anything, to improve British aviation safety.

I have laboriously read through the whole of the Public Inquiry transcripts which were a huge undertaking – in addition, I have examined the mountain of documentation, statements, correspondence and technical reports that were produced seemingly on a daily basis for consideration. It would be impossible here to record all the evidence, speeches and cross-examinations that were generated during the eighteen days of the inquiry; the witness statements alone run to some 1,000 pages. Consequently, I give here only the more pertinent points regarding the evidence that would be of interest to the reader.

It was a sunny but chilly morning when the Public Inquiry formally opened on Tuesday 28 November 1967, at 6 Burlington Gardens, Mayfair in London's West End, which, ironically is not far from Regent Street and Piccadilly, where at the time most of the national and international airlines had their headquarters. This imposing grade II listed building of architectural merit, certainly gave a sense of gravitas to the proceedings.

The inquiry was conducted by the Commissioner, Peter Bristow QC, with Captain Philip Brentnall and William Sturrock as assessors. Bristow was an affable character with a keen and irreverent sense of humour. He did not like the formality of wigs in court and for most of his career, he performed his judicial functions bareheaded. Fascinated by flying since childhood, he became a member of the University Air Squadron, qualifying as a pilot at the age of 21 and saw active service with the RAF during the war.

Captain Philip Brentnall, appointed as an assessor, was well suited to oversee the proceedings; at the time, he was the BOAC Flight Training Manager for the Boeing 707 aircraft, with 11,000 hours experience as a pilot on transport aircraft, 1,200 of these was on the Canadair C-4 Argonaut. He was also the famed captain on the jet Comet airliner's first commercial flight. His fellow assessor, William Sturrock, was also was well qualified to sit on the inquiry, being an aircraft maintenance engineer since 1940 as well as an Associate Fellow of the Royal Astronautical Society.

The last two public hearings into aviation matters in the UK – the Stansted Airport inquiry and the Heathrow Vanguard accident hearing – were conducted in such a shoddy manner as to bring the judicial process perilously near to falling into disrepute. It was hoped that these three individuals leading the Stockport inquiry would rectify the balance.

On the first day, the inquiry room was packed with over 200 people, which included barristers, lawyers and many others with an interest in the proceedings. The public area set aside was also crowded with relatives and friends of those who had lost their lives in the disaster and members of the press. In the days and weeks ahead, evidence would be given from the accident investigators, representatives of the airline, Canadair the manufacturers, lawyers representing various parties along with engineers and experts from every aspect of aviation. In all, sixty-three witnesses would be called to give evidence and be cross-examined.

The Attorney-General, Sir Elwyn Jones QC, the most senior lawyer in the country at the time, appeared on behalf of the Crown. He was appointed because of his vast experience having served as junior British Counsel during the Nuremberg War Trials and led the prosecution of the Moors murderers, Ian Brady and Myra Hindley; he was also credited with opening the inquiries into the Aberfan and Torrey Canyon disasters.

The inquiry room was still and quiet when he officially opened the proceedings with a tribute to Hotel Golf's commander Captain Marlow. He told the assembled in a slow measured pace that: "Argonaut Hotel Golf had crashed on one of the few open spaces in the heavily built-up area of Stockport town centre. There were no casualties on the ground. It may well be that credit for this should be given to Captain Marlow the pilot of the plane." He also went on to praise the police, fire and ambulance services, and said, "All those civilians in the area who, in circumstances of the deepest emergency, had done a tremendous job."

"Theoretically, the cause of the accident could be due to weakness of design, to the age of the aircraft, inadequate maintenance, pilot error, or to any combination of these four factors: I have little doubt that this court will explore all these possibilities. Nevertheless, I think it is right at the outset of this inquiry that the investigating officers consider that a shortcoming in design is probably the main causal factor in this case. If they are right, then a major and startling malfunction of the fuel system put engines number 3 and 4 on the starboard side out of action as the aircraft was coming into land through cloud, rain and drizzle."

Setting the scene, he proceeded to outline the sequence of events leading up to the accident. "The cause of the crash," he said, "was at first obscure. It was doubted at one time that the cause would ever be determined, however, thanks to the expert, painstaking, and thorough investigation carried out by the Accident Investigation Branch, it would seem likely that this court will be in the position in due course to make findings as to the probable cause of this catastrophe. For a catastrophe it was, resulting as it did in the loss of 72 lives – one of the highest death tolls in any air crash which has ever occurred in the United Kingdom."

Sir Elwyn continued, "There had been a great deal of public anxiety because this had been the third fatal disaster involving British registered charter aircraft engaged on holiday flights, and that there were widespread suspicions by the public that safety standards were not as high as they should be on charter flights, but this was untrue." He pointed out that charter aircraft were just as safe as those used on scheduled flights, for both were strictly examined for airworthiness and other safety aspects. "It would be," he said, "the task of the inquiry to determine whether the 18-year-old aircraft, which was bought by British Midland in 1961, was usable for the purpose for which it was employed."

This part of his opening statement was not strictly true. It was well known that the statistical record of the independent operators was without doubt far inferior regarding safety compared to that of the two British flag carriers – BOAC and BEA. The independents were involved in more incidents, suffered more technical delays and were involved in a higher proportion of serious accidents involving fatalities.

Much of the Attorney General's opening speech dwelt on the Argonauts fuel system, pointing out that the aircraft did not comply with UK airworthiness requirements, in that the fuel system was not designed in such a manner either to prevent fuel from being drawn from two tanks simultaneously, or to ensure that if this was a feature, that air could not be drawn into the system from a nearby empty tank. "Cross feed fuel lines," he said, "allowed for fuel to go from a variety of tanks to a variety of engines – a feature prohibited in British made aircraft and was only permitted in the Argonaut if placards warning against cross-feeding were prominently displayed in the cockpit." He said that the levers controlling the fuel cocks were badly placed in the cockpit, hard to move and gave the pilot uncertain impressions of what the crew had selected. "A slight error," he said, "in the position of the levers could lead to random cross-feeding from tank to tank. With so many inadvertent fuel transfer incidents on Argonauts and DC-4s uncovered during the investigation, it was only a matter of time before the inevitable would happen."

Referring to the need for exact fuel lever positioning, he said: "This is a most alarming design weakness and a built-in trap of which no one, apparently, was aware. They were not aware of it because of fuel gauge inaccuracies, which were a characteristic on old aircraft, masked the true cause of the aberrant fuel content gauge readings."

In a history of abnormalities recorded in Hotel Golf's fuel logs – the most dramatic being the Palma incident just seven days before the Stockport crash – was not deemed at the time worthy of reporting. Sir Elwyn said that this event only came to light in a voluntary statement more than four months after the accident by Brian Gifford, the engineer on that flight. This incident was not recorded, as it should have in the aircraft's technical log. At the time, Captain Fleming, the aircraft commander, claimed he could not even remember this incident happening.

Dealing with the question of crew fatigue, Sir Elwyn said the pilots had been on duty for 12 hours and 55 minutes when the accident occurred. Although this was within the flight duty rules in force at the time of the accident, this would not satisfy new regulations due to be introduced in January 1968. Captain Marlow had had 'very little' sleep in the 24 hours before the crash. He had cancelled a room booked for him in the Excelsior Hotel near the airport, and spent the morning before the evening flight playing golf. After a short afternoon sleep, he drove himself on the two-hour journey to the airport from Nottingham.

"The duty of this court," Sir Elwyn said, "was remedial not retributive. It was hoped that it might avoid accidents of this kind again or reduce the loss of life, injuries and damage likely to result from future accidents." He stressed that he and his colleagues representing the Crown were not there to make a case against anybody or to defend anybody. "We are here to represent the public interest and to assist this court to elicit the facts about this tragic accident." With those final remarks, the Attorney-General's two-day summary of the situation concluded and the inquiry settled down to the examination of witnesses and hear the technical evidence.

Of all the people assembled on that first day, there was one individual with more personal interest in the proceedings than anyone else – Captain Harry Marlow. He was effectively in the 'hot seat', his reputation and future flying career depended on the outcome of the proceedings. During the following days and weeks, he would sit in the inquiry room pale and stony-faced, listening to the background of that last flight. Every day, the evidence would be given and every known fact and relevant detail brought out and discussed.

One issue that was raised early on in the proceedings was the matter of pilot fatigue. In this respect, evidence was given regarding errors made by Captain Marlow in his transmissions with air traffic control during the final part of the flight.

As the aircraft passed Abbeville, the last reporting point in northern France at 8:36, the responsibility for control passed from French Air Traffic Control to that of London Airways who cleared the aircraft to proceed to Manchester by the usual route maintaining a height of 6,000 feet. At 9:32, Hotel Golf passed Daventry and control was then taken over by Preston Airways. At 9:46, Harry Marlow made a call to Preston Airways, it starts with 'Echo Golf...' which is a curious error. It may well be that Marlow had heard the reference over radio to Oscar Echo, another aircraft flying in the area and it was in his mind. But there it was clearly in the transcript; he calls his aircraft Echo Golf. Preston Airways answers as follows: 'HOTEL GOLF...' emphasising the call sign, presumably trying to draw Captain Marlow's attention to the fact that it was not Echo Golf but Hotel Golf. Marlow clearly gave the wrong call sign at the initiation of that transmission and it certainly indicates that there was some sense of confusion or muddle in his mind. Standing alone, of course, it may not be significant, but what was to follow may be.

At 9:53, Hotel Golf was handed over to Manchester approach control. As the aircraft was approaching the Congleton Beacon at 6,000 feet, Harry Marlow calls Manchester with the transmission: "Hotel Golf is just coming by Congleton, any instructions, over?"

Manchester replies: "Roger Hotel Golf, you're re-cleared to flight level five zero (5,000 feet) and turn right heading zero three zero."

Marlow repeats back the instruction given: "Right three three zero we're steering three two five now and we're re-cleared to five zero." The heading he repeated back is plainly wrong and Manchester immediately corrects him and says not three three zero, but ZERO THREE ZERO. Marlow, realising his error, transmits back: "Right zero three zero and down to five zero."

Then at 9:57, Manchester calls the aircraft with the instruction: "Hotel Golf Radar, continue descent to three five zero zero feet QNH (3,500 feet) and report passing five zero."

Marlow replies: "Roger three five on one zero two zero will check through five." This erroneous message is corrected by the traffic controller with emphasis: 'ONE ZERO TWO FIVE HOTEL GOLF!' Harry Marlow corrects himself again and says: "One, zero, two, five, SORRY!"

Regardless of permitted duty hours, most pilots find a full night's flying more tiring than an equivalent period of day duty. It is arguable, therefore, that trouble arising during the latter part of a night flight could take a pilot somewhat longer to analyse and correct than after a less onerous period of day duty.

Captain Marlow, questioned by Mars-Jones QC for Crown Counsel, put it to him: "A drive of two-and-a-half hours immediately before setting off on this trip was perhaps not the best prelude, it might be said."

To this, Captain Marlow countered: "I quite agree, but it could also be argued that ten hours in a strange hotel would not be the best form of preparation for a flight."

Either way, there can be no doubt that Harry Marlow would have been fairly tired after the long night flight – a not unusual situation in professional aircrews – and little importance should be placed on the errors made in the conversations with air traffic control. Such errors naturally occur with persons who are tired and relaxed when carrying out a familiar task. But it may be said that the fatigue factor at the end of the flight could have possibly contributed to the developing emergency and given rise to the difficulties in coping with the diagnosis and control of what may have been a difficult and complex situation. The errors of communications may well be another reflection of perhaps confusion and perhaps tiredness, and all this, of course, was before the dire emergency started that thrust high mental and physical demands on both pilots.

In 1967, and even today, it is almost impossible to prove conclusively that pilot fatigue was an underlying factor in the accident. Whatever effect fatigue had in this case, Captain Marlow finally managed to crash land the crippled Argonaut on one of the very few relatively open places in the town centre; an amazing piece of airmanship.

The most chilling part of the accident was why so few survived in what was a very survivable crash. Called to give his evidence regarding the medical aspects, was Group Captain Mason, who was brought in by the AIB on behalf of the Board of Trade. He presented his evidence convincingly; he was not only an expert in aircraft accident pathology, but also an expert witness who had the ability to hold everybody's attention. He said that the Stockport crash was a comparatively low impact crash and therefore a very survivable accident, in that the fuselage structure remained sufficiently intact to retain a protective shell allowing survivors to escape before flames or smoke kills them. In this matter, Mason stressed in his evidence, the large number of devastating lower leg injuries consisting of massive soft tissue damage with underlying fractures of tibia and fibula. In his opinion, they were the result of the crushing of the lower legs of the passengers against the metal structure of the seats in front.

Although the aircraft was eighteen years old, nobody realised, or even suspected, that the seats installed in the aircraft were potential killers. The seats had two metal strengthening bars between the uprights 9 inches above the cabin floor. The bar nearest the passenger seated behind is comparatively thin, the inner bar was massive. In the burnt out remains of the 66 seats recovered from the wreckage and examined, the thin outer bar was bent inwards or fractured in 38 cases, caused by the flailing legs of passengers as the seats broke away from the disintegrating floor on impact causing them to concertina forward. Mason told the inquiry that he had come across the same type of injuries when he investigated the Winter Hill air disaster of 1958.

It was these devastating leg injuries that prevented surviving passengers reaching safety by their own efforts and succumbed in the post-crash fire. Mason said he found that thirty-five of the seventy-two fatalities had died from burning, 15 were found to have died of typical deceleration injuries, seven from head trauma and the remainder from a variety of other serious injuries. With one exception, all the surviving passengers were seated on the starboard side of the aircraft between rows 2 and 7.

The thirty-five who died from burning alone was determined during the post mortems. For instance, those still alive in the cabin when the fire started, burns could be found in their air passages as far as the lungs. Also, examination of the victim's blood disclosed very large quantities of carbon monoxide, which proved they were still breathing when the fire took hold. It is difficult to imagine the sheer horror experienced by those unfortunate passengers who knew they had survived the impact yet found themselves trapped and knew they were going to perish in sight of their would-be rescuers.

The seats and their floor anchorages fitted in Hotel Golf were stressed to survive impact forces of 9g – a standard laid down in 1952 by a British Airworthiness Requirement – today regulations demand that seats have to withstand an impact shock of 16g almost double that of those installed in the Argonaut. It was calculated that the forward deceleration involved in the crash of Hotel Golf could have been in the order of 10g, but the dynamic or peak 'g' loadings may well have been much greater than this, possibly double. In addition to the forward deceleration on impact, there was a high downward deceleration probably in the order of 16g. These high impact forces disrupted the cabin floor and the integrity of the anchorages greatly in excess of their approved requirements.

The installation of rearward facing seats in civil aircraft was briefly touched upon, and according to AIB inspector, Eric Newton, if they had been installed in Hotel Golf, they would not have increased, to any measurable extent, the chances of passenger survival because of the unique circumstances of the accident.

The RAF, as a matter of policy, introduced rearward facing seats as standard on all their transport aircraft in the 1950s, and those airlines providing long-term charter aircraft for RAF trooping flights carrying servicemen and their dependents between Britain and her military bases overseas were obliged to have their aircraft seating reconfigured or lose the lucrative contracts. Even the United States Air Force opted for rearward facing seats in their belief that they are safer. Even today, in the absence of clear strong data and lack of airworthiness research; the jury is still out on the issue and the debate on rearward facing seats continues to rumble on to this day.

When Group Captain Mason stepped down from the witness box, attention focused on what had now widely become known as the Palma Incident. The Inquiry heard that it was some five months after the Stockport accident when the details of this incident first came to light when statements were volunteered to the investigators by the First Officer, Roger Wise and Brian Gifford the engineer on that particular flight. However, the aircraft's commander, Captain Fleming, despite the crew statements to the contrary, consistently denied any recollection of the incident. Although the Palma incident occurred just seven days before the Stockport crash, it went unreported. If the facts had been reported, investigated and corrective action been taken then most certainly, the Stockport disaster would have been avoided.

There were some lighter moments during the proceedings that gave some welcome relief and helped break the grim monotony of the courtroom atmosphere. When Peter Marks, a representative of the engine manufacturers Rolls-Royce, gave evidence about the reliability and excellent reputation of the Merlin engine, he said that they didn't habitually fail, and pointed out that the double engine failure was most likely due to fuel starvation alone and not a defect in the engines. He couldn't resist sarcastically adding, that as good as his company was, it had yet to design and produce an engine that didn't need fuel! This statement, delivered in a deadpan expression, caused howls of laughter in the inquiry room and made good copy for the assembled press.

The inquiry then moved on to the evidence regarding the cross-feed levers and how it affected the flow of fuel from the tanks to the engines. Geoffrey Wilkinson, the lead accident inspector told the inquiry: "I feel strongly that these two engine failures must have been closely related, and fuel starvation is the only root cause that seems to make sense in practical terms." Questioned about the positioning of the cross-feed fuel levers, he said he had personally tested the Argonaut cockpit layout whilst parked on the apron and found that when strapped into the co-pilot's seat, he had difficulty in operating the levers properly. When he had pushed them as far as he could, they were still about five degrees out of position. And until the accident, no one appreciated what a significant amount of fuel could pass unnoticed through a fuel cock to another fuel tank if the lever was not quite in the right position.

From this and other evidence, the fuel starvation theory now became the main thrust of the inquiry. Seizing on the importance of this evidence, the inquiry was adjourned for exhaustive testing to be carried out on the fuel system at the Aircraft and Armament Experiment Establishment (A&AEE) facility at Boscombe Down. It was hoped that these tests would support what had so far been mainly theoretical evidence. These experiments would inevitably take some considerable time and would most likely lead to the real answer to the causes of the accident. The investigation had rolled ponderously onward over the previous months at a huge cost to the taxpayer, and with these further tests, it was now going to cost even more.

British Midland Argonaut, Hotel Yankee, was flown from East Midlands Airport to the A&AEE facility at Boscombe Down. It was here that the fuel system underwent the most intensive testing that the 'boffins' could devise in a dogged pursuit of definitive answers that would hopefully solve once and for all the riddle of the Stockport air disaster. In a series of static tests, the engines were uncoupled from the fuel pipes and replaced with special pumps to draw off the fuel at the rate the engines would use in flight. With this test rig, they could discover not only how much fuel was being used from each tank, but if there was any cross feeding going on; where it was coming from, where it was going and how much. Flights were simulated with the cross-feed levers closed and with them just a quarter of an inch open. Fuel tank pressures were recorded and compared along with a mass of other data. All this was done to discover if a distinct possibility could be actually proved beyond doubt. They also conducted tests with the engines running live for long periods, tests that would have been impossible in anything but the freezing weather prevailing at the time, because the engines would have overheated. Even fuel lines were replaced by clear tubing to see if any air entered the system which might have been a possible cause of the inboard number 3 engine failing. The outcome of these experiments would be of great importance to Harry Marlow, who was invited to Boscombe Down as an observer. Perhaps, after these tests, he would know for certain what had happened during those last seven minutes of that fatal flight.

The results from the Boscombe Down tests were of the highest significance. It was found that the design and positions of the tank selector and cross feed levers were totally unacceptable and could easily lead to the failure of a flight crewmember to notice a malpositioning of the levers. It was also discovered that just a slight misalignment of the cross-feed levers – as little as a quarter of an inch – could lead to fuel starvation and failure of an outboard engine, but did not lead to any ill effects on the inboard engines, even with the cross-feed levers grossly open. During the static rig tests and ground running tests, no air was drawn into the system either before or after the outboard tanks ran dry. In the light of this evidence, the investigation team came to the conclusion that whilst it remained highly likely that Hotel Golf's number 4 engine ceased to deliver power as a result of fuel starvation caused by exhaustion of the number 4 fuel tank, they still did not know with any certainty why the number 3 engine failed twenty seconds later now that the air theory had been totally disproved.

In March 1968, the Public Inquiry was resumed and the results of the Boscombe Down tests were accepted without question. When the inquiry was closed on 1 April 1968, the assessors took over, and for several months more, they sifted and evaluated all the available evidence. Finally, on 22 August 1968, the Crown theory of the cause of the accident was published in a detailed and lengthy report. In summary, it reported:

In our view, there can be really no doubt that the number 4 engine failed first, and failed because of fuel starvation from an empty number 4 fuel tank due to inadvertent fuel transfer through an improperly open fuel cock. We find it impossible on all the evidence before us to determine why the second engine failed. Following upon the Boscombe Down tests, we considered the following possibilities:

When the number 4 engine failed, it was misidentified by the crew as number 3, which was then feathered and its fuel shut off. Captain Marlow then found that after cleaning up the number 3 engine, the aircraft had developed handling problems, and was losing height, which should not have happened with three engines under power, and so came to the conclusion that the failure was in fact number 4. Number 3 was then unfeathered and number 4 feathered, but because of the high workload encountered by the crew, power was never restored to the number 3 engine in time to prevent the crash.

It may well have taken Captain Marlow some time to recognise that he had misidentified the engine which had failed. Once the correct identification had been made, although ample time was in theory available to sort out the mix-up, the demands upon the Captain struggling with the controls with one engine feathered and one windmilling, coupled with the consequent workload of the First Officer who had everything else to do himself, make it quite understandable if they failed to carry out the necessary drills to restore power to the number 3 engine in time.

For example, the number 3 tank selector lever would have had to be opened and the number 4 closed, because Captain Marlow would have had both hands on the control column, and could hardly have leaned forward to reach the selector levers in view of the very high foot loads, he had to apply to the rudder pedal with his left foot. Chris Pollard would have had to release his seat harness before he could lean forward to reach the selector levers situated on the left-hand side of the centre console. If this is what happened, it would make sense of Harry Marlow's question to Geoffrey Wilkinson whilst under sedation in hospital on the day after the crash, 'Which engine was it?'

The second possibility was that the number 3 tank had also run dry because of inadvertent fuel transfer during the homeward flight, through fuel transferring across

166

ships to the port tanks. When the cross-feed lever was checked during the approach, fuel, until then feeding number 3 engine through the slightly open cock from another tank, was cut off, number 3 engine would then fail almost immediately.

Our conclusions on the cause of the failure of the number 3 engine accordingly must be, that it was either misidentified as the failed engine, feathered and subsequently unfeathered but not got under power in time to prevent the crash; or that it also failed through fuel starvation following upon inadvertent fuel transfer, and only connected with the failure of number 4, in that it was the landing check of the cross feed and tank selector levers during the approach which finally cut off its fuel. To choose between these two possibilities would on the evidence before us be speculation.

The possibility of losing power on both engines on one side in a four-engined aircraft are normally considered to be remote and highly unlikely. The majority of pilots faced with an engine failure will respond correctly and feather the appropriate propeller following the specified drill. However, if a second engine should fail almost immediately after the first engine, particularly if the precise reason for that failure has not been positively determined; it is possible that the pilot may not respond as promptly as he may have done to the first engine failure. If the RPM of the windmilling engine were to approximate to the RPM selected on the two 'good' (functioning) engines, as was demonstrated in the test flights undertaken, it would be quite understandable for a pilot to fail to identify the failure of a second engine quickly. It is also possible that the pilot was carrying out the drill for feathering the propeller of the first engine failure when a second engine lost power presenting him with a major handling problem.

In the annals of civil aviation, there is a long history of cases where the wrong engine has been shut down and its propeller feathered, and must be considered as a very real possibility in this case, especially in the critical circumstances of a flight which was conductive to pilot error.

If Captain Marlow did misidentify the troublesome engine – which from my research I believe he did – it is not surprising, because of the lack of power failure warning indicators. The instrumentation on the Argonaut was crude compared to today's hi-tech civil aircraft; in fact, the instrument panel and displays had changed little since the 1930s designed DC-3 Dakota. Many of the flight deck instruments for instance were dual pointer – that is two pointers or hands for two engines on the same dial – such as the RPM indicators, manifold pressure, fuel flow and oil temperature and pressure gauges. Experience over the years has shown that multi-pointer instruments are susceptible to being misread, as the following incident, ironically to another Argonaut, clearly demonstrates:

On the 21 July 1950, a BOAC Argonaut was flying over the South Atlantic on a flight from Dakar to Natal. Approximately, three and a half hours after take off, cruising at 20,000 feet in darkness and clear weather, an engine, which the pilot identified as number 4, over sped to 3,500 rpm. He shut down and feathered the engine and almost immediately after, the number 3 over sped to 4,000 rpm and caught fire and the emergency feathering and fire drill was carried out. This action momentarily checked the fire but did not feather the propeller and after a second unsuccessful attempt at feathering, speed was reduced to 120 knots. At 02:25 GMT, an SOS was transmitted, together with the aircraft's course, and position.

With only the 1 and 2 engines on the port side operating and the number 3 propeller windmilling, the aircraft developed severe handling problems and was unable to maintain height. Under the circumstances, the pilot decided to restart the number 4 engine, which he did successfully and the engine ran without further trouble for some four hours until he made a successful landing at Fernando de Noronha.

Subsequent examination of the number 4 engine showed no mechanical problems or signs of over speeding. The conclusions were obvious, the pilot had misinterpreted the warning of the over speeding due to the dual pointer instrument and shutdown and feathered number 4 when all along, it was really the number 3 engine where the problem lay.

The same again happened in November 1957. A Dakota of East West Airlines took off from Sydney on a night flight to Tamworth, carrying 27 passengers and crew. Shortly after the aircraft became airborne, the pilot-in-command detected severe backfiring and feathered the port engine. He attempted to return to the airport but as the backfiring continued and the aircraft lost height, it had to be ditched in a lake two miles east of Sydney Airport. Fortunately, no one was injured. The probable cause of this accident was that the pilot, on becoming aware of an engine defect, took action to feather a propeller on the basis of evidence that was insufficient to ensure correct identification of the defective engine.

Dealing with Marlow's decision to overshoot when the emergency arose, the report said:

At the height and position of Hotel Golf in relation to Manchester Airport at the time, it would have been possible for Captain Marlow to reach the runway – even with one engine feathered and one windmilling – if take off power had been applied to numbers 1 and 2 engines. But it is clear from the ATC recordings that he was perplexed by what was happening to his aircraft and took the deliberate decision to overshoot in order to try to sort it out. Although in the event this decision proved to be disastrous because power was never restored on either engine and control difficulties were so great that he was unable to maintain height sufficiently to reach the airport.

He was faced by a wholly unexpected situation which even the most alert crew might have been unable to combat, and we think it was reasonable on his part to have come to this decision to overshoot rather than to carry straight on for an emergency landing with both engines on the starboard side out of action, and that for making this decision, he was not to blame.

The report went on to list the following contributory causes of the accident:

1. The failure of those responsible for the design of the fuel system and the fuel cocks to warn operators that the failure to place the actuating levers in the proper positions in the cockpit would result in the risk of inadvertent fuel transfer.

2. The failure of British Midland aircrews and engineers to recognise the possibility of inadvertent fuel transfer from the evidence available in flight (The Palma Incident) and that contained in the fuel logs.

3. The failure of other Argonaut/DC-4 operators who had learned by experience of inadvertent fuel transfer in flight and had not informed the relevant bodies of those facts.

It is a sad fact to realise that because of the foot-dragging incompetence of the authorities governing air safety at the time that this crucial safety information was not delivered to the airline and its crews. The cost of this inaction? Seventy-two wasted lives.

Added to this chaotic mix was the astonishing ineptitude of the Air Registration Board to grant the C-4 Argonaut a certificate of airworthiness in the first place which allowed it to enter service with BOAC. This decision was evidently questionable, but because of the vestige interests of all the parties concerned – BOAC, the Ministry of Aviation and the ARB to name a few – no one at the time dared to query the decision. I find it amazing how it was ever issued with a Certificate of Airworthiness in the first place. It suggests to me that the ARB was nonchalant at best and negligent at worst.

The results of the Public Inquiry and its recommendations brought no consolation to those who lost friends and relatives in the disaster, but one thing the report highlighted, was to stress the human element in the matter of communications within the airline industry. To quote from the report: *Air safety is as much a communications problem as a technical problem. We think the present voluntary system of incident reporting is on the right lines and moving in the right direction.*

This statement was absolute madness in that after the tragedy at Stockport with massive loss of life, they still believed that voluntary reporting of incidents was still the best way forward. If mandatory reporting had been in existence in 1953, the information BOAC then had about inadvertent fuel transfer on their Argonauts would certainly have been disseminated to other operators of the type, and would have most certainly averted the Stockport disaster. It was the passengers who paid the ultimate price for the disastrous failure and ineptitude within the airline industry and the aviation bodies responsible for air safety.

A copybook example of voluntary reporting gone wrong concerns two serious failures of Viscount cabin blower fires in 1964. The two incidents were certainly not known by the Australian operator, Ansett ANA, which lost a Viscount, with tragic loss of life, after suffering a similar failure. The subsequent Australian report discovered that the manufacturer of the faulty cabin blower regarded the fires in the two previous incidents as isolated cases. Therefore, they did not think that a suggested modification to the cabin blower was necessary, or indeed that other Viscount operators should be notified of the incidents. This, of course, turned out to be total error of judgement resulting two years later in another accident with the needless loss of 24 passengers and crew.

The report concluded that in future, the Argonaut should be operated with a three-man crew – an additional pilot or qualified engineer – a recommendation which was now meaningless as the Argonaut was soon withdrawn from service by the airline, and worldwide the type was on the brink of being regarded as obsolete regarding the safe transportation of passengers.

Harry Marlow accepted that the Public Inquiry had treated him fairly and was certainly dismayed that he had to give up flying on medical grounds, which was his first love. Commenting to the press on the findings of the inquiry, he said: "I anticipated the report would say something like this and I am glad to know I have been cleared of blame. I think they have given me a certain amount of praise for getting the aircraft down in that particular place. If it had not been for post-crash fire, then certainly a lot more passengers would have been saved. That fuel trouble…there was no way of anyone knowing. I now only wish I could get back to flying which has been my life since I joined the RAF during the war, and I still think I could fly again. Apart from some back trouble and a knee injury, I feel physically and mentally fine."

With the publication of the report, the investigation was officially closed, although a number of loose ends were left unresolved and a number of questions still remained unanswered. The travelling public eagerly read and digested the published findings; but were the final conclusions as clear-cut as the evidence in the final report suggested?

Chapter Sixteen
Had It All Happened Before?

"Those who cannot learn from history are condemned to repeat it."
Old aviation maxim

In 1962, Britain's Minister for Aviation published a paper on aviation safety, which said in part:

Progress in aviation safety depends partly on foreseeing problems before they arise, and partly on learning the lessons of experiment and experience and spreading this knowledge to all those concerned, by *force* if necessary.

Clearly, in the light of what occurred in Stockport five years later, none of those recommendations were ever heeded or put into practice. The cost of this inaction – seventy-two wasted lives.

It seemed that nothing at all was learned from the prolonged investigation and demonstrates a certain amount of complacency surrounding the subject of air safety. It seems to me utterly incomprehensible, that after all the incidents of inadvertent fuel transfer recorded since the Canadair C-4 Argonaut entered service with BOAC in 1949, in addition to those incidents on British operated DC-4s, that nothing was ever done to 'root out the rot'.

If those persons responsible for analysing those incidents had been forced by law to pass on the information with urgency, it would have immediately highlighted the fuel related incidents caused by the flawed design of the fuel system. If a thorough in-depth investigation had been undertaken at the time, it would have unearthed the problem and disseminated to other operators of the type. If that had been done, then without any doubt, the Stockport disaster would have been averted.

The Board of Trade's safety officials stated at the Public Inquiry that they were totally satisfied with the voluntary system of incident reporting that was currently in place. This soft carpet slipper approach as against that of the jackboot was, it seemed, the gentlemanly and British preferred way of doing things. But this foot dragging approach allowed needless tragedy after needless tragedy to happen, simply because the lessons of an incident, that could quite easily have been an accident, were not seriously investigated and the results propagated to other interested parties.

The reasons behind the Stockport air disaster were never as straight forward or satisfactory resolved conclusively as the official report suggested. During my research, I discovered that inadvertent fuel transfer accidents and incidents involving the Douglas DC-4, C-54, the Argonaut, North Star and all its variants were commonplace. Incident reporting should never be neglected, because incidents – as aviation history tells us – are always the forerunners of serious fatal accidents. A noteworthy example of this, and certainly a precursor for the Stockport disaster, was the Starways DC-4 accident at Dublin in 1961.

I was alerted to this startling case by retired senior airline pilot Captain Douglas Wyles who served with BOAC and British Airways for some 25 years. Following up this information, my research took me into previously uncharted waters. Although reference to the Starways accident report was offered for discussion in the Public Inquiry, it was quickly dismissed and never alluded to thereafter. The parallels between the Dublin and Stockport accidents are astonishing. It is worth here taking a detailed look at the case.

On 19 September 1961, a Starways DC-4 departed empty on a flight from Liverpool Airport bound for Tarbes (Lourdes) in southern France where it would embark 69 Irish pilgrims and fly them back to Dublin. The aircraft was under the command of 34-year-old Captain Ian Johnson Maclean. He was a very experienced airline pilot and had been flying commercial transport aircraft since 1953. Besides being qualified to fly the DC-4, his licence was endorsed to command Viking and Dakota aircraft. Up to the time of the accident, he had an impressive total of 6,049 flying hours to his credit.

His First Officer assisting him on the flight was 54-year-old Bill Isaacs, who had first learned to fly in India in 1934; he too was also experienced on Viking and Dakota aircraft. By a startling coincidence, Bill Isaacs, the reader will recall, was the co-pilot killed in the Air Ferry accident at Perpignan the evening before the Stockport crash. Also carried on the flight were two stewardesses who were there to look after the catering and safety of the returning passengers.

The flight to Tarbes took four hours and five minutes and was in all respects uneventful. Captain Maclean assumed a round figure of 250 US gallons per engine as the fuel consumption for the return flight to Dublin, and requested Esso – the refuelling agents – to put 100 US gallons in each tank, which was roughly the amount burnt off during the outbound flight. After refuelling was completed, the tank contents were checked by dipstick and the figures reported to the captain. The amount of fuel uploaded was more than sufficient for the flight to Dublin with a reserve if they needed to divert to their alternate – in this case Shannon.

The aircraft took off at 17:10, and the flight was made under Instrument Flight Rules at a cruise altitude of 6,000 feet until some 10 minutes before arrival at Dublin when the descent was commenced. Operation was normal throughout the flight with each engine drawing fuel from its own tank. As it was still light and the visibility good, Captain Maclean informed Dublin control his intention of making a visual approach. On the downwind leg of the airport circuit, the routine approach check was carried out by the crew – just as Harry Marlow and Chris Pollard did on the approach to Manchester. This includes checking the fuel contents gauges, ensuring that the main tank selector valves were 'ON' and fuel cross feed valves 'OFF' and in addition switching on the fuel booster pumps.

Checking of the fuel contents gauges was carried out by Bill Isaacs who noted that the number 1 gauge was reading 80 US gallons with the needle fluctuating. As the aircraft turned onto the final approach to the runway, the number 1 port outer engine abruptly ceased to deliver power and the propeller spluttered to a stop. Captain Maclean assumed from his previous experiences flying DC-4s that fuel starvation was the root cause of the failure. In response, he immediately opened the number 1 and 2 cross feed cocks to try and maintain a fuel supply to the number one engine. Six seconds later as the turn was completed to line up with the runway, the number 2 engine – the port inner – also failed causing the aircraft to swing sharply to the left. With the loss of two engines on one side, Captain Maclean experienced severe control difficulties and all his efforts went into trying to keep the aircraft straight and level. He ordered his co-pilot to open all the cross-feed selectors. This was done, but there was no restoration of power to either port engines. Power on the two functioning starboard engines had been increased to 2,550 RPM after the first engine failure and now had to be further increased to full take off rating to avoid losing air speed and sacrificing height. In this condition with both port propellers windmilling in the airflow, control of the aircraft was becoming critical even with the First Officer assisting. Even with full right rudder applied, the aircraft swung appreciably to the left away from the line of approach. Height above the airfield after the second engine failure was estimated at less than 300 feet. Visibility was reasonably good and Bill Isaacs saw to the left a group of illuminated hangars and a stretch of green fields beyond. He pointed this out to Captain Maclean, who then allowed the aircraft to swing further left skirting the northeast end of a large hangar. An aircraft engineer working on an Aer Lingus Boeing 720 on the apron was alarmed to see that the DC-4 was 'clearly way off course and in difficulties' heading for the area between two hangars. It then made a turn of increasing steepness in order to clear the gable end of the hangar and was at this point so low that eye-witnesses describe the port wing as 'hedge clipping'.

After safely clearing the hangar, Captain Maclean managed to level the aircraft and make a successful belly landing in an open field. After ploughing through a hedge, the aircraft finally came to rest across the main Dublin to Belfast road. Unlike Stockport, this accident did have a happy ending. Damage to the aircraft was minimal and with the help of the cabin crew and passers-by, all 69 passengers managed to evacuate the aircraft via the main cabin door and emergency exits without serious injury – which goes to prove the old aviation adage that: 'a good landing is one you can walk away from!'

Given that this was a charter flight from Lourdes, it could truly be said that all those pilgrims on board had a truly miraculous escape. One devout and pious couple from County Offaly told a reporter that they attributed their survival to bottles of Holy Water they were carrying at the time. One very nervous priest accompanying the party was observed in the final seconds of flight with a rosary in one hand and a glass of whisky earnestly gripped in the other! It is in situations like this that the passengers – and even the crew – become very religious.

The Dublin Airport fire service arrived at the scene within minutes; fortunately, there was no post-crash fire. Because of the failing light and the onset of heavy rain, it was decided to defer the detailed examination of the aircraft until the following morning.

Given the circumstances of the accident, the investigation immediately focused on the fuel system and a dipstick examination of the fuel remaining in the tanks was made. It was discovered that the number 1 tank supplying the number 1 engine – which failed first – was completely empty. The number 2 tank contained 120 gallons; number 3 – 230 gallons and number 4 tank 106 gallons. At the same time, fuel samples were taken to check for contamination, the results of which were negative. The accident investigators found no evidence of failure or defect in the aircraft or in its fuel system, and the total fuel load on board was of the correct grade and sufficient for the flight.

The published report on the accident concluded that: *'shortcomings in fuel management (by the flight crew) were the major contributory factor in the accident...which resulted in partial loss of power and control and a forced landing outside the airport'.* The wording is suspiciously deceptive given the fact that on this particular flight the aircraft was operated on a tank to engine basis involving no cross feeding. The only other possibility for the double engine power loss was inadvertent fuel transfer during the flight due to an improperly closed cross feed lever. This is exactly what occurred to Hotel Golf on its approach to Stockport.

What the inquiry never asked – and the published report does not even attempt to answer – is why an experienced aircrew, who knew the DC-4 fuel system inside out, could possibly have mismanaged the system. The verdict was, in other words, 'pilot error', which was particularly hard on Captain Maclean, who had previously enjoyed an unblemished professional reputation.

After reading and studying the Dublin accident in depth, I had an ominous feeling of *déjà vu.* Looking a bit more deeply into the circumstances, the evidence suggests to me that fuel starvation – like Stockport – was the real factor in this accident and the 'fuel mismanagement' by the flight crew in my view is questionable.

Checking the transcripts from the Stockport inquiry, I found that the Dublin accident report was offered in evidence on day fifteen of the inquiry and was briefly alluded to when William Tench, an extremely knowledgeable expert from the AIB took the stand to give evidence. There is no doubt that he knew a great deal more about the Dublin incident than he was willing to disclose. When cross-examined, he was extremely careful to skirt the real issues surrounding the Dublin accident; in fact, all his replies were evasive and non-committal. When directly asked that fuel starvation, caused by a miss-aligned levers was the possible cause, he became evasive and would not be drawn to give his opinion:

Q. Have you considered the findings into the accident to the Starways Douglas DC-4 at Dublin, which occurred when the aircraft ran out of fuel on two engines on its final approach to the airport?

A. With respect, I think this was an Irish inquiry, was it not?

Warming to his task, the questioner pressed the point: It may well have been. I am just wondering if you have applied your mind to it?

A. I would certainly hesitate to criticise anybody else's report. I think this is not our purpose at all.

Q. Could you say anything as a result of reading that report as to whether or not it will assist this court?

Tench was not the type of individual to be easily intimidated and give in under pressure; refusing to be browbeaten, he replied, "I do hesitate to intrude upon a report written by another authority."

Despite the robust probing from the questioner, Tench steadfastly refused to be drawn to comment, making it perfectly clear that the matter, as far as he was concerned, was not up for further discussion. With that brief interchange, the subject was dropped and the Dublin accident never alluded to again. Tench stepped down from the witness box and left the room still smarting from the cross-examination.

There can be no doubt that Tench was trying to distance himself and the AIB from the Dublin incident. On the face of it, his answers – or lack of them – were rather odd. It was quite clear that he knew the full details of the Dublin incident, as representatives from the AIB Farnborough assisted the Irish authorities in the investigation. In June 1963, they issued their findings in the UK report – CAP 190 published by HMSO – available to members of the general public for the princely sum of three shillings and sixpence. As I type these words, a copy of the report from my own technical library sits on my desk and the evidence within is there for all to see.

Throughout the questioning, Tench made out to be ignorant of any details regarding the Dublin incident. He certainly showed reluctance to reveal what he and the AIB already knew about the causes of the Dublin incident, and by implication, knowledge of the dangers of fuel starvation on the DC-4/Argonaut type at least six years before Stockport. Understandably, Tench was very cautious and careful not to say anything that would embarrass him and the AIB which he represented.

It is interesting to note that the Dublin accident report gives the following recommendation:

Particular care should be taken, especially in the case of aircraft of this type (DC-4/ Argonaut) which has seen considerable service, to establish by physical test the actual capacities of fuel tanks and the accuracy of dipsticks.

This recommendation certainly suggests that during flight, fuel was migrating from tank to tank via partially open fuel cocks.

If the Dublin accident report had been studied closely by the aviation safety authorities in 1961, it would have pre-warned of the possible dangers of inadvertent fuel transfer and fuel starvation on aircraft of the DC-4/Argonaut type and further investigation would have most certainly brought to light the BOAC incidents in 1953/54.

The evidence in the Dublin report is damming. For me, this was the clinching evidence that the Starways accident was not caused by fuel mismanagement by the crew but by inadvertent fuel transfer during the flight – it was too great a coincidence. The Dublin accident, to all intents and purposes, was a carbon copy of the Stockport disaster and should have been investigated further.

The parallels between the Dublin and Stockport accidents are startling.

1. The aircraft was a Douglas DC-4, almost identical to the Argonaut with an identical fuel system.
2. Both aircraft at the time of the emergency were on the approach check when the emergency began.
3. In each case, an outboard engine failed first, followed seconds later by the failure of an inboard engine on the same wing.
4. After the loss of two engines, both aircraft suffered severe control difficulties and began to rapidly lose height.
5. The captain had no alternative but to put the aircraft down in the nearest open space.

Added to all this was the disturbing fact that BOAC, Invicta Airlines, Aer Lingus amongst other DC-4, Carvair and Argonaut operators had experienced and reported incidents of inadvertent fuel transfer to the relevant aviation authority years before, and in BOAC's case, the manufacturers Canadair. Knowing something was seriously amiss with the design of the fuel system, the aviation authorities failed to truly understand the ominous significance; they sat tight and did nothing.

As far as Canadair were concerned, the BOAC incidents were, in their view, just isolated incidents and felt there was no necessity to pass on this information to other operators, nor did they make any efforts to have the C-4 Argonaut operating manuals amended to warn flight crews of the problem. In addition, those authorities governing air safety failed miserably to assess and heed the very real implications of these incidents. The end result was that it took 18-years of Argonaut and DC-4 operation before the tragic loss of Hotel Golf highlighted the very real design faults in the fuel system.

There is enough information from the Starways Dublin accident alone to cast doubt on the findings of the Stockport Public Inquiry – enough doubt in fact to press for a new investigation. But after half-a-century, there is of course the temptation to say 'let the victims rest in peace'. But the issues raised are far too important, indeed the victims, relatives and the people of Stockport will not rest until they are fully satisfied that all the facts about the disaster are fully brought out. Perhaps there is the view, because it all happened so long ago, that there is little that can be done to address these issues and no doubt after fifty-years, it would be pointless and distressing for both survivors and relatives of the victims.

All the evidence I have uncovered suggests that inadvertent fuel transfer goes back many years. For example, there is the testimony, not widely reported at the time, of a former RAF flight engineer who served on the Merlin-engined Lancaster bombers during the Second World War. He lived a few miles from the threshold of runway 24 at Ringway. He clearly heard the Argonaut's faltering engines when it initiated the overshoot – the cloud base was too low for him to see it. On hearing the discordant sounds, he knew instinctively from his wartime experience that: "The sound of the spluttering and popping was unmistakable classic Merlin engine fuel starvation noises that I knew so well from my time on the Lancaster. I found it amazing that the crew risked an overshoot. I'd have thought that any shot at landing would have been preferable if the engines are giving up like that."

One of the earliest incidents I came across directly attributed to inadvertent fuel transfer causing fuel starvation occurred as far back as 1948.

On 7 January of that year, a Coastal Airlines Dakota was *en route* between Charleston and Savannah, Georgia, when both engines suddenly stopped. Multiple attempts to restart the engines failed and the crew prepared for an emergency landing. Unfortunately, before the pilot could get the aircraft on the ground it stalled and crashed killing 18 of the 27 occupants. The subsequent investigation concluded that because of a misaligned fuel cock, both engines were being supplied fuel from a single tank which, in due course ran dry causing fuel starvation to both engines.

Another incident a year later involved a Douglas C-54 – the military designation of the DC-4. The aircraft had been chartered from the British independent operator, Skyways, by the War Office to transport military personnel from Nairobi back to the UK.

Early on the evening of 4 February, it landed at Khartoum for a refuelling stop and departed at 1905 hours to make the 1,700-mile direct crossing of the Libyan desert to Castel Benito. Most of the flight was flown at 8,500 feet in clear weather, but thunder and rain were encountered for the last 200 miles. After flying over Castel Benito, the pilot began his let down to the west of the airport in heavy rain and poor visibility. At approximately 700 feet whilst descending downwind towards the airport, the port outer engine suddenly failed, followed approximately 20 seconds later by the port inner. The aircraft immediately lost height, became uncontrollable and crashed killing the pilot.

The report into the accident attributed the cause to the failure by the captain to maintain a safe height after the emergency arose by utilising the available power of the starboard engines. The power failure in both port engines was undoubtedly caused by fuel starvation. This fuel shortage was the result of the port wing tanks being allowed to become progressively unbalanced during the latter stages of the flight. An attempt by the flight engineer to cross feed the port engines from the starboard tanks failed owing to the full operation not having been carried out in time.

Another classic fuel related case occurred in 1955 to a DC-4 operated by the Flying Tiger Line flying over the Pacific Ocean. The number 1 port outer engine without warning spluttered to an abrupt stop. The captain mistakenly placed number 2 and 3 fuel selectors to the near empty auxiliary tanks and shortly thereafter, numbers 2 and 3 engines also ceased to deliver power. After failing to restart engines 1, 2 and 3, the propellers were feathered and full power was applied to the number 4 engine. During the descent, numbers 1 and 2 propellers were unfeathered and separate attempts to restart the engines were unsuccessful. The number 3 propeller was then unfeathered and the captain was attempting to restart that engine when the aircraft struck the water.

The board of inquiry determined – unfairly in my opinion – that the probable cause of the accident was the loss of power in three engines was due to incorrect fuel system management and faulty restarting methods by the crew. Studying this case, I believe the fuel starvation to the engines caused by inadvertent fuel transfer was the primary cause.

It will be recalled by the reader that the day following the Stockport and Perpignan disasters, questions were raised in the House of Commons following public concern over the recent crashes. For his part, Douglas Jay, the President of the Board of Trade announced that a 'special review' into the performance and safety of all British airlines. But two weeks later, it emerged that the review was going to be a hush-hush affair. No evidence would be taken from outside aviation experts or from airline pilots and no formal report would be published – it was going to be purely interdepartmental.

The Board of Trade 'secret probe' was undertaken by the Directorate of Flight Safety, which at the time vetted all British airline operators. It was a department that was totally understaffed and overworked and it was difficult to see what facts it could uncover that it didn't already know. It looked to the jaundiced eye as if, after the Stockport and Perpignan disasters, the government departments responsible for air safety had to be seen by the public to be doing something worthy of their existence.

Many in the aviation industry with very real concerns about safety and the lack of enforcement of the regulations by the Board, would have welcomed a thorough review and overhauling of the entire system by which British airline safety regulations are made and policed. In the end, no doubt due to pressure from other quarters, the Board of Trade did publish a report of sorts in 1968, entitled – *The Safety Performances of United Kingdom Airline Operators.* Surprisingly, the report was a frank and critical examination of the whole of the British airline industry and the government departments overseeing their regulations. The report's conclusions refer to the operational record of the then forty-one operators of public transport aircraft; varying in size from the two national flag carriers – BOAC and BEA, the larger independents right down to the small companies operating a handful of light aircraft. The report did little to enhance air safety.

I conducted my own research into the British aviation standards of the period and it didn't take much digging to uncover a disturbing situation. If the truth be known, it was in a shocking state of disarray which greatly compromised the safety of the British travelling public. I found a truly bizarre situation in place where safety standards were maintained almost on a basis of trust between the airlines and the regulatory body concerned. For example, routine checks on the maintenance of aircraft and the standards of pilots were overseen by employees of the same airline – a sort of police policing the police situation.

I discovered that the Board of Trade was supposed to have at least a minimum of 30 flight operations inspectors, all of whom had to be qualified pilots with airline experience. In 1967, there were just 20, and it was virtually impossible to recruit the full complement because of the low salary offered, which was substantially less than an experienced pilot could earn with an airline. The Board was also supposed to make routine and snap checks on all British airlines operating services all over the world. I found that there were in fact only 16 flight examiners on the books with the ultimate responsibility for checking up and maintaining the required flying standards of some 4,000 pilots holding British commercial licences – an impossible task for an understaffed department of that size to carry out. For example, after first obtaining his commercial licence, a pilot may never be checked by a Board of Trade examiner in many years of airline flying, if at all. His six-monthly competency checks would be overseen by a 'check' pilot – approved by the Board and employed by the same airline. The Boards own flight examiners were only in a position to 'check the checkers' and approve them to vet the pilots in their own airline. This was a system that was inherently unsafe. During the 1960s, proposals to make government examiners do *all* the checks on pilots were turned down largely on the grounds of cost. To do this, the Board would have needed to employ several hundred pilots to undertake and keep pace with this monumental task.

Ensuring that aircraft, engines and equipment installed in the aircraft are serviced and kept in good order – in other words fit to fly – was the responsibility of yet another government department – the Air Registration Board – this, the reader will recall, was the very same department responsible in 1949 for cutting corners and issuing the Canadair C-4 with its British certificate of airworthiness, so clearing it to carry unsuspecting passengers. Here again was a delegated system, in which licensed engineers within an airline can check and pass the work of their colleagues.

I also found that a Certificate of Airworthiness could be renewed before the necessary test flight had actually been made and reported upon. It was the legal duty of the ARB to see that the test had been carried out and not rely on or trust the operator to make the test *'as and when it considered it convenient'* and to submit the results of test to the ARB *'as and when airline thinks fit'*. Both for pilots and engineers, there were fears that this divided loyalty – a man being both an airline employee and a government inspector – could be a dangerous thing and somewhere along the line lead to accidents.

Another safety issue under serious discussion at the time was the excessive number of flying hours a commercial pilot was subjected to by his airline. Throughout 1967, a fierce row ensued between the British Airline Pilots Association (BALPA) and the British aviation authorities over pilots' duty hours; a dispute that had rumbled on for almost two years.

A French civil aviation accident investigator said at the time: "Our knowledge about air crew fatigue may well prove to be the chief explanation of accidents that have been put down in the past to 'pilot error' or the 'human factor' simply because we don't understand what makes an experienced, well qualified and conscientious pilot commit almost unbelievably stupid mistakes." Those stupid mistakes include, misreading instruments, failure to recognise the causes of a sudden emergency and delay in reacting to it, trying to land in low visibility instead of diverting and miscellaneous general bog-standard errors, especially at the end of a long tiring period of duty.

A proposal, originally suggested by Board of Trade officials, to cut maximum flight duty hours from 15 to 12, was suddenly shelved after protests from the airline operators, who, of course, were concerned less about the safety of its passengers and more about their profit margins in what was at the time a very competitive industry. Having given way under pressure from the airlines, the Board had to be seen doing something useful to justify their existence, so they issued a set of watered-down guidelines which were nothing more than a face-saving exercise. Some pilots called these recommendations nothing more than a 'licence to kill'. It was beyond stupid.

It was well known at the time that extreme accumulative fatigue could leave a pilot drunk with exhaustion, with fatal consequences. One of the most fatiguing factors – which at the time affected the majority of charter flights – was that of night duty. It was certainly known from all the research and studies previously undertaken, that alertness and the speed of mental reactions fall appreciably during this period.

One experienced, and very much overworked charter pilot responded to the Board of Trade recommendations with scorn and angrily commented: 'What the operators and legislators don't seem to take into account is the accumulative factor. After three hectic nights flying backwards and forwards to the continent with holidaymakers, fatigue is quicker to take effect. After one particular busy week during a long night flight when the autopilot was engaged, I told my co-pilot I was going to have a quick nap. Suddenly, I woke up to find him asleep as well. There we were with 12,000 horsepower thundering through the night sky at 400 mph and everyone on the flight deck asleep! If the man responsible for coming up with this legislative shambles regarding flight duty time was willing to take the risk and board my aircraft, I would look him straight in the eyes and yell at him in no uncertain terms: "SIT DOWN MAN... YOU'RE A BLOODY DISGRACE!"

A controversial report issued by BALPA in 1973 gave added impact to the growing concerns regarding crew fatigue. The 150-page document blamed six of the ten major crashes of British airliners between 1966 and 1970 on nothing more complicated than pilot exhaustion. It noted that all six accidents, in which 257 lives were lost, occurred during take off and landing, *'when workload is highest and fatigue at its worst'*. In five of the accidents, *'the flight crew apparently flew a perfectly serviceable aircraft into the ground'*.

One of those accidents, a Britannia carrying British holidaymakers crashed on the approach to Ljubljana, killing 98 passengers and crew. In this case, fatigue was a pertinent question. According to the accident report, the aircraft crashed because the captain failed to adjust his altimeter setting, resulting in the approach being made approximately 1,250 feet lower that the safety altitude. Because of the good visibility in moonlight, the crew could not distinguish any landmarks which might have alerted them to their low altitude. Although the inquiry found no direct evidence to prove fatigue, it could not be excluded. The captain had flown close to the then maximum legal limit for the previous two months before the accident and the co-pilot's duty time was also close to the limit.

One captain on an intercontinental flight to Darwin, Australia, reported that after 14 hours of continuous duty and 25 hours without sleep 'my first officer fell asleep more than once – in fact I had to wake him to give him the approach briefing'. In yet another case, a pilot dozed off at the end of the runway whilst awaiting clearance to take off on a London to Frankfurt flight. In another instance, an exhausted flight crew missed an airport altogether and landed at Sharjah on the Persian Gulf rather than at Dubai, which is six miles away.

But all this was nothing new. In a Commons debate on civil aviation back in 1959, *Hansard* reported that opposition MPs claimed that the Ministry of Aviation had not been tough enough in regulating the airline industry; not robustly policing maintenance requirements and not closing the legal loophole which allowed fatigued pilots to continue flying during what should have been their designated rest periods.

One must ask what was contained in that inter departmental 'hush hush' review undertaken in 1967 as a 'knee jerk' reaction by the Ministry of Aviation to the Perpignan and Stockport disasters that was deemed too unpalatable for the travelling public's consumption. The answer was simple and straightforward: *The vested interests of other parties involved* – in other words 'profit' for the airlines and their shareholders. Airlines in the 1960s, especially the independents, may well have wanted to operate safe services, but their primary aim above all else was to make money and stay in business. When it comes to safety versus profit, profit will win out every time.

Looking back over the years, we have seen tremendous advances in air safety; it seems laughable now that the whole Argonaut saga was one long catalogue of poor legislation poor overseeing of air safety and probably above all bloody-minded institutionalised complacency that led to the 72 tragic deaths at Stockport. The fact that this could have occurred in a Britain where air safety legislation was assumed to have the highest level of professional competency is astounding.

In truth, safety in civil aviation is only secured once enough people have died to convince those with their hands on the chequebook to splash out on better safety standards. There is no doubt in my mind that all safety standards and improvements over the years are built on the remains and memories of the unfortunate victims.

Sadly, as it always is, it took a totally preventable accident that unnecessarily took the lives of 72 men, women and children and the subsequent public outcry for the authorities governing air safety to react and make the necessary changes to prevent such disasters happening again. As ever, hindsight is a wonderful thing, but it begs the often-repeated question: why does it always seem to take accidents with accompanying massive loss of life to get anything done?

Another issue raised in the immediate aftermath of the Perpignan and Stockport accidents was the age of both aircraft involved. When does an airliner become old you may ask? There is no magic formula to determine this, everything depends on the types design, the individual airframe history and its maintenance record; it is certainly not just a geriatric problem. Take for example the ubiquitous Douglas DC-3 Dakota, regarded as the most significant transport aircraft ever produced, outselling any other type. It first entered service way back in 1936 and immediately revolutionised civil aviation and soon became standard equipment of most of the world's airlines – in fact, it was the only aircraft at the time capable of making money for the operators. It was very advanced aerodynamically, versatile, rugged and simple to fly and operate with a reliability that kept the airlines in business. Even to this day, there are still a handful of trusty old DC-3s in revenue earning service around the world and no doubt, there will be a few airworthy examples still flying when it reaches its centenary in 2036. One Dakota pilot is reputed to have said to one of his passengers after querying the age of the aircraft: "Lady, do you really want me to answer you if this old aeroplane is safe? Just how in the world do you think it got to be this old?"

Over the years, a number of attempts have been made to design and build a DC-3 replacement. The aircraft manufactures saw a huge potential market for such an aircraft. The British Hawker Siddeley 748, Fokker F27 Friendship and the Handley Page Herald are just a few examples that were successful in their own right, but none of these came anywhere close to matching the versatility or reliability of the original. In the end, the DC-3 Dakota outlived them all. Aircraft come and go, but very few have left such an indelible mark as the DC-3 has on aviation history and it is the perfect example that age is no barrier to a proven, reliable and safe aeroplane. There is a saying in the aviation industry that the only replacement for a DC-3 is a DC-3!

However, the Canadair C-4 Argonaut did not fare so well in the long-levity stakes. Besides the fuel system design fault, it had many other shortcomings and it is clear that if the type had been offered up for certification in the UK in 1967, it would, under the higher standards then set, have been rejected outright as un-airworthy and therefore unsafe to carry passengers. However, this was not retrospective legislation and the ARB – which is empowered to withdraw certificates of airworthiness at any time if they believe an aircraft, or part of it, does not come up to the required standards – continued each and every year since 1949 to give the type its annual certificate of airworthiness enabling British Midland to keep their Argonauts flying and allowing unsuspecting holidaymakers to happily go off on holiday believing that the aircraft was safe and airworthy.

Chapter Seventeen
In Memoriam

All were faced with the true horror of tragedy and did not turn away.
Memorial inscription

Life moves relentlessly forward, and we as humans tend to forget those disastrous events in which so many tragically lose their lives, and it is particularly disturbing when the cause of those deaths was totally preventable. Today, the disaster is a distant memory for most. If you ask, the average Stockport senior citizen if they recall the air disaster, they either have vague memories or none at all. For those born after the event, there is of course no recollection. As each year passes, those directly involved diminish and gradually, the memory fades from Stockport's collective consciousness. One day soon, perhaps very soon, there won't be anyone alive who was around at the time to remember. As one of Britain's worst ever civil aviation accidents, it has disappeared entirely from the national consciousness. Yet despite the passage of fifty years, there are a handful of individuals still alive who will never forget that day and its immediate aftermath; for them, the anniversary on 4 June each year rewinds like a grainy black and white home movie.

In some respects, the disaster has cast a shadow over the town that the local authority has found difficult to dispel. It has been suggested by some that the civic leaders have done their utmost over the succeeding years to play down the event, for the simple and understandable reason that whenever the town features in the national news, it is almost inevitable that the subject of the accident crops up. Clearly, they did not want Stockport to be known only as a disaster first and a town second, or to be constantly referred to as that 'bad news town'.

However, considering the sheer enormity of the tragedy in the annals of British civil aviation and the fact that it was Stockport's greatest catastrophe in its 1,000-year history, there wasn't a single volume which chronicled the events. Even books detailing the history of the township gave the disaster little more than a few lines in passing – giving the briefest of details, which for the most part were erroneous. The Central Library in Stockport does hold a mediocre amount of yellowing newspaper clippings and press photographs. Apart from these negligible items, there is little else.

As the thirtieth anniversary approached in 1997, there was not only renewed interest in the events but controversy also. Many questions were asked by survivors, relatives and others directly involved, as to why the crash site had lain unmarked all these years. This is a question I couldn't answer, but during my research into the local authority archives, I uncovered documentation and plans that had been drawn up in 1977 for a proposed memorial garden to be built on the site to commemorate the tenth anniversary – but for various undisclosed reasons, these proposals were never carried through. It is rumoured that some civic leaders and a number of councillors secretly blocked the plans in the belief that it would only bring renewed notoriety to the town and wanted to erase this part of the town's history. And if possible, sweep the subject under the carpet as if it had never happened and hope that in time it would just go away. In the following two decades, the subject did indeed go away, but as the 30th anniversary approached in 1997, local baker and rescuer, Brian Donohoe and I joined together and formulated a campaign to have a permanent memorial erected on the site. We were initially met with resistance from a certain number within the local authority, but with the publicity generated in the media, they were quick to come onboard. With the tremendous support of survivors, relatives and others, the campaign for the memorial quickly gathered apace.

The author with rescuer Brian Donohoe at the memorial unveiling in 1998 (author's archive).

On a Sunday morning in June 1998, the rain fell again at Hopes Carr, just as it did thirty-one years earlier, reviving sharp painful memories for those assembled at the crash site. Some 400 invited guests – made up of survivors, relatives and friends, along with those members of the emergency services and civilians directly involved in the rescue and recovery gathered on the corner of Hopes Carr and Waterloo Road to remember.

It was oddly disturbing for some of the survivors returning to the crash site where their memories after thirty years remained fresh and vivid. For many of the relatives, it was the first time they had visited the scene where their loved ones perished. They came in trepidation in what for them had been at the time a living nightmare. For others, it was a personal exorcism, a cathartic exercise, a way of finally coming to terms with those events and to lay the ghosts and personal demons to rest. It helped them close the circle and draw a line under the tragedy enabling them perhaps for the first time to live in the present and concentrate on the future.

Because of his close association with the accident, it was appropriate that the Reverend Arthur Connop officiated at the unveiling and service of commemoration; his presence lending eloquence and gravitas to the occasion. Despite a torrential downpour, the service was a moving, dignified and uplifting occasion. At 10:09, the precise moment Hotel Golf plunged from the sky, Vivienne Thornber, alongside fellow survivors Harold Wood and David Ralphs unveiled the memorial in memory of all those who would never fly again. The memorial in the form of a rough-hewn stone, inset with a bronze plaque bears the simple legend:

IN MEMORY
OF THE SEVENTY-TWO PASSENGERS
AND CREW
WHO LOST THEIR LIVES
IN THE
STOCKPORT AIR DISASTER
4th JUNE 1967

Memorial unveiling in June 1998. L to R: David Ralphs (survivor), Steve Morrin (author), Vivienne Thornber (survivor), Brian Donohoe (rescuer) and Harold Wood (survivor).

Following the unveiling, a civic reception was held at the nearby Town Hall giving those attending the opportunity to renew old friendships that had fallen into abeyance and in many cases form new ones. The close bonds forged between the survivors and their rescuers were apparent as they met again for the first time. Arthur Connop believed that for the relatives, the unveiling and commemoration had enabled them, after more than three decades, to come out of the shadow of their grief and associate with others, making a transition from a 'Fellowship of Suffering' to an alliance of 'Thankful Remembrance'. As a passionate campaigner for the memorial, I was immensely proud to be part of their day.

A week after the service, Bertha Thorniley of the Salvation Army told me of the personal comfort that she and her husband, Arthur, gained from attending the ceremony and having the opportunity to meet some of the survivors for the first time: "The thing I appreciate about all this," she said, "was being there at the memorial unveiling and meeting three of the survivors and being able to talk to them. Because those are the three people I will hang on to and remember. Arthur and I have talked about this, and we both agree that this was the best thing that has happened to us – the fact that we were able to meet and talk to some of those who were rescued and survived, instead of having the awful memory over the past thirty years of the people who didn't."

One individual who has been consistently overlooked for his part in averting an even far greater loss of life on the ground was Hotel Golf's commander, Captain Harry Marlow. It was clear from all evidence and eyewitness accounts that when he realised an accident was inevitable, he showed great coolness in the face of overwhelming odds and deliberately aimed his stricken aircraft towards the only relatively open space in the town centre. His split-second decision and airmanship ensured that there were no casualties on the ground. If he hadn't carried out this manoeuvre, then it would have been far worse. For beyond the crash site, in the aircraft's direct flight path, are four 150-foot residential tower blocks housing scores of families, police headquarters and the infirmary. We should be grateful to Harry Marlow.

One would have expected recognition of these facts to follow swiftly, but this was not to be. Over the coming decades, his part in the events was largely forgotten. With this in mind, I took the opportunity of the approaching 35th anniversary to put forward a proposal with the local authority to recognise his exemplary piece of flying that day.

His son, Robert, was one of the hundreds who defied the bad weather to attend the service of remembrance at the memorial site in June 2002. He received from Stockport Mayor, David Brailsford, on behalf of his father, a silver plaque engraved with the simple words: *To Captain Harry Marlow, with thanks from the people of Stockport.* Robert commented: "My father is a shy man, but he appreciates this kind gesture. He would also like to thank all those Stockport people who at the time sent him their good wishes."

To be fair and balanced, I must mention at this juncture that there are those directly involved with the accident that vehemently hold the view, despite the evidence to the contrary, that Captain Marlow alone was responsible for the accident and will not be challenged on the issue. I only hope that my many years of research to unearth the real truth behind the disaster as detailed in this book are sufficient for them to reconsider their long-held beliefs.

Having achieved the erection of the memorial to the victims in 1998, it was clear that there were those individuals who were never given any official recognition for their outstanding and selfless contribution they made on the 4 June 1967. They, of course, were the members of the emergency services; the Stockport Police and surrounding forces; the Stockport, Manchester and Airport Fire Brigades, the regional

Ambulance Services, Civil Defence Corps, the Red Cross and Salvation Army. These uniformed organisations had no choice on the day disaster struck but to get involved. But few people today have little idea of the extraordinary selfless role of the rescue work undertaken by ordinary Stockport folk, who on that overcast suburban Sunday morning came together in the most horrendous of circumstances and found themselves faced with unimaginable horror and danger. It was extremely traumatic for them, having no training in such situations, to be confronted with victims who were trapped, still alive and dying horrifically before their eyes. All these individuals stood out above the crowd because they were willing to make the supreme sacrifice and risk their own lives to save the lives of those they didn't know. On that day, they became super-human and performed tasks which later they could hardly credit themselves of being capable of doing. It was a day that saw individual acts of kindness and powerful heroism all driven by a collective sense of duty and humanity. Of course, they all felt fear but the bravery and courage they demonstrated was without question.

Heroes and cowards are not preordained; when people are suddenly faced with life threatening situations they have only split seconds to react. And until that happens, its futile to speculate what the response will be. But what can truthfully be said is that when the ordinary townsfolk were put to the test, their character was not found wanting and clearly demonstrates the remarkable heights to which human nature can attain in adversity. Some of their remarkable and inspirational stories of bravery and courage are recounted elsewhere in this book.

In this modern age, it is something of a cliché to wax nostalgic about simpler times when the word heroism was used for those who saved lives rather than to describe the antics of some overpaid footballer or talent less 'air-head' celebrity. None of those involved in the rescue would class themselves as heroes, but truthfully, these ordinary people like Bill Oliver, John Heath, Ernie Taylor, Brian Donohoe and countless others were just ordinary people who did extraordinary things. Many were haunted and traumatised by the horrific carnage they witnessed chose, for their own reasons, not to come forward and make themselves known. Many of those I contacted declined to be interviewed for this book because they couldn't bear to relive their memories. Some even denied being involved – despite evidence to the contrary.

Throughout 2002, a campaign was launched by the *Stockport Express* newspaper to create a further memorial on the site dedicated to the heroic role played by the rescuers. It was a campaign, that over the coming months, quickly gained momentum and even got the backing of the then Prime Minister, Tony Blair.

On Sunday 13 October 2002, survivors of the tragedy joined with relatives to recognise the heroism of those who came to the rescue. The Reverend Arthur Connop – about to bow out of public life – again officiated at the commemoration and unveiling. It was he, amongst others, who gave so much personal and pastoral time in his capacity as a Methodist minister to all those devastated by the disaster. He told the gathered crowd that the town would always remember the efforts of the heroes of Hopes Carr: "It is precisely the fact that they have not sought for our desired thanks that we place this memorial here to remind ourselves and future generations how generous the human spirit really is and that in the face of demand, there are self-effacing people who humble us by their devotion, sacrifice and willingness to care for others."

Vivienne Thornber and fellow survivor, David Ralphs, unveiled the memorial to the rescuers at 10:09, the precise time that Hotel Golf plunged to earth. The poignant inscription on the bronze plaque says everything anybody needs to know about all those official, and unofficial individuals who rose to the challenge of a difficult rescue operation with guts, courage and compassion in an attempt to save a few of those lives that had been rudely shattered on that Sunday morning.

THIS MEMORIAL IS DEDICATED TO THOSE INVOLVED IN THE RESCUE AND WHO GAVE AID AT THE STOCKPORT AIR DISASTER 4th JUNE 1967 ALL WERE FACED WITH THE TRUE HORROR OF TRAGEDY AND DID NOT TURN AWAY THEIR COURAGE SAVED TWELVE LIVES

Vivienne commented: "I feel very privileged to have unveiled the plaque with survivor David Ralphs. I am sure that the volunteers and everyone that came to our rescue on that awful day appreciate the fact that they have now been recognised."

David added: "I am very appreciative to the people who got me out and saved my life. It must have been quite a shock for them. I always find it somewhat upsetting coming back to scene, but it serves a purpose; being a survivor people naturally want to talk to you and I am extremely grateful that I am able to do so."

Ex policeman, John Heath, who travelled from his home in Anglesey to attend the ceremony. He told me:

I had not been back to Hopes Carr since leaving the police force in 1969. The site has changed little in the intervening years, and it seeing closely again all these years later brought back so many heartfelt memories of that tragic day. It was good to meet Brian Donohoe again, a civilian who had no responsibility to help at the time, but like many others, got stuck in and assisted in the rescue work as much as anyone from the statutory emergency services. It was also reassuring to meet survivors Vivienne and David who were so gracious and thankful for our efforts on the day. Although the gathering was a somewhat sombre occasion, it did personally help me to put my reflections of the time into a positive framework.

Since the day of the accident, I have always attempted to put the dreadful memories behind me, partly because it was such a horrific event and partly because I often wonder if I could have done more. Although one tries to feel that we did all we could to save as many people as possible, I have always had a feeling that has never gone away that I could have done much more after the aircraft exploded and burst into flames. Perhaps we need not have jumped out of the fuselage too soon. I know speaking to my colleague Bill Oliver in following weeks and months that he too had exactly the same feelings of frustration and he too felt he could have done more. However, at the unveiling, those feelings of 'not doing enough' were challenged. The Mayor of Stockport and the Reverend Arthur Connop were complimentary and positive towards all those who took part, and for me, and undoubtedly for others, the ceremony was comforting and reassuring.

A few weeks after the unveiling, radio and TV presenter, David Hamilton, who reported from the scene in 1967, returned to Stockport to present a short documentary on the disaster for the BBC which gave him the opportunity to meet again some of those involved. "Thirty-five years later, I met up with ex policeman, John Heath. After some filming and interviews at the site, we both walked over the road to the Waterloo Hotel, where on the day of the disaster, I bought him a stiff drink to steady his nerves, now 35-years later in that same public house, John was able to reciprocate."

David Hamilton met up again with ex-police officer John Heath at the Waterloo Hotel in 2002 (author's archive).

Chapter Eighteen
At the End of the Day

"I was one of the lucky ones."

Survivor – David Ralphs

Today, if you walk down Waterloo Road and turn into Hopes Carr, you will find little to indicate that this corner of central Stockport bore violent witness to one of Britain's worst urban air disasters. But there are still subtle signs from that harrowing Sunday morning if you know where to look. The electricity substation that was partially destroyed when Hotel Golf's starboard wing and engines impacted was rebuilt and still stands, and if you know where to look, you can faintly define where the new brickwork interlocks the old. The garage forecourt area surrounding the sub station where the main body of the aircraft came to rest, is now nothing more mundane than a 'pay and display' car park. The garage directly opposite the site, which was put to use as a makeshift mortuary has in recent years been demolished to make way for a modern, rather soulless flat block. The steep grassy embankment leading down to the Tin Brook where Hotel Golf's blackened tail section lay, has been reclaimed over the intervening years by trees and dense undergrowth hiding all traces that a disaster ever occurred there.

No doubt the readers curiosity will want to know what has become of those people whose individual stories are described in this book. The passing years, of course, has exacted the inevitable toll on many of those directly involved. Of the ten passengers and two crew members who survived, only six are still with us and they will all tell you that they were very lucky to come through the ordeal alive.

All airline pilots like to retire having beaten the odds – in that, their number of landings equals their number of take offs. But unfortunately for Hotel Golf's commander, Harry Marlow, this was not the case. Because of the injuries he sustained in the crash, he was deemed medically unfit for flying duties and his licence was revoked. Swapping airliners for washing machines, he invested in a laundry business in Borrowash, Derbyshire, which was the first of many successful business ventures he undertook in the following years. In the summer of 1974, he studied accountancy, a job he continued until his retirement. According to his family and friends, he remained socially active and still retained his passion for golf and aviation.

The story of Captain Marlow has never been anything more over the years than a marginal component in the saga of the Stockport disaster. Since the accident, he consistently refused to give interviews to the media, and on the few occasions, I spoke to him he was, understandably, reluctant to discuss details of the crash itself, although he freely chatted with me on other topics, including flying and aviation in general.

His son, Robert, told me in 2002:

My father never talked to us about the accident in any detail, besides, in later years, he could not remember anything about the return flight beyond Paris. There is little I can tell you about the crash itself – I was only nine years old at the time. On that

Sunday morning, I was at the weekly Boys Brigade meeting and was collected by an aunt. I have vague memories of my mother seeing me and saying: "Dad's had a flying accident, but he's all right." So clearly, the initial panic and worry had died down somewhat by then. The next time I saw him was when he was transferred from Stockport Infirmary to Nottingham General Hospital, by this time, he was on the mend and had just one or two scars.

Later, when I heard about the technicalities of the accident, my reaction was – remember I was only nine – 'those rotten little levers' and 'what bad luck'. I didn't think then, like I do now, that the crash needn't have happened. I can remember some negative comments my mother made at the time about the Public Inquiry looking for 'pilot error'. You can imagine this caused a great deal of resentment in the family after it became clear the skilful actions my father had taken in those final moments to put the aircraft down in that small open area without loss of life on the ground. We received hundreds of thank you letters from the residents in the nearby tower blocks – an incredible response – they knew their lives had been saved that day. I think the fatigue factor that was brought up at the inquiry was an irrelevancy, he was well aware of how to prepare for a flight. I remember he once told me: "You can't store sleep."

Although I was very young at the time, I did feel the collective family shock, and to me Stockport became 'that bad place', not in the sense of the town or anyone who lived there, but just a place I personally wouldn't want to visit because of what occurred there on that Sunday morning in the summer of 1967.

I remember Julia Partleton, the stewardess, who was a great friend of my father, at several parties and get-togethers we had at our house in Queens Road, Nottingham – I was probably about ten at the time. I remember she was the first woman I ever saw wearing trousers. I thought she would be angry and resentful towards my father for causing her legs to be so badly scarred – of course, she wasn't. Julia wasn't the sort of person to hold a grudge; she just got on with life no matter what was thrown at her.

I must admit to feeling a bit apprehensive coming to Stockport for the first time to attend the commemoration for the 35th anniversary in 2002 to accept the engraved plaque on behalf of my father, but I felt it was something I had to do as a way of thanking everyone for their kind wishes at the time of the accident. The balance between going and leaving it all in the past was a difficult one, but in the end, I felt I made the right decision and it gave me the chance to meet and talk to some of the survivors and those involved in the rescue.

For the Marlow family, the ghost of Hotel Golf was to haunt them in the years and decades following the tragedy. In a letter, Bobbie Marlow wrote to me before her death in 2006, she said of her husband: 'For Harry, flying was his whole life, and all that came to an abrupt and tragic end on Sunday 4 June 1967 with the deaths of 72 passengers and crew. Nothing, of course, could ever be the same again, and as a family, we will always have to live with that'.

The Marlow's eldest son, Stephen, added: "Regretfully, for the remainder of us, although the passage of time has dimmed our memories, we remember the disaster and its aftermath as a period of great distress and sadness in our lives. We believe that now after half a century, this story should finally be laid to rest."

Harry Marlow lived out his final years quietly in his native Nottingham. He passed away peacefully at his home on 4 August 2009 after a long and courageous battle with cancer – he was 83.

Hotel Golf's Stewardess, Julia Partleton, is perhaps the ultimate survivor. In the accident, she suffered a serious back injury and first degree burns to thirty-five percent of her body and endured months of plastic surgery. Indeed, she showed remarkable courage, when on the day she was discharged from hospital, she immediately went straight to the airport and flew as a passenger, ironically to of all places – Majorca.

Once fully recovered – if one ever truly recovers from the physical and mental trauma of such a horrific accident – she showed no fear and with great fortitude resumed flying duties with British Midland Airways and later with Kestrel Aviation and Air International. After leaving flying, she returned to secretarial work and also had an interest in a furniture business in Ilkeston, Derbyshire, with her long-time partner, David Thorpe. At the same time, she worked hard restoring an old cottage in Castle Donington which became her cherished home.

In the 1970s, Julia was driving on the M1 motorway when a lorry travelling in the opposite direction careered over the central reservation and collided head on with her vehicle. Miraculously, she walked away shaken but unharmed. In a second accident, the steering on her Ford Capri failed and it careered down an embankment. Again, she came away unscathed. Amazingly, she told friends that she had a charmed life.

Ironically, Julia died prematurely on 20 October 1996 in Derby Royal Infirmary aged just 54, when on the following day my request seeking her whereabouts appeared in the *Derby Evening Telegraph*. A few days later in response to the article, David Thorpe, her partner of some thirty-years, told me:

I first met Julia in the early 1960s during her Derby Airways days, I immediately formed a rapport with her because, like me, she was an animal person; she was very caring in that way. It will always remain a question of debate as to how Julia would have reacted to the 30th anniversary commemoration of the disaster and the general publicity surrounding it, as she rarely spoke of the accident. Having said that, I found that she left a very comprehensive scrapbook of all the cuttings of the day, as well as saving all the cards from all the flowers she received, but again, she never showed them to anyone.

My own feelings when I travelled up to Stockport in June 1997 to attend the service, was of still being very upset by her untimely death. I nevertheless felt some gratitude for the extra thirty-years which Julia had, if she hadn't in those final moments of the flight unfastened her seatbelt and walked down the cabin to the galley to fetch a passenger a glass of water.

Her death occurred two-years after suffering a stroke to the right-hand side of her body, which seriously affected her speech and movement. As a very proud and independent woman, this came as a devastating blow. I can well remember the day she came out of hospital – where she had spent four months – and came face-to-face with all the aids which had been made ready pending her return home. She took one look at the commode which had been installed downstairs, whereupon she literally forced herself upstairs, despite the fact she had only the use of one arm and one leg. I recall another incident which clearly demonstrates her fiercely independent nature. One day, I found her trying to get ready to go out, and when I asked her where she was going, the answer was that she had to try and get back to work. Many people in similar circumstances would probably have been thinking about benefits, allowances, insurance claims etc., but to Julia, all these were offensive words as they denoted dependence on others, or even failure.

I remember taking her Christmas shopping in Derby – she loved Christmas – and she was so eager to make sure she had a present for everyone, even the cats. As we all helped with the wrapping up, I remember looking at her and wondering how many of us would have been so keen to buy presents for everyone whilst suffering so many afflictions ourselves.

It was the last three months leading up to her death that she began to plateau in her recovery process, eventually becoming breathless with increasing frequency. The doctor said she was hyperventilating and advised that she breathe into a paper bag! When her breathlessness clearly became unacceptable, she was admitted to the Derby Royal Infirmary where she was diagnosed as having possible pneumonia and transferred to a chest ward. In the month that followed, she seemed to deteriorate, and indeed relied totally on her oxygen mask. Two days before she died, it was eventually established that she had a tumour on her heart. This was not malignant, and although its removal would have involved open-heart surgery, it would have been a very survivable operation. Sadly, she died the day before its planned removal.

David Thorpe, a tenacious man, wanted some kind of redress for what he calls this 'sadly mismanaged affair' in which incompetent doctors 'failed to find a growth the size of cricket ball and a profession with an equally incompetent system of accountability'. He went ahead and took legal action, first against Leicester Royal Infirmary, where Julia was admitted in 1994 after suffering a stroke. It was there she underwent an echocardiogram which should have diagnosed the tumour, but nothing was found.

It was nearly four years after her death that the Leicester Hospital finally admitted that its staff had not diagnosed the tumour that eventually killed her. David was awarded £10,000 in an out-of-court settlement; the money going towards animal welfare in her memory as she passionately loved animals.

David's efforts failed to bring any individuals to account. He commented on how the doctors closed ranks: "I used to work in the airline industry," he said, "and when a pilot had a near miss he would be grounded pending an inquiry. It would then be investigated by the airline concerned and the Civil Aviation Authority. Even if cleared, it would still be on his records; certainly, it would not be left to the passengers to investigate."

"I have to thank both hospitals involved for being so devious, obstructive, and even unprofessional – had they apologised to me in the first place, I might not have troubled them. In the event, I requested an Independent Review of the situation, which confirmed beyond doubt that there were sufficient early warning signs for the specialists to have taken earlier action. It seems very sad that such a kind and caring person should have died through the carelessness and incompetence of others, particularly as she had survived the Stockport air disaster and two serious car accidents."

Julia is buried in Castle Donington Cemetery, which ironically backs on to the perimeter of East Midlands Airport. It was from here that she flew so often, during what must have been the happiest years of her life.

For the few passengers who escaped from Hotel Golf, it was the most dramatic and traumatic single event in their lives; the numbing horror of which will stay with them in some form for the rest of their days. Counselling, of course, didn't exist at the time and all those exposed to the trauma were expected to just get on with it. Eventually, they all recovered in their own way with the help of family and friends and carried on with the rest of their lives as best they could; but they could never forget.

When people survive life-threatening situations, they often become more positive and grateful in the aftermath. That life-changing experience at Stockport certainly will stay with Vivienne Thornber. What she endured in the disaster and its aftermath, both mentally and physically, gave her a totally different outlook, it caused her to think deeply about the fragility of life and made a courageous effort to rebuild her future.

I was in and out of hospital for twelve months and the disaster haunted me with nightmares and flashbacks. But I was determined not to let it rule my life. Even today, I still have nightmares from time to time, although physically I have recovered remarkably well. The doctors at the time thought that I might lose my leg, but thankfully, they managed to save it and today I don't even have a limp.

Susan and I started mulling over the idea of going on holiday again to Majorca. My mum and dad didn't want me to fly obviously, but Susan said, "Oh, come on, we can do to his." I thought, *Can we?* So, I summoned up the courage to take to the air again. This time we went on a British Caledonian Boeing 707. I had never been on a jet before and it was huge. I thought, *Oh, what have I done?* and Susan said, "Do you want a fag?" I have never smoked before or since, so there I was two years after the accident on this gigantic Boeing 707 puffing away on a cigarette. I clung to my seat all the way there. It was wonderful flight and we had a really fabulous holiday.

Now, half a century later, Vivienne is treading the boards as an award-winning actress on the local amateur stage and shows no sign of slowing down. She adds:

I married my husband, Chris, in 1971, four years after the crash, and we have flown every year since. I still fly because I love travel and the sun. Considering I survived an air disaster, I cope fairly well, but I always, if possible, prefer to sit in the same seats Susan and I occupied on the Argonaut on that fateful day. It feels strangely comforting knowing they were lucky for me then. Unaccountably, it is the take off which is my worst moment, but I am reasonably calm on landing which seems strange given the circumstances of the accident. Once I'm up in the air and we level off, I am absolutely fine and particularly when flying to Majorca, which I have done about fourteen times since the crash. When I see the windmills coming in to view on the approach to Palma Airport, I think: *Vivienne, you're coming home.*

Today I am living a very full and active life. It was inconceivable, considering the state of my completely shattered left leg, that I would be even able to walk again, let alone live life at the hectic pace I do now – looking after my home and having my musical and theatrical hobbies. Since the accident, my motto is: Life is most certainly not a rehearsal – this is the real show. Get all you can from life whilst you have it and live it to the full.

Each year on the anniversary, I go back to the crash site and lay flowers – not just for the 72 who died, but to say thank you to all those rescuers whose selfless heroic acts undoubtedly saved my life that day. It is also an opportunity to reflect, to say thank you that I am alive and to remember those who did not survive. I don't find it easy going back; it's an emotional journey every time. I think about the people and children who lost their lives and the town's people, many passers-by who did what they could to rescue the passengers. How can you say thank you for your life?

Vivienne still has in her possession – what she refers to as her lucky charm – her red plastic passport holder which was the only thing returned to her following the crash and which she still uses to this day. It helps remind her of her fortuitous escape and the thanks she owes to those who saved her life. It remains her only memento from that unforgettable flight.

Survivors: Vivienne Thornber and David Ralphs seen here at the Stockport Hall on the 30th anniversary (author's archive).

For anyone who survives a deadly air disaster, life will never be the same again, and she truly believes that in some sense, she owes it to those who didn't survive that she should make the most of this life.

David Ralphs, the last passenger to be pulled alive from the blazing wreckage, knows that he cheated death by the slimmest of margins that day. He suffered horrendous burns in the accident and was hospitalised for many months. He then endured a series of painful skin graft operations over a three-year period. Today, he feels he was incredibly fortunate to be rescued and has unfailing gratitude to those who saved his life. Although he has moved on from the tragedy in a spirit of optimism and confidence, he knows full well that the events he endured have shaped his life and outlook:

As a survivor of the disaster, I have thankfully few memories of that awful and traumatic day. But one vivid memory I do have is somebody dragging me out of the burning wreckage, and I showed my gratitude by swearing at him! My seat and clothing was ablaze and as a result, I needed lengthy treatment for third degree burns on my back. I spent just a week in Stockport Infirmary before the Minister of our church in Stoke-on-Trent arranged to get me transferred to the burns unit at our local hospital.

It was only later that I discovered that I was the last person to be pulled out of the aircraft alive, so the unveiling of the second memorial dedicated to the rescuers and helpers is of special significance to me. At home, I have a scrapbook containing newspaper cuttings and photographs, which various people gave to me to keep as a record. But I have learned far more of what happened during and after the crash thanks to the hard work and dedication of the author of this book.

My wife, Rosalie, and I attended the short service held at the crash site on the 30th anniversary in 1997, and the following year, I helped to unveil the memorial to all those who perished. Many of the relatives of those who tragically died were present and we were humbled by what they told us and how the disaster had deeply affected their lives. We also spoke to some of the helpers, including Arthur Thorniley and his wife, Bertha, of the Salvation Army – what a tower of strength they must have been in that difficult time. It reaffirms your faith in people and humanity that so many people came to help that didn't have to. I appreciate that because I have been given a second chance.

Because of the accident, I was reluctant to fly for many years, preferring to take holidays by car or coach. But after a holiday flight to Italy some years later, I have not looked back, and have since flown all over the world with Rosalie and our two grown-up daughters, Debbie and Helen. Even the terrible events of 9/11 have not deterred us and we thank God that we are able to lead full and meaningful lives.

I was one of the lucky ones.

David is now retired and living in Staffordshire. His friend and holiday companion, Alan Johnson, who survived with minor injuries, lost his life in a bizarre and tragic accident in 1995. Whilst walking his dog, he slipped on a patch of ice, suffering a fractured skull in the fall. A few days later, complications set in and he collapsed and died from a brain haemorrhage – he was just 48.

Harold Wood and his brother Billy miraculously came through the crash relatively unscathed; their father seated just yards away died instantly. Their mother, Gill, remained at home to run the family public house; otherwise, it could have been so much worse. Reflecting on his fortuitous escape, he told me:

I too, along with my brother, was one of the lucky ones to get out of the aircraft alive. I went blind in my left eye due to concussion which cleared up within a week and today still suffer from partial deafness in my right ear. The last memory we have of our father was of a man enjoying himself on holiday, that's how my brother Billy and I want to remember him.

The experience of being involved in the air crash and a near brush with death has not put me off flying and since the accident, I have flown all over the world – I have even piloted a glider and enjoyed a ride in a hot air balloon. Today I am married to Linda and have two grown-up children, Matthew and Christina and together we have been running the Cross Swords – a country inn and restaurant in Skillington, Lincolnshire for the past twenty-five years.

Looking back at the circumstances of the accident, I feel a lot more people would have been killed that morning if it hadn't been for the skill of Captain Harry Marlow putting the aircraft down when and where he did.

All these years later, I still get occasional flashbacks. My worst fear is being trapped in a burning aircraft. I tend to get them just as I begin to wake up in the morning. I kick off the bedclothes and dive out of bed with an unreasonable and overwhelming fear that I've got to get out of here.

Harold's younger brother, Billy, was deeply traumatised by the accident and is still affected to some degree today. Because of this, he declined my invitation to be interviewed for this book. He is now retired and lives happily in Malta.

Local girl, Fiona Child, who was pulled from the wreckage by Brian Donohoe, was shielded by her parents from all publicity at the time and in the years following. She quickly disappeared from public view and became something of an enigma. She has never spoken publicly about the disaster which killed her best friend. Over the years, I made numerous attempts to track her down and interview her for this book, but she has, for whatever reasons, chosen to remain for the most part silent. She continued to maintain her self-imposed anonymity and isolation for over four decades. She briefly and unexpectedly appeared at Hopes Carr with her rescuer Brian on the 40th anniversary commemoration in 2008. But even then, she was hesitant to discuss with anyone her memories of that awful day.

Brian Donohoe with Fiona Child, the girl he rescued (author's archive).

Of the other remaining survivors, Linda Parry has since died. Her friend and holiday companion, Mary Green, is someone else who prefers to remain silent. At the time of writing, I was reliably informed by a contact that she is still alive and living in the Preston area – she will be now in her nineties.

Albert Owen from Eastham on the Wirral, who lost his wife Eva in the accident, passed on at some stage. Despite a great deal of research over the years, I have been unable to discover anything about him and he remains the only survivor I have been unable to trace. If anyone reading these words has any knowledge of him, I would be interested to speak to them.

Motorcycle patrolman, Bill Oliver, who witnessed the crash whilst out on patrol and sounded the alert, was, like so many others, deeply affected by the events he witnessed. He said it was the most distressing moment he had been involved with in the whole of his police career. He continued as a motorcycle patrol officer before moving on to Panda cars. In December 1976, he collapsed at his home after suffering a heart attack a few hours after coming off duty; he was just 42.

Lifelong friend, James Beard, who grew up with Bill told me:

Billy – as we all called him – was a Hazel Grove lad where his parents ran the Liberal Club. When he was called up for National Service – being in the Transport Police – he served as a Military policeman in Vienna working alongside a Russian, a Frenchman and an American in the four-man Police Commission. Following demob, he joined Stockport Borough Police as one of the first motorcycle patrolman in the force. A job for which he was well suited as he was a keen motorcyclist, owning a Vincent HRD when the rest of us were only pedal cyclists! I kept in touch with Billy right up until his untimely death. I still cannot understand to this day why he and others were not honoured in some way for their selfless endeavours on that tragic day.

For John Heath, the second police officer to arrive on the scene and join his colleague Bill Oliver in the rescue, was, by his own admission, traumatised by his experiences and the spectre of Hotel Golf was to haunt him for many years to come. Now retired and living in Anglesey, he told me how he was affected by the events.

I must admit that I suffered quite badly over the days and weeks following the disaster. I could not eat or sleep properly and I had painful feelings of guilt that I could have done much more for the passengers trapped in the aircraft before the fire took hold. When I travelled down to London with Bill Oliver to give evidence at the Public Inquiry, he shared with me that he too had suffered terrible nightmares and he also felt he could have done more. Bill was a calm, collected and efficient police officer who I greatly admired and respected. More recently, I have wondered if Bill's traumatic experiences that day had contributed in some way to his sad and premature passing. He will always remain very much a hero to me.

Apart from the support of my section sergeant and my constable colleagues, there was, unlike today, no organised counselling or support. I don't think Post Traumatic Stress Syndrome had been considered at the time, or even heard of. One of the recommendations that came out of the subsequent inquiry was that all police forces surrounding the airport should be informed immediately whenever there was a potential emergency. This resulted in there being a few notifications when on duty and did not make for a stress-free shift for any of us. Because of this, I left the police force in the summer of 1969 and went into welfare work and have since retired.

Even today, I am still affected to some degree and even now have occasional flashbacks and nightmares. I have not been in an aircraft since that day and cannot contemplate flying at all. I am sure that everyone closely involved will have been distraught to some degree, including all those heroic Stockport civilians who had no responsibility whatsoever to help, but spontaneously, without concern for their own safety, got stuck in and I am sure positively helped to save many of the twelve survivors.

Stephen Clegg is another police officer who still retains vivid and troubled memories of the time. He told me in 2015 that:

In the days and weeks after the disaster, life slowly returned to normal. There was no such thing as counselling back then, we were simply told to 'get on with it' and we did. I don't recall seeing or hearing about any of my fellow officers being adversely affected, nor do I ever remember any mess room conversations about the crash, but I was never a party to any of their innermost thoughts, recollections or demons. It was an event; the event passed; we moved on.

On the 18 June 1972 – ironically, another Sunday – a BEA Trident airliner crashed shortly after take off from Heathrow killing all 118 people on board. The images broadcast on television from that crash site had a deeply profound effect on me and I recall being so overcome by the memories of Stockport that I was reduced to tears. I should say in conclusion, that I have not wept over the Stockport air disaster from that day until the day the author of this book asked me to record these memories for posterity.

Station Officer Fred Matkin, who was in overall command of the Stockport Fire service on the day disaster passed away in 1978. His son, Barry, told me of his father's long career in the service

Dad joined the Stockport Fire Service in September 1939; they were preparing for war and it was a busy time. In 1941, he was sent with others to fight the fires in the blitzes in Liverpool, Manchester and Coventry. During one raid, fifty percent of the firemen were killed. My mother tells the story that he was called out one day and didn't return for three weeks as they were going from city to city wherever they were needed.

He was then called up for army service and posted to Crawley. As he walked through the camp gates for the first time, he saw one of the huts on fire. Using his fire-fighting experience, he quickly found the fire hose and had put out the fire before the campfire tender arrived. When the officer in charge asked who had put out the fire, Dad proudly stepped forward. The officer then bellowed: "Well, you'd better light the ruddy thing again so we can continue with our exercise!"

After the war, he returned to the fire service and at a major fire the following year at Wellington Mill, Dad was trapped and seriously injured along with other firemen. He suffered serious burns and a broken back and was in plaster for almost a year. The doctors told him that his injuries were so serious that he would have to retire from the fire service, but undeterred, he fought hard to regain his fitness and eventually returned to the service becoming officer in charge at Reddish station.

He attended many incidents during his service, including a plane crash at the nearby Woodford Aerodrome, train crashes on the Stockport viaduct and Cheadle Hulme station. In 1952, he volunteered to go with a crew from Stockport to help out during the Lincolnshire floods. He was deservedly awarded the Queens Medal for his outstanding service in 1959 and retired in 1970 with 31 years of dedicated service.

The Stockport air disaster distressed him more than anything else he had experienced in all his years in the Brigade, he was on the second appliance to arrive, and he told me that the men from the first were already inside the blazing aircraft attempting to rescue passengers at great risk to themselves. There were fires and explosions all around and he said that his men were just turning their backs on the blasts and carrying on with the rescue work. It was only when the heat became so intense and they were literally blown out of the aircraft that they reluctantly came away. In his report on the incident, he recommended five firemen for outstanding bravery awards, but his recommendations were rejected, which made him very angry. In fact, no fireman received any award of any kind. One can imagine the awesome responsibility of knowing that you are in charge of such a catastrophe with so many dangers, and so many lives at risk. He always said that all the firemen to a man were magnificent that day.

Fire Officer Mike Phillips who turned out from the Whitehill Street station with Fred Matkin is alive and well and still living in the Stockport area. He told me that nothing in his long career with the service will come anywhere close to what he encountered on that ill-fated Sunday.

Since the disaster, whenever there a full emergency alert for a possible aircraft emergency, we had to change into full firefighting gear and stand by the appliance until it was over. This action would have probably saved perhaps a minute or two in an attendance should we have been needed – this practice was later disbanded as impracticable.

The nightmares and flashbacks I suffered in the aftermath stopped after about a year, and as time went on, I thought about it less and less.

I was operational for 26 years and in fire safety for a further six. Looking back on my career, there were many incidents which stand out, not forgetting the fireman's strike in 1977/78 which was very hard financially. During all my years of service, I have attended many large fires and uncountable accidents and incidents, but nothing has come anywhere close to compare with the events of Sunday 4 June 1967.

The impression you get when speaking to Brian Donohoe is of an affable, modest, self-effacing Stockport baker and granddad. Yet he has one of the most dramatic and unbelievable stories of tragedy and survival to tell. The sights and sounds he experienced continued to haunt him for the rest of his life. Whenever he was interviewed by the media about his part in the rescue, he spoke in a quiet voice of modest detachment as if he has done nothing more than help somebody off a bus.

Heroes are not preordained, but when put to the test his character was not found wanting and his actions on that tragic day clearly demonstrate the remarkable heights which human nature can attain in adversity. Brian, like all those others involved in the rescue attempts, received no recognition, no honours, no awards, no medals or citations. In the wake of the disaster, like many others involved, it was a strange and emotionally turbulent period. In my interview with him in 1998, he recalled the aftermath:

In the days and weeks immediately following the crash, I was a mess, a terrible mess – everyone who knew me says so – especially at work in the bake house. I remember going out on deliveries and forgetting to bring the breadboards back, in fact if I'm honest, I didn't bring anything back – my mind was elsewhere.

Even now, it still hurts to think about the disaster. It was a traumatic experience for me and all concerned, but I am glad that we were there to do what we could for the survivors. People have talked about us, the police and fire service being brave or even heroes. Even today, people say what a good job we did, but we didn't think about that at the time, we just did what had to be done. I only wish we could have done more to rescue more people but it wasn't to be. I'm thankful for the twelve lives we did save.

On New Year's Eve, 2008, at the age of 75, Brian baked his last loaf and at the end of the day, closed and locked the doors of his shop on Middle Hillgate for the final time after 60 years serving the local community. "The business has always been very much a family affair," recalled Brian nostalgically, where he always worked side by side with his wife Florence, daughter Margaret, and their next-door neighbour, known to one and all in the area as Auntie Joan. "My Hillgate shop has been so good to us," reflected Brian, "you treat people as customers but you don't realise that as the years pass they have become your friends as well."

Since the dark day of the disaster, Brian took on the self-imposed role of guardian of the memory of those who perished and those who survived. Although he never opposed the planned redevelopment in the Hopes Carr area, he vehemently opposed any plans to relocate the memorials for the sole purpose of profit.

Brian sadly passed away in February 2016 aged 82.

The Reverend Arthur Connop, having to deal with the spiritual and social effects of the disaster gave him a unique insight into the disaster's impact in personal human terms. He was an incredible man, a one off, with a natural gift for dealing with people. He is not only remembered for his outstanding work during the time of the accident, he will be remembered by the town for much more. As the police chaplain, he devoted more than forty-years to consoling Stockport police and families affected by crime and personal tragedy. It was Arthur's compassionate face that knocked on many a front door to break the news of a loved one's death to more than 1,700 families across the town. He earned the respect of all the emergency services from the highest officers to the lowliest of recruits.

He retired from the police chaplaincy and mainstream public life in 2003 at the age of 86 and received a lifetime achievement award from the Chief Constable of Greater Manchester, in recognition of a career which lasted far longer than any other police chaplain in the country. He said at the time: "I have been tremendously privileged to have had the opportunity to be linked through my work to the police who are the most wonderful people. I came into this job to try to help people and that is what I hope I have done to the best of my ability."

"I am full of admiration and affection for the people of Stockport who have shown wonderful kindness and support for me, and for the remarkable courage they have shown in some of their darkest hours."

Arthur, supported by his devoted wife, Alice, during 67 years of marriage, died peacefully in Stockport in August 2008 aged 91.

In the aftermath that followed, it was a grim and grievous time for all those who had lost relatives and friends in the disaster leaving them with emptiness and despair; many fell into a cataclysm of depression and felt that they too had died on that dreadful Sunday.

Few felt the impact of the crash quite like Pauline O'Sullivan, who suffered the devastating loss of both parents, brother and cousin. She knew that life had to continue, but for Pauline and her sister, Marilyn, they knew it would never be quite the same again. Since the accident, Pauline had always wanted to make a pilgrimage to Majorca and to try if possible to capture something of the enjoyment they had found on that last holiday together before disaster struck.

Mum had sent us two postcards whilst on holiday in Majorca and over the years, I have always wanted to go there someday to retrace their steps, see the places they had visited and, most of all find the hotel were they all stayed. But since the day of the air crash, I was terrified of flying. My husband, Ted, was always reassuring me how safe flying was as he has flown all over the world with his job. I must admit that every time we said goodbye before those trips, I wondered if he would come home safe – still vividly remembering that day in 1967 when I said my last goodbye to Mum, Dad, brother David, and cousin, Philip. Eventually, in October 1995, I finally managed to summon up the courage and flew over to Majorca with Ted.

We stayed in the beautiful resort Pollensa, in the north of the island and hired a car to visit all the places mentioned in the postcards. Valldemosa was one, a spectacular village in the mountains. One evening, we went on an excursion to an old Mallorcan palace for a meal and variety show – possibly, this was the very same one the family had visited to see a display of Spanish folk dancing.

On one of the postcards was a picture of Cala Mayor and this was where we began our search for the hotel Bon Estar. We asked hoteliers, bar owners, the tourist information centre and even the Federation of Hotels, but we drew a complete blank – no one had ever heard of it. I knew that after so many years it could have changed its name or maybe no longer a hotel. Even so, I was really disappointed. However, on the flight back to Manchester, I got chatting to lady passenger – Dee Wade – she had been living on the island for seven years with her family and was travelling back to the UK for a holiday and meet up with old friends. During the flight, I told her all about the air disaster and our fruitless search for the hotel. Before we went our separate ways at the airport, she promised me that on her return to the island, she would try and discover the hotel's location.

Several months later, to my surprise and delight, a bulky letter arrived from Dee. After a series of appeals in the Mallorca Daily Bulletin, the hotel was finally located in Ciudad Jardin, to the east of Palma near the Airport and was in the first stages of demolition. Dee even sent me a postcard of the hotel in its heyday.

For Pauline, finding the hotel was the last link in the tragedy, and now it has been found, feels she has completed a cycle. In so doing, she has moved on with her life, laid some ghosts, overcome her fear of flying, discovered a beautiful island and acquired some happier memories.

For British Midland, the Stockport disaster was a defining moment in the history of one of Britain's longest serving airlines. It was their worst fatal accident, although the crash of one of its Boeing 737s on the M1 Motorway near Kegworth in January 1989 came close when 47 were killed; if there had been a post-crash fire, it would in all probability have had a greater death toll than Stockport.

For the two remaining Argonauts in the fleet, the writing was well and truly on the wall. Their time with the airline had not been a happy or prosperous one. After being used for flight and ground testing by the AIB, they continued flying to European and domestic destinations for the remainder of 1967. The last operation recorded was a freight flight from Aldergrove to East Midlands Airport on 3 November of that year.

The records show that both aircraft were officially sold on 19 October 1968 to a hitherto unknown British operator, Chartwell Aviation. In fact, Chartwell had no connection whatsoever with aviation; it was in fact a Kent-based car retailer who had agreed to put up the finance to cover the purchase of the two aircraft. The actual operation of the aircraft was in the hands of a broker, Templewood Aviation, who had already applied to the Board of Trade for an export licence for the two aircraft on the strength of a lease-charter agreement with the Biafran's – the Biafra war was raging at this time – Templewood hired four ground engineers and two flight crews.

The Biafra Airlift originally came about simply to bring humanitarian relief to those affected by the ravages of the ongoing civil war. However, there was the belief – which turned out to be true – that some aircraft and crews supposedly engaged in genuine relief work were flying arms and ammunition into the country compounding the suffering. There was some suspicion by the British authorities about the true nature of the operations the two aircraft would be undertaking.

The first of the Argonauts, Hotel Sierra, attempted to depart East Midlands Airport on Sunday 21 October on a clandestine flight. The flight plan filed by the crew simply showed a positioning flight to Zurich, but its ultimate destination was widely believed to be Lisbon, via either Prague or Vienna, where the aircraft would uplift an undisclosed cargo – no doubt, this subterfuge was devised to confuse the authorities. As Hotel Sierra taxied out towards the runway threshold, suspicious HM Custom officers – having received a tip-off as to the precise nature of the flight – ordered the captain to return to the terminal where the aircraft was detained and the crew questioned. In the end, no charges were brought against either the flight crew or Templewood. All that Customs wanted was a signed declaration that neither of the two aircraft was destined to be used in the airlift. Templewood flatly refused to give such an undertaking and abandoned any further attempt to fly the aircraft out of the UK.

In the end, both Hotel Sierra and Hotel Yankee never flew again and languished on the edge of the airfield as testament to a dark period in British civil aviation history. Both aircraft were finally reduced to scrap in 1970.

In commercial operations, the Canadair Argonaut and its variants had a relatively lengthy career as a civil airliner and freighter. For example, Trans Canada Airlines flew their North Stars from 1946 right through to 1961, and BOAC from 1949 to 1960. After service with major airlines, they extended their careers with secondary operators. In military service, the Royal Canadian Air Force operated the type for 18-years, clocking up an estimated 193 million miles. Cargo conversions of available airworthy airframes extended their service life still further. One of the longest-lived aircraft – CF-UXA, an ex-Royal Canadian Air Force machine – was the last DC-4M North Star in airline service, carrying out its final flight on 19 June 1975 from Miami, Florida.

At the beginning of the 1967 holiday season, Harry Bowden Smith, the founder of Arrowsmith Holidays who chartered Hotel Golf for that fatal flight, had been seriously considering selling the company that had made him a multi-millionaire. Having seen so many of his clients – including infants and children – killed in the disaster, and the fact that his wife, Edna, had died the previous year, finally tipped him over the edge. Losing all heart to continue on with the business, he sold out to the flamboyant airline and travel pioneer, Freddie Laker. Harry Bowden Smith retired to the Wirral where he passed away in 2003 aged 85.

For many, it was inescapable that Hopes Carr was, and still is, haunted by so many ghosts and memories. If you stand on the corner of Waterloo Road and Hopes Carr today, the disaster site is eerily quiet. I have in the course of my research visited the site on countless occasions and I have always found it has an atmosphere that I couldn't quite explain; a feeling of something not quite right. Even on a sunny day in the height of summer, it has certain silent quality about it. It took many years before I eventually came to the realisation that it is a place where the birds don't sing.

In 1968, the famous Strawberry recording studios opened in a converted warehouse directly opposite the Waterloo Hotel. It has been used over the years by a wide variety of recording artists, such as the Bay City Rollers, 10cc, Neil Sedaka, New Order, The Smiths and Paul McCartney and Wings amongst many more. Interestingly, Paul McCartney and his wife, Linda, were frequent customers at Brian Donohoe's shop where they would call in for tea and sandwiches during their breaks in recording and thereafter became great friends.

Stockport has seen many changes in the five decades following the disaster. Like many other towns and cities across the country, wholesale demolition and modernisation was the order of the day. Many new public buildings had already been erected and during that early summer of 1967, the bright modernistic Mersey Way Shopping Precinct – in sharp contrast to its industrial surroundings – was nearing completion. If you stand on any vantage point around the town today, you will be hard pressed to spot a factory chimney that was once the familiar industrial backdrop that defined the town.

In the 1970s, the town council and planners, having no interest in its heritage, wanted nothing more than wholesale demolition – a sort of knock it down and start again mentality. There was a desire to leave the past behind, and Stockport was radically transformed by grandiose modernistic architectural projects born of an unholy alliance between greedy developers and town planners who believed that anything old should be bulldozed and replaced with what they erroneously believed was something better. Beside the blanket demolition of the Portwood district – which was undoubtedly the right decision – the rest of the town remains a tribute to the worst excesses in town planning, a policy that has seen much of Stockport's heritage ripped away without thought or consideration to be replaced by a brutal modernistic mix of concrete, glass and steel – clinical, undistinguished and heartless. Even the landmark viaduct underwent a £3 million restoration programme in 1989, a process that included, not only cleaning the brickwork of a hundred and thirty years of industrial grime, but also adding floodlights to illuminate the western gateway to the town. Despite all the changes the town has seen in recent decades, it still remains the town's iconic landmark of distinction.

Hopes Carr, the focal point of the air disaster, has changed little over the past 50 years. Today the ravine, or dell, as it is sometimes referred to by locals, is semi-derelict and overgrown and the once sparkling waters of the Tin Brook that meanders below is home to old car tyres and an assortment of discarded rubbish. Overall, the crash site has remained undeveloped since 1967, but in recent years, the Stockport Metropolitan Borough has embarked on an ambitious regeneration scheme for the area to attract people to come and live in the town centre. The redevelopment when completed would include 250 flats, a 100-bed hotel, pubs, cafés, retail outlets and a fanciful landscaped water park.

Stockport Infirmary, where the survivors were taken for treatment closed its doors in 1996. Now Grade II listed, it was purchased by a developer and renovated into office space. Now known as Millennium House, it still retains its handsome brick frontage.

Other buildings that have changed their usage include the Salvation Army Citadel. Because of the escalating costs of repair and upkeep of the building, the Corps had no alternative but to relocate to modern premises elsewhere in the town. The building was sold off to a housing association and converted to contemporary flats. The restored frontage of the building, including the foundation stone and Salvation Army lettering cut into the sandstone was conserved in compliance with heritage regulations.

The Stockport and Perpignan disasters marked a turning point in civil aviation safety and how the travelling public felt about old lumbering piston-engined aircraft being operated on their holiday flights. The Perpignan crash highlighted the dangers of night charter flights to secondary European airfields tucked away amongst mountainous terrain with poor landing aids and other disadvantages. It became a highly charged issue at the time and forced the tour operators to radically change their operating practises. To allay public anxiety, they rejected the old Dakotas, DC-4s and anything else powered by piston engines in favour of modern turbo props and pure jets that the public demanded. The jet engine generation of airliners were undoubtedly much safer, more reliable and, with a greater range eliminated refuelling stops at problematic airports like Perpignan and elsewhere. Within a few years, the piston-engined airliners were either scrapped or relegated to cargo operations. But even with modern equipment, the sky can still be a hostile place as the continuing number of aircraft accidents following on from Stockport and Perpignan testify.

Compared with the pioneering days of the package holiday, the modern-day era of 'cheap and cheerful' holiday flights to Spain and other Mediterranean destinations has sanitised of all fun and romance that the 'golden age' of flying had in abundance – stewardesses in white gloves, ex RAF pilots with magnificent moustaches, starched linen, silver service and good manners shown by all. Now the package holiday is homogenised and where passengers have the understandable tendency to think of themselves as neglected human cargo.

Millions of us today take the package tour holiday every year, but it bears little resemblance to those relaxed and peaceful family holidays enjoyed in the pioneering days of the '50s and '60s. In the modern era, people now have for the first time the opportunity to travel to exotic destinations they would hardly have dreamed of fifty years ago. But there has been a downside to the modern 'cheap as chips' holidays on offer. In the main, they appeal to the hedonistic young Brits – especially holidays to the Spanish Costas – they have become so popular in recent years that many of these once peaceful and innocent family resorts now resemble the sordid base culture that exists in many parts of the UK that are the catchment area for these brash young Brits. Typically, on offer are English themed pubs, 24-hour drinking, all day belt-busting English breakfasts, drunkenness, yobbish behaviour, sex on the beach and vomit splattered streets. Because of cheap booze freely available at any time of day or night, getting wasted, it seems, has become the British national sport. It is in these resorts throughout the year that you can find British boys and girls behaving badly and it's a common sight to see shoeless and dishevelled girls slumped on the streets muttering helplessly about how smashed they are. There is even a dedicated website for the more refined holidaymaker that gives tips and advice on how to avoid the badly behaved drunken British on holiday!

Within a decade, destinations like Majorca morphed from holiday idyll to tacky resorts with associated dubious pleasures. One ex pat describes his happy and memorable Spanish family holidays back in the sixties compared with what's on offer today:

I was a teenager when my parents took us off on holidays abroad. All the resorts were still quiet fishing villages back then and there were no drunken British lager louts and associated behaviour to contend with. I remember my dad worked overtime until he nearly dropped to take us on holiday to Spain – it was he who gave me my travel bug. I fondly remember the airlines we flew on – British Eagle and Channel Airways. Many years later, when my children were young, I went back on a nostalgic day trip to Benidorm and I stood on a street corner and began crying. I couldn't believe what it had been turned into.

Epilogue

In the main, this book has been about the Stockport air disaster and all those directly caught up in the tragedy; a story of those who died, those who survived and those relatives and close friends left behind to grieve. It is also the story of the technical failings of the airline industry and the government departments who did not fulfil their responsibilities for maintaining air safety in the UK and, if truth be told, were indirectly responsible for the deaths of 72 men, women and children.

But it must not be forgotten that 88 others died in an almost identical aircraft just 12 hours earlier in the unforgiving darkness of the high Pyrenees. In terms of fatalities, the Air Ferry crash was far worse. Even in terms of those hard-to-qualify elements of grief and loss, it certainly had far deeper repercussions than Stockport, and statistically, it was also the worst loss of life ever to occur in a DC-4. Both accidents, with the loss of 160 lives, made it the blackest weekend in British civil aviation history, and thankfully, it has never been equalled.

A feature article in *The Daily Telegraph Magazine,* entitled *The Black Mountain,* published a few weeks after the Air Ferry disaster, emphasised that nine airliners had crashed in the vicinity of Perpignan since 1951. The article, by journalist Andrew Duncan, reads:

The forlorn remnants of this summer's first air crash in which 83 holidaymakers and 5 crew died still litter the slopes of Mount Canigou in the Pyrenees. A stream struggles through the centre of the wreck, lazily carrying with it the occasional crushed carton of duty-free cigarettes. Lumps of fuselage are lodged in the scorched trees, and mementoes of individual disasters lie untouched nearby: children's water wings, a pair of new white high heels, unopened packets of cine film, combs, bathing costumes, a crumpled bucket and spade...

It is an unpleasant and unforgettable sight. But for people in nearby villages, it is not unusual. This year's crash – on June 3 – was the third on or very near Mount Canigou since October 1961. A total of 162 people, mostly Britons heading for holidays on the Costa Brava, have died. All three crashes were at night and involved charter planes about to land at Perpignan, which has an unmatched record of catastrophe. Nine planes have crashed in the past 16 years in the mountains surrounding the airport – known somewhat dramatically as 'the graveyard of airliners'.

On summer weekends, 8,000 people land at Perpignan and take a two-hour coach trip to Spanish resorts. They pay from 30 guineas for 15 days, all-inclusive, to fly by DC-4, the type of aircraft that crashed in June. A jet flight could be £10 more, but not necessarily any safer. Perpignan Airport itself is not considered dangerous and has a category A classification which means the procedures are straightforward. London, New York and Hong Kong, for instance, are category C.

Why, then, have 219 people been killed in the vicinity?

"There are 1,001 reasons," said Andrew Burns, British Eagle station manager for two years. "The approaches are difficult, but not dangerous. I've seen plenty of worse ones, such as Naples or Berlin where you descend between blocks of flats."

Investigations have usually produced one of three answers: navigational error, bad weather or interference from the radio stations at Madrid, Andorra or Pals. But in the villages surrounding Mount Canigou, there are those who think the coincidences are too awesome to be explained in any of these ways. Moreover, the last crash took place in perfect weather.

"I don't know what to think anymore," says Henriette Touron, who runs a cinema in Prades, a few miles from the most recent accident. "I used to believe there was something in the mountains that affected navigation in bad weather. That was because our car radio never worked during a storm. But now...who knows? The only certain thing is that when one hears an aeroplane flying low one thinks, 'Oh no, not another accident.'"

Superstition is not a common characteristic of the Catalans. "We are very objective, like the Chinese," says Louis Monestier, mayor of Prades. "We don't believe in miracles or mysteries." And yet, in the case of Mount Canigou, 9,137 feet, some people have begun to wonder.

By night, during the frequent thunderstorms, Canigou provides a spectacle that would effervesce even the most blasé psychedelic. Sheer lightning illuminates vast areas of gaunt cliff. Rust-coloured rocks jut out on all sides of you. Thunder echoes down the valleys. And then, everything is eerie and still and you hope the next lightning bolt won't be too close. A fox rushes frightened through the trees. Then more lightning just ahead. It is a virtuoso performance.

"People speak of the magic of Canigou," says Anna White, a 71-year-old widow who has lived at Vernet-les-Baines since 1924. "There must be something strange here because no one can understand why the crashes happen. I think there is an easy explanation somewhere. They say that signals coming from Perpignan are not clear because of mineral deposits left over from the iron mines."

"The terrible thing is that before all three crashes we have heard the planes circling overhead, looking for a way out. You despair because you know in a few minutes they are going to crash, and you are lying in bed, and can do nothing. It's terrible, worse than a nightmare, and it feels as if danger is all around. Before the last crash, the pilot seemed to speak to me, 'Where can I go?' Then there was an awful boomf as the aircraft hit the mountain."

At the tiny village of Py, half a mile from the last crash, some of the inhabitants agree with their mayor, Rene Pedeil: "There are iron deposits in the mountains, but it has nothing to do with the crashes. It is simply that the Pyrenees are a barrier. I saw the plane come over and thought it would hit the village. Then it turned away, the wing tip hit a ledge, and it plunged on to the mountain and caught fire. It was like an atomic explosion lighting up the sky."

The Air Ferry accident was duly investigated by the French Ministry of Transport, assisted by UK accredited representatives and advisors from the Accident Investigation Branch, Farnborough. The wreckage was, of course, searched for clues, but it was the toxicological examination of the remains of the crew which revealed elevated levels of carbon monoxide in the blood, indicating that there must have been an unusual high level of the gas present in the cockpit. In September of that year during a fresh search of the wreckage, the remains of the cockpit heaters were found. Expert examination of the equipment established with certainty that burnt gasses passed into the cockpit and concluded that was the main cause of the crash. The report said that carbon monoxide intoxication from the leaking heater 'very probably impaired the powers of the crew members and affected to a greater degree the judgement of the aircraft commander who, occupying the left-hand seat, was in the best position to observe, allowing for the visibility, that the aircraft was deviating abnormally from the coast'.

Some of the senior engineers at Air Ferry were quite vehement that all the blame should not be apportioned to the heaters. They were widely known to give trouble on the DC-4 and the engineers always paid particular attention to them prior to a flight. If they found any hint of leakage or trouble, they would have them disabled which led to bitter complaints from the flight crew at being cold. Many tests were carried out on the heaters, including one where the engineers bored holes in the casing, after which the heater was refitted into the aircraft and a ground run carried out without registering a significant amount of carbon monoxide. It was also mentioned in the Perpignan inquiry that the flight crew of Yankee Kilo travelled to Manston Airport together by road and were caught up in a slow-moving traffic jam which lasted for half an hour. There was no wind and with the windows of the vehicle open, it was suggested that they could have picked up significant quantities of the gas during that period. Nothing could be proved of course, but nonetheless, it was still another factor to consider in the build up to the accident.

The very comprehensive French report revealed no evidence of mechanical failure in the aircraft itself – apart from the cracked heater – and no significant outside factor which could have contributed to the accident. On an apparently normal flight, the aircraft was descending from 7,000 feet when it hit the foothills of the Canigou massif at approximately 4,000 feet. It seems that at the last minute, the crew switched on their landing lights and realised their proximity to the high ground. This, the report says, was only the final phase of a series of incidents which led to the accident. Reconstructions of the DC-4s flight path from the flight recorder and from the ground radar recorders shows that shortly before the aircraft passed Mende, it began to deviate from the normal flight track. At Papa 3 – a reporting point north of Perpignan – the deviation was 15 kilometres west of the reporting point and increased appreciably later when the aircraft began what the report states: 'might have been an approach and landing procedure'.

Radio communications between the aircraft and Perpignan control show that there were obvious misunderstandings which led on two occasions to the aircraft being asked to report downwind for landing. Another theory put forward was that the crew mistook a line of lights at Vernet les Bains for the Perpignan runway lights and that Prades was mistaken as being Rivesaltes.

The report went on to criticise the ground controller at Perpignan for not checking the bearing of the aircraft during the last few minutes of the flight – an omission brought about by the fact that the controller believed the DC-4 had the airfield in sight. On this point, the report says that if the bearing had been checked, the controller would have immediately noticed the error and would have informed the aircraft and possibly prevented the accident.

There were other factors to consider. There were some who felt that there was an element of bad crewing for the flight. Captain Pullinger, although a very experienced and well-regarded pilot, was still relatively new in command of a heavy four-engined transport aircraft, the flight was at night and whilst Perpignan may not have been categorised as an exceptionally difficult airport, it was an airfield surrounded by forbidding terrain. It had a challenging approach without decent landing aids and other basic amenities. Added to this were the questionable standards of the Perpignan Air Traffic Control where their knowledge and standard of English was deemed by pilots to be very poor and unacceptable. The fact that there are reputed to be some sixteen crash sites in the mountainous vicinity must have some significance.

At the time, Perpignan was considered by pilots and others in the aviation fraternity as an unlucky airport. The surrounding mountainous terrain has always been a hazardous feature of the airfield, ready to catch the unwary and fatigued. One inspector recalls an occasion when they were departing Perpignan early one morning in a Bristol 170 Freighter and climbing out through mist. After what seemed an eternity, the Bristol finally emerged into clear air and sunshine but the surrounding mountains still menacingly towered all around them.

The Air Ferry accident evoked the hypotheses that magnetic interference – caused by unique geological conditions created by iron mines in the area – disrupted radio communications and flight instruments, was a possible cause of the accident. This of course totally conflicts with the official findings of the inquiry, but nevertheless, provides another interesting theory.

There is an eerie and somewhat chilling postscript to the Air Ferry disaster that occurred many months later. It happened to one of their engineers working far away in Kabul, Afghanistan, and is best described in his own words:

Once upon a time – there's a beginning for you – an aircraft engineer was standing on the tarmac at Kabul, doing watch duty whilst one of his company aircraft was being ground run. It was a long engine run and as a small distraction, the engineer almost subconsciously noticed a small ball of paper being blown towards him by the ever-present breeze that one finds at a location nearly 6,000 feet above sea level.

Some seven months prior to this time, another aeroplane operated by the company had been prepared for a night flight to Perpignan in southern France, taken on a full load of passengers, and in the early evening eased its way south from its airport in Kent. It never landed in Perpignan, crashing instead into Mount Canigou in the Pyrenees. All 88 people on board lost their lives. Only the very public crash of a similar aircraft type at Stockport the following day prevented the usual all-engulfing press attention making more of the disaster in France.

Meanwhile, back in Kabul, the engine run was still roaring on, and the little ball of paper was blowing nearer to our engineer, who by now was wondering how close to him the breeze would bring it on its journey along the great stretch of tarmac, he was determined not to take a step forward or back to make it 'happen'.

A look up at the flight deck showed the two men were engrossed in the interior of the cockpit and their instrument readings. A glance to the left showed the windblown object to be moving by the starboard wingtip. Another glance to the cockpit, the propeller discs slowing showed the engine run was complete, silence at last, now where was that piece of paper. Good Lord, just there in front of me. Bend down, pick it up, unscrew it, flatten it out, read it.

IT WAS THE REFUELLING CHIT FOR THE FLIGHT FROM MANSTON TO PERPIGNAN, SEVEN MONTHS BEFORE THAT ENDED IN TRAGEDY HIGH IN THOSE MOUNTAINS SO FAR AWAY.

I know this is true. Because I – Paul Noller – was that engineer.

All in all, 1967 had been a terrible year for Air Ferry. It started badly when on Saturday 21 January, one of their DC-4s – call sign Oscar Golf – departed Manchester at 01:09 on a cargo flight to Frankfurt. At 04:14, in darkness, approximately 2,700 metres from the runway threshold the aircraft struck trees before hitting the ground. The aircraft was totally destroyed by the impact and ensuing fire killing the two pilots, Captain Adcock and First Officer Gutteridge. As it was an all-cargo flight, the accident attracted little attention in the press. The accident was duly investigated by the Federal

German authorities who established that the probable cause was a wrong altimeter setting leading the crew to believe they were flying at a higher altitude that they actually were.

Just four months previously, a Bristol Britannia, operated by Britannia Airways carrying 110 holidaymakers and seven crew on a night flight, was lost in almost identical circumstances on the approach to Ljubljana airport in the then Yugoslavia, with the loss of 95 lives. The inquiry blamed the accident on 'pilot error' and said that the aircraft altimeter had been incorrectly set for the airfield elevation. It was a case of another British airliner being at the wrong place at the wrong height.

For Air Ferry, the tragic loss of Yankee Kilo at Perpignan brought with it serious consequential problems, it left them with just one remaining DC-4, with the almost impossible task of carrying on with its contracted services for the rest of the season. It cannot be underestimated the effect of the loss of two aircraft in such a short space of time on a small airline operating on a shoestring, it could have quite easily brought about their immediate collapse.

Like so many of the British independents, Air Ferry had a long struggle to remain viable. In order to compete with its rivals, they had no choice but to negotiate the lease of two Channel Airways Viscount turbo-prop airliners to operate its contracted charter services for the summer of 1968. Both aircraft were sprayed up in full Air Ferry livery and flew many thousands of passengers from Manston, Gatwick, Newcastle and Manchester on behalf of several large tour operators. However, Air Holdings, the parent company, seeing its profits slump announced that Air Ferry would be closed down at the end of the season, with all its passenger and freight services transferred to British United Airways.

Consequently, on 31 October 1968, the airline operated its last revenue earning flight. The leased Viscounts were returned to Channel Airways and the remainder of the Air Ferry fleet were sold off. In its short history, the company had flown 40,314 hours over six years of operations and carried 834,931 passengers.

Besides the demise of Air Ferry, it was a turbulent year all round for the British independents. The Wilson Government, having devalued sterling the previous year, decided in its fiscal wisdom to impose a £50 cash limit that anyone could spend abroad on a foreign holiday, which not unnaturally discouraged many prospective holidaymakers to shun the package tour and instead take their annual holidays in the UK.

For British Eagle, the country's second biggest independent airline at the time, with a long-chequered history stretching back to 1948, this financial restriction led to the cancellation of inclusive tour holiday bookings worth over £1,000,000. Then, to compound matters, on 9 August, the airline suffered the tragic loss of one of its Viscounts on a holiday flight from Heathrow to Innsbruck in the Austrian Alps.

Whilst flying in cloud, in the region of Langenbruck, Bavaria, the aircraft suffered a complete electrical failure resulting in the captain being left with just an airspeed indicator and turn and slip instrument. As a result of disorientation on the part of the crew, the Viscount entered a high-speed dive and plunged with disintegrating impact into the side of an embankment carrying the Munich-Nuremberg autobahn, exploding in a fireball killing all 48 passengers and crew.

In the wake of the accident came the first signs of the airline's impending collapse. British Eagle's bankers were not convinced that the company, with debts of over £7 million, could survive the financial crisis and withdrew their support. So it was on the afternoon of Wednesday 6 November that the British Eagle board announced that from midnight all flying would cease. It was a sad end for an independent airline that from the very beginning had to fight for its very existence and was thwarted at every turn by the very bureaucracy that would finally bring it to its knees. Later that same month, Transglobe suffered the same fate after two of its major shareholders introduced winding-up proceedings.

In the following years, because of their weak financial position, many other famous names disappeared from the British aviation scene, such as British United Airways which was bought out by Caledonian in November 1970. Channel Airways also went into receivership in 1972, whilst Skyways, another independent with a rich and colourful history, was absorbed by Dan Air a few months later.

The demise of these pioneering independent operators brought to an end the glamour and romance associated with post-war air travel. Despite the well-publicised dangers associated with flying, it will always be remembered as the 'golden age' – a nostalgic era of well-appointed airliners with plenty of legroom, five course meals served on fine china, silver cutlery and starched linen tablecloths. It was a time when stewardesses wore white gloves, were adept in mixing cocktails and knew how to address a titled passenger.

What is largely forgotten by most air travellers today is that in the immediate post war years flying was never less than a hazardous business, but the risk was stoically accepted by aircrews and their passengers. There was good reason for this, aircraft operated by the independent charter sector tended to be second, third or even fourth hand. They were heavily overworked and by the end of the holiday season, the airframes were overstressed and the engines grossly overtaxed and in desperate need of maintenance. Flight crews too were fatigued and overworked – especially during the busy summer season when the independents made their money.

Because of simple economics, these charter companies tended to operate out of secondary inferior airports and mostly at night when landing fees and other operating costs were much lower. Pilots, using these airfields frequently, reported radio beacons suddenly going off air, poor radio communications, serious deficiencies in air traffic control and the poor English spoken by the controllers. Added to this mix was poor navigational and other equipment fitted onboard their aging aircraft.

But it would be unfair to lump all charter companies together. In 1967, there were some very good independent airlines operating to the letter of the law whilst there were others that were undertaking barely legal operations. There is enough evidence to show that throughout the 1950s and 1960s, some of the latter indulged in the dubious practice of cutting corners, although these companies preferred to term it as 'efficiency'.

By any yardstick, 1967 was a particular bad year for civil aviation safety. In all, there were 57 reported accidents to commercial airliners – including Stockport and Perpignan – with a total of 1,323 fatalities. In the following years, aviation accidents and incidents continued with frightening rapidity with corresponding loss of life.

Accidents that were feared and predicted with the introduction of the high capacity wide bodied 'jumbo' jets have come to pass with great loss of life. Perhaps the most memorable of these being the Tenerife disaster of 1977. On 27 March of that year, two fully laden Boeing 747 passenger jets collided on the runway at Los Rodeos Airport. The crash killed 583 people making it the deadliest accident in aviation history. The findings of the inquiry firmly placed the blame on poor communications between air traffic control and the pilots causing one aircraft to commence take off without proper clearance.

Besides commercial operating accidents, there have been other truly horrific disasters, caused entirely by the sheer perversity of human nature – that of wanton terrorism and sabotage – best described as mass murder for political and individual personal ends. It may seem that these malicious acts are a recent phenomenon, but in fact, they are nothing new and recorded incidents go back much further than people think.

In October 1967, a British European Airways Comet 4B was blown up by an explosive devise whilst cruising over the Mediterranean at 29,000 feet. Although no suspects were ever apprehended, the motive may have been an attempt to kill General Grivas – the controversial Greek Cypriot and former leader of EOKA. The accident immediately caused alarm amongst Comet operators and passengers reviving fearful memories of the series of Comet I disasters in the 1950s. Proof of sabotage in this case was eventually provided by the post mortems carried out on some of the passengers and the recovery of a small amount of wreckage and explosion torn seat cushions that remained afloat.

Air India Flight 182, a Boeing 747-237B, was another airliner ripped apart by a terrorist's bomb on 23 June 1985, crashing into the Atlantic Ocean off the south west coast of Ireland killing all 329 passengers and crew. Investigation and prosecution of this atrocity took almost 25-years to complete.

The Lockerbie catastrophe in 1988 is another case of ineffective security that enabled a bomb to be placed aboard a civil airliner. The Pan American Boeing 747 had taken off from London Airport on the evening of 21 December bound for the United States. Forty minutes later whilst cruising at 31,000 feet over Lockerbie, the airliner disintegrated after powerful explosion in the forward cargo hold, scattering wreckage over an extensive area killing all 259 people on board and eleven on the ground. The airline was harshly criticised for lax security after receiving a warning that a sabotage attempt was highly likely.

The 9/11 attacks on the World Trade Centre in New York and the Pentagon are yet another example of how terrorists utilise aircraft for their own political and theological beliefs. It is these acts that are the real dangers to commercial flying in the modern era that demand evermore vigilance and counter measures by governments, airlines, airports and indeed members of the public.

Total safety in air travel will always be an unattainable objective; pilot error, maintenance, design faults, collisions, weather, bird strikes and terrorism are but just a few of the potential hazards that will never be fully eradicated.

The present-day mandatory reporting of all incidents by pilots, however minor, that have the potential for catastrophic accidents and great loss of life, certainly had its genesis in the Stockport accident, which highlighted all that was wrong with the airline industry and government regulatory bodies.

Since the crash of the British Midland Boeing 737 at Kegworth in 1989, Britain has enjoyed an unprecedented period of airline safety with not a single major accident to a British airline, and bears testimony to the high standard of safety now enjoyed by the travelling public. The airline industry knows that its future success depends on convincing the public that flying is safe…never an easy task. When news of a major air disaster breaks, it impresses itself intensely on the public consciousness, no doubt, because they are extremely rare events and always associated in people's minds with mass violent death and destruction.

Today those who take to the air do so in comparative safety. Modern airliners are powerful, reliable and equipped with state-of-the-art electronics, navigational and radio aids, and multiple backup systems if anything should fail. All the available statistics are unequivocal and reassuring making commercial flying the safest form of travel, a triumph of organisation and regulation. In fact, the chances of an individual getting anywhere close to an air crash are infinitesimal, even for air crews, who spend the whole of their working lives aloft. The probability of a passenger being killed on a single flight is now estimated at approximately eight million to one. Looked at another way, if a passenger boarded a flight at random once a day, every day, it would statistically be over 21,000 years before he or she would be killed. Another way to describe this amazingly high safety level is the formula that: If a baby who was born and grew up without ever leaving an airliner in non-stop service, he or she would not be involved in a fatal accident before their seventy-sixth birthday. These reassurances sound convincing, but the average passenger is more interested in the numbers that reflect his or her prospects of completing their flight safely.

In reality, flying will never be totally safe and statistics can be notoriously manipulative and deceiving. On that note, I will close this story with one further statistic for the reader to ponder. ***The vast majority of those passengers who booked on those two holiday flights in June 1967 and tragically lost their lives were first time flyers.***